Live in the Present and Learn Valuable Life Lessons to Improve Any Relationship

"Did You Get That Monkey Off Your Back?"

JOSH R. HIMMELMAN

BALBOA
PRESS
A DIVISION OF HAY HOUSE

Copyright © 2012 by Josh R. Himmelman.

All rights reserved. No part of this book may be used or reproduced by any means, graphic, electronic, or mechanical, including photocopying, recording, taping or by any information storage retrieval system without the written permission of the publisher except in the case of brief quotations embodied in critical articles and reviews.

This book is a work of fiction. People, places, events, and situations are the product of the author's imagination. Any resemblance to actual persons, living or dead, or historical events, is purely coincidental.

Balboa Press books may be ordered through booksellers or by contacting:

Balboa Press
A Division of Hay House
1663 Liberty Drive
Bloomington, IN 47403
www.balboapress.com
1-(877) 407-4847

ISBN: 978-1-4525-4992-7 (sc)
ISBN: 978-1-4525-4990-3 (hc)
ISBN: 978-1-4525-4991-0 (e)

Library of Congress Control Number: 2012915970

Because of the dynamic nature of the Internet, any web addresses or links contained in this book may have changed since publication and may no longer be valid. The views expressed in this work are solely those of the author and do not necessarily reflect the views of the publisher, and the publisher hereby disclaims any responsibility for them.

The author of this book does not dispense medical advice or prescribe the use of any technique as a form of treatment for physical, emotional, or medical problems without the advice of a physician, either directly or indirectly. The intent of the author is only to offer information of a general nature to help you in your quest for emotional and spiritual well-being. In the event you use any of the information in this book for yourself, which is your constitutional right, the author and the publisher assume no responsibility for your actions.

Any people depicted in stock imagery provided by Thinkstock are models, and such images are being used for illustrative purposes only.
Certain stock imagery © Thinkstock.

Printed in the United States of America

Balboa Press rev. date: 10/03/2012

What readers will learn?

The purpose of this manuscript is not the final word regarding any given advice and or advice discussed at length from indicated sources. Its purpose is to provide additional information and avenues for you to seek your own answers. If unable to do so, then you should seek expert advice from a competent professional. By reading this book, I trust it has provided you with the correct thoughts and terminology to gather the appropriate additional information you need to be happier and at peace in the present to live your life.

This book is meant to provide a general informative, teaching discussion of relationship topics that you choose from to help you start to understand your own living situation. The education provided here is only the beginning to start opening discussions within your own relationship and improve your LIFE.

These issues are common to all intimate relationships, whether gay or straight, so all readers will benefit in learning from the relationship experiences. Within each lesson there can be and should be seen by the readers, parts that apply to them. The same problems are common but may have different causes.

All the self-help ideas provided here are areas that started to give me answers. The reasoning for me providing these avenues of help are simple. Most people do not know where to begin and or are afraid to seek professional help due to believing there is a stigma attached. In today's society more people than you realize seek help professionally. Do not be afraid to reach out.

INTRODUCTION

I suggest, especially in today's ever changing world that you keep a record, a set of dates and times to keep your memory in focus like the proverbial elephant. Elephants cry, play, have incredible memories, and laugh. Even the elephants seem confused today. Once studied and found to be nuclear families co-existing side-by-side, peaceful, with an inherit purpose for their day and family, some think of them as destructive mammals destroying the forest. Elephants are sensitive fellow animals where if a baby complains, the entire family will rumble and go over to touch and caress it. Elephants have greeting ceremonies when a friend that has been away for some time returns to the group. We however, live by blackberries or hard covered personal agendas to be organized and not to forget and yet the next day becomes a confusion of unexpected experiences and old memories of "How did that happen?" it was not in my schedule. Where did our ceremonies go? Do we need to schedule in happy moments, a time to laugh? Why do we need to tell our loved ones tomorrow is my birthday, our anniversary is today or Christmas is next Tuesday? Myself, envied as the elephant man of remembering every detail always thought what a great gift I have been given. Through experiencing this book, it is my hope that you will find ways of creating ceremonies that celebrate friendship, happy times in your relationships and peace in your life.

TABLE OF CONTENTS

SECTION ONE

CHAPTER ONE 3
Life Living Lesson: Attitude 14

CHAPTER TWO. 18
7 p.m. Friday, November 20, 2007—3:30 am. Sunday,
November 22, 2007 18
Life living lesson: When does the pain turn into hurt?. 22

CHAPTER THREE. 25
12 noon, Sunday, November 22, 2007—Saturday,
November 28, 2007 25
Life living lesson: Are we having the act of sex or truly
making love to each other? Does one or both as a couple
forget intimacy?. 36
Life living lesson: From birth, our brain is a library of
our life. There is no eraser for our memory! 47

SECTION TWO

CHAPTER FOUR. 53
Sunday, November 29, 2007, 11:30 p.m. 53
   Note 1—Folder 1 created November 16, 2007, notes. 54
   Note 2—Folder 2 created, November 18, 2007, notes.. 58
   Note 3—Folder 3 created November 29, 2007, notes. 60

Life living lesson: Who says it really is a lie? 63
Life living lesson: Can verbal abuse vs. physical abuse be
more significant in a relationship?. 70

CHAPTER FIVE 76
Sunday, November 29, 2007, 11:30 p.m.. 76
Life living lesson: Being afraid cripples your decision-
making process. 92
Life living lesson: Do not get angry 95

CHAPTER SIX 99
Monday, November 30, 2007. 99
Life living lesson: Friendship. 99

CHAPTER SEVEN 118
Tuesday, December 1, 2007 A.M.—to—Thursday,
December 31, 2007 118
Life living lesson: Suicide. 134
Life living lesson: Cross-cultural love 141

SECTION THREE

CHAPTER EIGHT—The BEGINNING of Jill and John. 159
Saturday, January 10, 1997—March 2003 159
Life living lesson: Can you feel alone and be in an
intimate relationship?. 170
Life living lesson: Do not argue in closed, restricted
spaces, or with your back against the wall.. 173
Life living lesson: Time out! Giving space and freedom
in arguments—is it a must?. 176
Life living lesson: Cocaine 187

CHAPTER NINE 190
Sunday, March 27, 2005—Thursday, November 19, 2007 190
Life living lesson: Crystal Meth and Methamphetamine. 194
Life living lesson: Does cheating really improve your
sexual relations at home? 195
Life living lesson: (Needs vs. wants) and their effect on
honesty, respect, and trust).. 201
Life living lesson: When it is time to give up on a relationship? . . 205

SECTION FOUR
RECOVERY PERIOD

CHAPTER TEN 213
January 01, 2008—Depression 213
Life living lesson: Depression. 214
Life living lesson: Does running away from you help? 218
February, 2008—Co-Dependency 225
Life living lesson: Co-dependency, Parts One to Eleven. 226
Sunday, February 28, 2008. 231
March, 2008—and still learning. 234
Life living lesson: When you need time for yourself, take it. 235
Life living lesson: Religion and spirituality 237
Life living lesson: Visualization will help. 240
Life living lesson: You can create and live your reality 247

SECTION ONE

CHAPTER ONE

How do you define happiness in a marriage? Maybe you have to try and retry until what you perceive as happiness comes to you. But it should never come to just you, but be a part both of you. John seemed to lack that concept, hence moved through two marriages, Cheryl and Mary, until he finally meets Jill. Failures in a marriage are of many different sources and unfortunately can change even a seemingly gentle person into someone even they themselves do not recognize. Is it the marriage that caused John to be a drug abuser or was it already programmed into his character?

John was already twenty-four and desperately wanting a wife and a family. Up until this point in his life John had no admiration for cheating on a loved one or a craving for drugs. John was very passive, but never overlooked any faults in the personalities of others. When he meets Mary, John's supposedly active ego changes as she become his catalyst for changing his mind in believing marriage should be his future. She was the opposite of what society had taught in these years, which was a woman should be outgoing and independent. Mary's demeanor was shy and not the young party scene girl. Because Mary simply came across as shy, he thought Mary was exactly what he needed to enjoy life. John outwardly was seen as a statement of confidence and comfortable in all social situations. Unfortunately John forgot to look within at his own belief system that said opposites attract and complete each other and if he had honestly looked inward, he would have acknowledged that he wasn't as confident and outgoing as he appeared on the outside. He continued to date Mary not realizing that who he perceived her to be was in fact who he was deep down. Mary was someone who represented what he always wanted to be and actually was. This kind of union of like attracting like should be effortless and pleasant. The reality was that things didn't run smoothly. Mary wasn't in love with John and would do things to push him away. This made John more desperate to have his picture of the perfect life with Mary.

They had dated for only sixteen months, with John being very impatient to be engaged and plan a wedding. Even before being engaged, he bought a twelve-room small mansion sitting on a large river. With the mansion went a wharf, a boat and a new sports car. His plan was in place to give a ring with a future that no one could refuse.

Blinded by his own heart, he overlooked many indicators of Mary's doubts about the marriage because of her uncertainty concerning John. Her sixth sense told her that the likelihood that John's perfect married life with her was questionable given her doubts about her love for him. It was suggested, by her mother, that John should move into the family home with Mary, her mother, father and brothers for them to be closer together. Her mother could not see the true John or was blinded by his charm and good looks as a man.

Each day John came home for lunch, which was nicely prepared by his soon-to-be-mother-in-law. Mary never wanted to prepare meals or help her mother, or do laundries or anything for John. But one day she did prepare something: his packed suitcase sitting on the front stoop at lunch time, a not-too subtle request to please get lost. Mary did not feel love for John as she thought and dreamed love should be. With much pleading from her mother who pointed out what a catch and provider John would be, Mary conceded. But in her heart there was no remorse for packing his suitcase and she felt a fight within her to continue to try and love John.

The problem for John was what forgiveness should he be giving and for what purpose? John did not care as long as he was back in her home allowing him an opportunity to work even harder for her love. When would John learn the word "resentment" and why he lacked it towards her actions? Where was his resentment for Mary's lack of love and her cruel message to get out of her life? Why do we not feel indignation when a person insults or even injures us? It should have been John resenting Mary, not Mary resenting him. His first experience of drugs he blamed on Mary. At work he came across a little white powder that his friends promised him would help make life more pure and loving. John was not ignorant of what he was about to do, just selfish not thinking about Mary and the consequences. What they didn't tell him was that this perception would only be on his part and no one else's and would be a very expensive way to understand loving another person, such as Mary. John joked with his friends saying this will not be a problem because he is strong willed and would not need this on a regular basis. But cocaine has a mind of its own and takes over your thoughts and desires.

Understanding what is happening will help us see how the other person is feeling. To forgive, you must first understand their motives. Is love really that blind that you cannot be angry? The blame for the choice of taking drugs and illusion instead of the reality of his and Mary's parts in their relationship lay with John. He needed to be clear to himself about his relationship, which would ultimately lead to no forgiveness, for both parties.

John always saw himself as in control of his thoughts and actions. With the drugs this proved not to be true. For someone like John, can you be taught that you are pitiful? To be told this would cause anyone to lash out, because their ego is now injured. An outsider would do well to remind John of his responsibilities to himself, his own worthiness and his need to control his responses. But, John pushed forward in his own drug induced bubble of reality.

Soon as possible the flashy ring was offered, and Mary's mother rushed the wedding plans into action. The whole town heard of the news and the home quickly became filled with enormous presents. Both were separately well-known from their careers, and everyone thought, what a union! John was a grand thinker, and Mary's mother knew there would be over six hundred people at the ceremony, standing room only in and outside the church. John almost fainted and had to be held as he saw his bride enter the church because he dream was finally becoming a reality. Unfortunately, John's parents, who were skeptical about the union and Mary's feelings, were too afraid to speak out to him, hoping that they were wrong about it being a loveless marriage for Mary. After the honeymoon through Europe, Mary was very quiet and she began to resent being a new bride. John learned that on the wedding day, she had not wanted to get married or even see John anymore. Her mother's persistence sent her walking down the aisle to meet her unwanted destiny.

The new marital home became a tomb of passionless love. Life did not continue as in Mary's family home where they appeared to others to be in love. Mary was trying to love John and his gift of a family home. Everything that represented the union of man and wife she started to resent. John tried to please his young bride by ensuring that they attend local dances as a couple and had dinner parties in their large home meant for entertaining. People were soon led to see that it was just a house and not a home as John's personality began to change, slamming doors and starting arguments for no reason.

Mary was very reserved and often embarrassed by John. She loved to sew her own dresses and to please John as much as possible, they were fashionable and dignified. John's nickname however became "Flaunt and tease!" He acted and felt like he was a lady's man. This was too much embarrassment for a quiet girl like Mary. Then it started, every time John came home from work Mary would be gone. John would drive around and would find her walking home to mother's house. Relatives of John would come to visit the home only to find him there by himself, a newlywed with no wife. It soon became a sexless marriage. Then one day when Mary wasn't home, John went to her mother's house looking for her and was informed that Mary was in hospital. John arrived at the hospital only to find that Mary didn't want to see him. John went to their reverend and asked him to advise them what to do to encourage a better marriage. The response was not at all what he expected. The reverend shook his head and said "Sometimes two people are on different paths and we have to let them go their own ways". Before being married, they had seen this same man several times to discuss their union. Why the sudden change? Again, with more shocking and disturbing news to come, John left to see their family doctor. It was as if the doctor was enacting a scene from some drama lesson on how to be timid. He literally stood in a corner of his office, protected by his desk, and said he was not at liberty to discuss Mary's illness. At twenty-four, how was John to understand all these issues coming at him? Back to his cocaine, a little more white powder helped to ease the pain of rejection for which he was responsible. We never see who is truly responsible because we live by our egos, living a life to expect and not accept.

Enough! John filed for a divorce; Mary was dismissed from the hospital. She returned the divorce papers having written on them,

"Divorce is based on my husband wanting too much sex." In haste, John padlocked the home to keep Mary from entering. Today, John realizes that this was unlawful. What was once a peaceful man had now turned into a vengeful, angry, I'll-get-even guy. He moved back home with his parents after he sold the house. He found his parents were ashamed of him. Before he had been the son who could do no wrong and now he was an embarrassment to the family.

Very quickly a court date was assigned, and John went to court along with his entire family. In the divorce process, Mary had stated that the reason for the divorce was that John made too many sexual demands. When the grounds for divorce were read, John just pleaded with his parents not to be upset. These court cases are nothing new. Mary did not appear and did not contest the divorce. The judge made an immediate ruling that John had an instant divorce, no waiting period, and please go find a new life where someone cares about you.

Within a month, John learned that Mary was pregnant with twins and had complications, eventually losing the babies. John developed depression, smoking one cigarette after another, not eating and almost lost his job. Eventually he collapsed and spent a month in his parents' home bed-ridden and receiving personal care from his mother. This changed his parents' view of him, and as a result they didn't care what others felt or had to say about their son but felt that he should start over in another place.

Left to be alone, John moved into a two bedroom apartment, purchasing everything new to escape any memories. He felt lonely and didn't know what was wrong with his life. He sought and found a roommate and ran the bar scene. Within three months, of running the bar scene while his roommate was never to be seen out, he had some questions for his co-dweller. "I never see you with a girl or in a bar; why not?" John was still disturbed by his life and became a little edgy about what he would do. The roommate admitted he was gay and was sorry that he had not been honest. He went on to ask John if he wanted to see the difference between sleeping with a man as opposed to with a woman. John answered with a "No" filled with deep agitation. Falling asleep, morning came too quickly. John was riddled with guilt now living with a gay man and what his parents would think. He was tortured by his religious principles, and thoughts that his family once again would be embarrassed by him. His own beliefs and morals were tested yet again in his so far short life.

The failure of marriage was not a practical problem for John, but became an emotional problem—depression. How could he resolve this mistake? Or was it a mistake? At first he felt confusion, and then conceived the idea that this had been an experience and could easily be understood and that marriages fail. But, this soon became ineffective, and his lifestyle seemed in jeopardy, out of control and impossible to resolve. Once again John needed to look at his internal strength to achieve emotional freedom and a more positive attitude. Not aware of what was happening; John was now faced with self-acceptance.

John transferred his job to another city, leaving behind memories that he knew were killing the real him. Now he started over again trying to figure out his new life and the path he should take for happiness. It took a year, but finally he met Cheryl, a woman he thought was a committed, permanent life-lasting relationship. Their pasts had strong parallels and both decided it was best to move as far away from families that their jobs would allow. In their relationship, John and Cheryl realized the issues were the same as they would have been in a partnership back at home. With similar issues about communication, honesty, trust, and commitment, it was no easier.

At the start of the relationship, John felt he pursued an honest and trusting woman. In fact, still religious; John would pray each evening for this to be the one for him, like an answer from God. What John was doing, and what we are all capable of, was to align his thoughts to the emotions of what he desired and deserved. At the time, John was very unaware of visualization, but was actually practicing the format. He saw himself in love and feeling an attachment to another person who felt the same way toward him. His demeanor and facial expressions changed, and he appeared to be in love and in harmony with his new emotions. According to the law of attraction, you reap what you sew. In this case, as he thought, love with Cheryl.

John and Cheryl were close in age but they had totally different earlier life experiences. From his childhood John was considered to be very dominating, both at home with his twin sister and out on the streets with his friends. He was also sexually active at a young age, first experiencing sex with his baby sitter. John's past was most definitely a very colorful past in comparison to Cheryl's grey, foggy, shallow experiences in relation to sexual encounters.

John boasted of having conquered at least fifty women. He had finally married the one he felt would keep him satisfied sexually, Cheryl. Cheryl's sexual appetite matched John's. It was evident sex played a huge role in John's life, both past and present.

In the first few years of their marriage, life was truly fun: lots of travel and no real marital problems. But Cheryl made sure her husband was put on an allowance not large enough for one of today's teenagers.

Cheryl suggested they take a trip together to a retreat. Unbelievable to John, the women were separated from the men. These guys were already converted to this cult affair and expected John to join in the nefarious activities like dancing naked around a fire. He managed to escape and quickly got back home. There were no fights resulting from that weekend. Actually, Cheryl was even nicer and daily, in fact as often as possible, wanted them to be intimate. John believed he was in heaven and that maybe she should do more retreats. Cheryl had a plan in place and that was to become pregnant. John learned later that her intention of bringing him to a distant place from his parents had been to start a family and then send him back home. However, a baby girl named Lauren was born. John dreamt the dream of a beautiful home and a well-paid job to provide for his family. But soon, there was no love from his wife, only anger and resentment which was building up against him. Realizing this was happening, John bought a bigger house, believing that a second baby would please Cheryl. For a time, he was right.

John made more trips up north to his friend's cottage, but this time to discuss how to save a failing marriage. There were no good answers, because he knew Cheryl was vengeful and on a different path from his own dream which was to be part of a family.

John, once again a dominant guy, became disillusioned by his disappointment with his American family. This was no longer a nuclear family but a broken one. Eventually Cheryl, with her large income, hired a great lawyer and divorced John. He was left with no assets and very bad resentment. He agreed not to fight the divorce if he could have partial custody of the girls. It was obvious that Cheryl would use this tactic to blackmail John.

Self-concept, "the person you think you are", is the main factor in determining one's personal choices. It evolves from what other people say and instills a new thought or brings to light something you already know but which was hidden deep within you. You live trusting the society that is saying you are okay and that everyone is truly sincere. But, if you allow negative thoughts to creep in, then no matter what is said about you, you will choose to believe the negative thoughts and opinions to be true. There can be an increase or a decrease in your self-esteem depending on the response from people who depend on you and care most about you. The image in the mirror and self-image can agree or disagree based on your own self-assessment.

To be well-adjusted and fit into society John needed to feel acceptance. Based on his responses in therapy, John was told he would never feel fulfilled. He would live in constant confusion. The one thing forgotten in that therapy was that self-concept can be learned and best yet can be changed. Still, John wondered who he really was and never really accepted himself and the drugs he was using were beginning to consume him.

Weirdly enough, John who went back home to his family after his break up with Cheryl, came to the same conclusion as his parents, that he should start over in a new city to avoid the embarrassment of what others would think of their son. There was no question in John's mind that he wanted to leave, and did so.

A mirror is an excellent treatment for looking at one's self-concept and making one's self-assessment, because the only "me" there is yourself. You must face yourself and the idea of maybe changing your appearance. If you find yourself smiling at your reflection, that is an indication of self-acceptance. Live and grow with the obvious. You can look yourself in the eyes; see your strengths without speaking or discussing out loud with yourself. This is different than what you are thinking. Verbal communication is like someone else speaking, a voice easily swayed by others' opinions; you may be swayed by your own verbal talk. The true understanding is within your thoughts—the house of who you really are as a person.

Once again, John went through such a similar departure in his life towards a new destiny. After questioning himself, he needed to know, was he ready for the reaction? And there would always be a reaction from family, co-workers, society, neighbors and the church. We all question life when a strange life-changing decision has to be shared in all parts of our life.

If you do not realize yet, you are constantly told who you ought to be, what you ought to do and how you ought to feel. Just about every individual around you will take part in one or all of the above when giving you advice. The question is how do you combat them and be yourself? See yourself in the mirror. As you stare, the inside of you will be revealed. In general, we all feel we are not good enough. Now this feeling and its intensity will differ from individual to individual. Who you are for everyone will depend on your own self-concept.

Talk about consciously finding yourself very tense and scared, scared of living life in your own eyes and in the eyes of the world. Does that apply only to heterosexuals or to homosexual males and females? The most scared are those who live only a half-life—they lose out on experiences. Do not be afraid to be judged. Do not even judge yourself, for you consciously make your decisions. Those decisions are yours to keep and once acted upon cannot be taken back.

In life, it is okay to be imperfect and we do not imply life is an imperfection. Life will definitely be more fun and fulfilling if you dance through it and if you wish, grab a partner to share your dance.

January 1997, two seemingly mature young people meet, John and Jill. They didn't know that each had been unhappily married before. These two were born into and had childhoods from two different worlds. John is a North American, full of dreams and aspirations of success with no inward capabilities to achieve success. Jill, years before, had crossed the Atlantic from her homeland, with her brother, to settle in a new country for a better life and to find the family she thought was her dream. Newly divorced and faced with her family's disapproval, she decided to leave and embed herself into a new culture.

These two have quite different cultures motivating their thoughts and actions. The exterior, or as I call it, the façade of both is very appealing, sexy and definitely charming. There is absolutely no evidence of either ever being in loveless marriages. Both are very desirable; one could say "head turners." Each had a definite appeal to the other.

John is very easy to describe to you. He is a strapping guy of six feet three inches tall, a perfect weight of two hundred and twenty pounds, and has muscles popping through his clothing. Everything he wears makes him look like a GQ man but his personality is not, he is self-indulgent. Dark hair and dark hazel eyes complement a groomed "stache". No tattoo adorns his naturally olive skin that has its share of body hair. The chest is covered in a wave pattern that is like watching the waves release on a natural peaceful cove, spreading outward in perfect symmetry. When John and Jill met, two things observed by John immediately made him very jealous or uncomfortable with her. This is when he realized there is a jealous side to his character. Jill was admired not for her beauty but for her natural giving of kindness. She never had to try to be beautiful and charming, she just was. Jill was not only in control of her life but shared her life with those she loved. John unknowingly set out to destroy a perfect dove in Jill. I cannot tell you which one of these emotions, kindness or lovingness, were missing in John. I would rather that no jealousy had taken up residence in his thoughts; those thoughts causing the beginning of tension between the two of these great people.

Jill, a beautiful woman in her own right, never did and still definitely does not see her own beauty. She is a woman who was devoid of self-respect and who realized she needed to find that within herself. By doing this she would be able to see herself, and get herself to see how great a person she is.

Trying to describe Jill and speak about her only to attract another's attention is very easy. You often hear the word angelic and wonder what the meaning for this description is. As one would see Jill, you saw a face full of sunshine flickering off the still lake water. Definitely no make-up is ever needed and she would never be described as a plain Jane. It was a natural beauty starting with her coal black hair, shoulder length and styled like Mrs. Clever of Leave it to Beaver TV program. The constant smile and outward reaching, helping hands made you feel completely embraced by her kind and loving spirit. There was no denying that both outward and inward personality traits were complimentary to the impression of a nurse caring for a World War I injured soldier. John and Jill on the outside physically complemented each other perfectly but by unfolding their inner personalities, one would see the differences. What John had for himself was his ideal compliment. A woman who was caring, giving to a fault and co-dependent hanging on until the walls would crash down. Jill demonstrates her qualities one incident at Christmas. Jill would invite friends to spend the day and have dinner, not unlike a family. They would watch television, play games, and sometimes she would buy little gifts as a welcome to their home and then they would be stuffed like big birds. She would create massive paper dinner plates of everything she had prepared, one for each person to take home and several for all of them to take to city hall to feed the homeless on Christmas night.

To formulate a picture of John in your mind, you must remember it is tainted with Jill's love for him. Beauty is in the eyes of the beholder—a true and honest statement. However, in this case the description of John really is that of the exterior of the man. As you read ahead, how can a person like Jill make someone like John see what great qualities he has? John believed he was never good enough in any part of his life.

Definitely, Jill loves John and for many reasons, one being his outward appearance but not his inward personality. His character was sometimes undeniably giving. Over the years Jill would watch John buy a minimum of one thousand dollars worth of drug store items and send a massive box overseas to the unfortunate. How can you not love such a heart! On special family days, far in advance, John would shop for beautiful clothing and ship them off to his relatives. Only once did Jill mention that this was pushing the limit on his credit, and the resulting look of disappointment on John's face left Jill speechless. John had a tremendous amount of kindness until later on when things changed. John had kindness for others, but only attitude for Jill.

Josh R. Himmelman

Life Living Lesson: Attitude

What exactly is attitude? The word "attitude" means a way of thinking, acting, or feeling. It is shown in many ways. Attitude can be positive or negative. Negative attitudes lead to negative results, so a positive attitude is necessary for you to make the most of your life. Attitudes affect every aspect of our lives. It can be mental with regard to a fact, a feeling or an emotion resulting from a situation, usually created by someone you know and or love. Attitude can also be how your body is positioned in a stance, on purpose to look threatening or accepting. Therefore, your attitude is in constant change, unlike your personality, which is constant like the spots on a leopard's skin, and mostly cannot be changed. It is hard work, but if you love your partner enough, you can begin changing his or her attitude simply by communicating with them. Be realistic. That means giving calm and understanding messages, which are not blaming or accusatory. You need to know what your partner's buttons are so that you can positively affect their emotions and then begin approaching the changing of attitude. You know your partner well; therefore you can choose the right words to persuade him or her because you are one step ahead. Use your intuition to predict their reaction and be ready with positive reinforcement to assist in changing this negative attitude.

> *"Attitude is a little thing that makes a big difference." (Winston Churchill)*
> **Churchill, Winston: Thinkexist. Retrieved February 2012 from http://thinkexist.com/quotation/ attitude_is_a_little_thing_that_makes_a_ big/219106.html**

> *"Keep a green tree in your heart and perhaps a singing bird will come."*
> *(Chinese Proverb)*
> **Chinese Proverb: Bing. Retrieved February 2012 from http://www.bing.com/search?q=%E2%80% 9CKeep+a+green+tree+in+your+heart+and+per**

haps+a+singing+bird+will+come.%E2%80%9D
+++++++++%28Chinese+Proverb%29&src=IE-
SearchBox&Form=IE8SRC

In Jill's relationship, the most annoying attitude was the conscious one. A scowl on the face and a refusal to reply to a question always gave it away. Be ready. If the person is driving a car, then you put up with the jerking motion of the car being manipulated—an extension of this attitude. Then there is the unpleasant closeness, the kind where you smell the tension in the air you have to breathe. It feels like you are absorbing their attitude in your lungs, no escape. You say something to create a smile or some kind of pleasant atmosphere. All you ask is for some kind of recognition that you are there too and please let this not be my fault again. It seems when a person has a lot of negative attitude around you, they choose to always make it your problem. How nice to have yet another problem thrown into your lap! You just want a nice day with the one you love.

> "Let us rise up and be thankful, for if we didn't learn a lot today, at least we learned a little, and if we didn't learn a little, at least we didn't get sick, and if we got sick, at least we didn't die; so, let us all be thankful." (Buddha)
> **Buddha. Thinkexist. Retrieved February 2012 from http://thinkexist.com/quotation/let_us_rise_up_and_be_thankful-for_if_we_didn-t/199980.html**

Jill visited many religious buildings; seeking answers in any religion that could help her understand John. The most rewarding of all was the Buddhist Temple.

The only escape from a car is to physically get out. You watch, and it is not the car spinning away but the person inside controlling the car. The same happens when you watch then, full of negative attitude; walk out the door, or away from a restaurant. It is them walking away, not you. How quickly things can change when not confronted! And shortly afterwards, you receive a call asking for a favor. Now one wonders, is this to check on you to see if you are where you said you would be or maybe to check on your mood? Adverse attitude brings on a state of confusion for the recipient. They are hoping you are all hyped up, because they are ready now to have that argument that they obviously want. But, now it's the "Ah" factor. You have the opportunity to ask what is wrong. The famous answer is the ten seconds of silence and then the word, "Nothing!" How do you respond to this act of "Talk to me but do not talk to me"?

If you are left standing alone, get out of there fast. Too much pleasure is derived for your partner to drive around or walk back and see you in despair. That equals more power to them. Go home if you can. It is the best place to go, not with friends, not to a movie or on a long walk. Even though you are seeking solace with someone you know, it puts you even more in a defensive state like a charged criminal needing an alibi. You should never need an alibi in a loving relationship.

You make it home, and for sure, the phone will ring. Part of you does not want to answer because there is still some satisfaction derived by your partner that they have put you in a place. Guaranteed, the first question is "What are you doing?" At this point no matter what the personal appearance is of this individual, being handsome or beautiful or just ordinary, they now appear unattractive; their voice is becoming annoying, and you wish their undesirable attitude would all go away. It is okay to have those feelings. You are dealing with someone who is very confused about you or themselves. Oh, you get an answer to your question about "What's wrong?" and they say, "Well, you taught me to react and be this way!" What is it now they really want from you and this relationship? Is it a drawn-out fight? They are looking for an intense argument, where of course, now you are the starter of the argument, because they opened the door to your emotions. Yes, and now they have the power to blame you for starting an argument and not getting along. Is this rational or irrational thinking? Obviously irrational, and how do you cope with irrationality? Rational is easy because it is the sense and feelings where you are in command and can be understood. If faced with an undeniable irrational scenario, realize that you have no control over it, all you can do is change your perception of the situation.

"If you don't like something change it; if you can't change it, change the way you think about it." (Mary Engelbreit)

Englebret, Mary: Sand 1.wordpress. Retrieved February 2012 from : http://sand1.wordpress.com/2008/06/17/69-if-you-dont-like-something-change-it-if-you-cant-change-it-change-the-way-you-think-about-it-mary-engelbreit/

End of Life living lesson: Attitude.

CHAPTER TWO

7 p.m. Friday, November 20, 2007—3:30 am. Sunday, November 22, 2007

Did you ever ask yourself, "Why is it my darkest moments seem to happen at night?" Night, when the sun disappears, taking its warmth, brightness and that happy feeling that everything will be fine; and then you realize out of your fear everything will not be fine. Then in those passing seconds comes forth another thought. Wait, tomorrow is another day, and it is a chance to redo or change. Cannot change it tonight but as I live it tomorrow I can act on my new thought and behave according to how I am thinking on this new day. Sounds quite wonderful and it lightens your heart. You relax, but joy is killed. There are always new hurdles, whether you created them or someone else created them for you, to challenge once again, your perspective on living.

Thoughts are speeding through Jill's head. John is gone and so little time was spent together this fall. John recently bought a house as an investment and he left on Friday to spend time there. As had been happening recently, Jill did not go with him. Whenever Jill arrived at John's home, she immediately became a workhorse. So, she stayed in their own home and in John's mind that was because Jill was cheating on him and using chat lines to do so.

Jill had the best friend anyone could ever ask for. Her name was Lori and she was a truly gentle woman who was very easily taken advantage of and had already been married twice. Lori had maintained her gentle nature in spite of marriages to two husbands who failed to love her as she deserved.

Sleepless at 3:30 a.m., Jill lay awake eating a Nutty Buddy ice cream in bed, and for some strange reason feeling good. Her perspective was about to change but not through her own volition. With fifteen years of insomnia, the bad habit—having a sweet snack in the middle of the night—seemed normal to her. The pleasure of sweetness, a cozy bed sheet and being smothered in a goose down duvet, was all she needed to finally fall asleep. The bloody phone rang. She answered in a mild voice with "Hello". A huge force of anger in a wild, bellowing scream yelled down the line, breaking the silence. It was John. The bedroom was in darkness with black-out curtains, in an attempt to help Jill sleep. She had heard this voice too many times before. It was the worst voice John would use with her. She has never seen or heard John speak on the phone to anyone else in this voice that he used with his loving partner, Jill. Do married couples often hide behind a barrier such as a phone to exert a force way out of line? For John it was the way he treated his wife. This could explain his behavior now? If Jill were a child and he was her father, that darkened room would have been filled with monsters, the kind that eat you with their slime. There is always a façade to every individual, and this was the one John kept for Jill only. Later in this read you will be quoted *verbatim* how John can crush and almost send Jill's soul racing for the Afghan caves. Over the phone loudly and roughly he says," You changed your passwords. Higher even still, "Change them back now or I am going to take you to court and sue!" There was little bit of ice cream on Jill's chin that was making her feel like that little girl again all snuggled in bed for night time. The child-like pleasure of illicit snacks in a cozy bed was transformed into being in a coffin. Jill said, "What are you talking about now?" and the phone receiver smashed so hard that there wasn't a clicking sound so much as the sound of a forceful explosion. At first Jill was at a loss with what had just happened. "Why is he this way?" Then she remembered that voice in the past, the voice that you will come to know later. She just lay there numb, once again beaten by the verbal abuse. Hurt or pain, which one is it now that John managed to use to control her feelings? For seconds she truly did not know what John's accusation was referring to. Then, not with a smile of, "Oh now I remember!" but rather, "Damn, I was right." Jill knew that John had found access to one chat site of hers on the computer, but she wasn't sure about the rest. John was very smart with electronics and computer equipment. Today everyone seems to have a chat site somewhere. The internet has become part of social media where you can connect and discuss issues with anyone in the world. Better to tell your partner than to hide your internet activities and your reasons had better be good.

This is how Jill was certain John had found this one chat line she had started. Jill is truly lost on a computer and navigating a chat line was nearly impossible. All the guys trying to chat with her would say, "Can't you even send a picture?" Nope, she was quite inept and did not know how to make these sites work properly. One day during the past two weeks, John, in his snoop mode, accessed this chat line on Jill's computer. Jill did not even know how to retrieve messages, let alone their attachments. John could do this and the attachment was a picture of this guy naked. John turned that picture into her screen saver and made it appear as a multiple of fifty times on her screen. It was disgusting and shocking to anyone to see her computer screen turned into a porn page. During the morning, John called her at work and asked when she would be home. Ignorant of what was awaiting her, she said "The usual, around 4 p.m." No gym for her that day. Then he asked her if she would wait for him to come home—as always. Where else would Jill be going? Jill arrived home, settled in, and decided to turn on her computer. There was John's gift. Seriously, she felt a nauseous tingle like you do just before you vomit. The phone was ringing and yes, it was John. Jill didn't even hesitate to answer, "What and why, John, did you do this? This is SICK! To leave this for me to find, therefore letting me know that you are invading my privacy. And YOU have done much worse for a much longer time to me! Why are you acting so ignorant of your own misdoings?" Silence prevailed and then John said, "Look on your desk, there is a piece of paper folded. Open it and read it, Jill." And he hung up. Jill watching her own hands unfolding the piece of paper, shaking and with no feelings, read a very simple line of text. "Jill, after I saw this message on your computer I began to feel hurt. Something I haven't for a long time. It made me realize I am jealous and I still love you." He signed the note unlike ever before, with two sets of Xs. It's amazing how such a symbol can change more than fifty per cent of your negative thoughts

John's mid-morning phone call just confirmed that Jill needed to change her passwords. That is why, before Jill went to bed that evening, she changed every one of them. Jill was not sure if John had the right to go through her personal computer in their home. Is that an invasion of privacy or an eye opener that there was cheating going on. When you are a loving couple, is everything in your life theirs to know? Again, should he be allowed to cruise through the links, documents, files and whatever else is on your computer?

Sleepless, not in Seattle, which was a fun movie to watch more than once, Jill lay in bed confused and thought, "What reaction am I going to have when he walks through the door tomorrow?" John played out the scenario knowing it would be him acting and, as always, ignoring the whole incident. Not a word would be spoken about that phone call and sweet co-dependent Jill would offer dinner and dessert. The rest of the evening would continue in the same pattern, like a continuous sequence of numbers. John would make believe he fell asleep on the sofa and Jill would sit in the big chair, glancing over every few minutes wondering how she could fix the two of them. Really, she saw a relationship as something that needed fixing, like an old car getting a new engine to put it back into service. Putting a relationship back into service? What were she seeing, butterflies and daisies?

Josh R. Himmelman

Life living lesson: When does the pain turn into hurt?

One can easily say pain is the unpleasant feeling common to such experiences as stubbing a toe, burning a finger, putting iodine on a cut and bumping the funny bone. The International Association for the Study of Pain defines pain as "an unpleasant sensory and emotional experience associated with actual or potential tissue damage, or described in terms of such damage. Pain is a single sharp and distinct feeling, a form of physical suffering; hurt is an injury that can be either physical or mentally inflicted."

When we experience pain it motivates us to withdraw from damaging or potentially damaging situations, to protect the damaged body part while it heals, and avoid those situations in the future for any human body part. Are my brain and my heart body parts? In my biology class it certainly appeared that was the case. Why then, when such pain is caused by a partner; we tend not to protect ourselves from it happening again and again. The medical world and its terminology mean little to us, like "nociceptors in the peripheral nervous system." Most hurt resolves quickly once the painful stimulus (that would be the partner) is removed and the body (heart or thoughts that cause behavior of emotions and feelings) has healed. But, sometimes, hurt persists despite removal of the partner. To heal the body or the emotions created from a trauma caused by a partner is a gamble. I will not even venture today into my experiences on whether my partner being gone or whether forgetting the feelings he aroused would help me to heal my pain and hurt. Some victimized women in shelters say they just became numb. Sometimes hurt arises in both your heart and thoughts without your partner even being present or if present, he can pull a trigger like that of a Colt Thirty-five to set you off into distress or even agony. And why does this happen? I believe it is mostly from unresolved issues of the past for both heterosexual couples and in same-sex couples, the dominant one of the two being in the power position. One Big Horn sheep has to rule the hill—it's quite simple. The other is me, I will just show more love in what I do for him, and tomorrow he will see how important I am in his life. Equality, yes, equal partners tomorrow we will become equal partners. Just as a side note, social support in your partner's life, their cultural values, events that give them excitement are all theirs. A sport or just any distraction in your partner's life takes him away from you and makes your hurt significantly deeper and more unpleasant. Does this hold true for both people in a marriage? Of course it does. The husband can wait many times for his wife to return from her weekly social gathering of the girls. Resentment can build and if not resolved, carry over into the next relationship?

Pain is a major symptom in many medical conditions and can significantly interfere with a person's quality of life and general day-to-day activities. Your question may be, "What is the medicine I can use to alleviate this pain of neglect from my partner?" Good old—fashioned COMMUNICATION and not going to bed with issues unresolved can provide relief but it may become daunting to your inner self, the fear that the pain will never go away. The pain burns hotter and runs faster, like your body inside is doing its own marathon. At this point, you both need pain medicine in the form of a third party such as group therapists, family counseling or psychotherapy.

Is it accidental or true sabotage by your partner that causes you to feel hurt? Hit yourself physically in the chest area. This is a little punch in comparison to what you feel is the empty cavity left by the loss of a once loving relationship. What you are actually doing is beating on two body parts that happen to control a great part of your life. First; the emotions of love or lack of love felt in your heart and second; physical tension in the chest, whether it is chronic or episodic, caused by anxiety of the unknown new future.

I have never in my life hit another person and I even have difficulty smacking a fly or a spider. Now ants are a different story, as invaders of my home, my place of family. So why do the ants get the physical attention? Because they are doing physical damage, tearing down my physical support structure, the framing that holds up my home and keeps my loving family safe. A fly or a spider does not physically destroy the framing structure around me. Who cares about the fly and the spider? An abusive partner is like the ant and can be the one tearing down your structure of thought and behavior, your feelings and emotions, leaving your present in some sort of hurtful and wrongful state.

Does an abusive partner give me the right to retaliate with both physical pain and emotional hurt? If I physically strike back, will it stop the abuse? Like killing an ant to stop my physical home from crumbling? I do not think so. Retaliation will never work in any situation. The physical blow is only a bruise on the surface, a pain that heals and dissipates. It's a combination of physical and verbal abuse, the words and their tone as they strike, that tears your bodily frame down. It is thanks to all those loud-mouthed, abusive-talking partners who know exactly what to say, where to say it and when, that can, yes, destroy you or yet another piece of you.

Are we suffering from pain or a hurt? Both can be physical. A pain causes physical suffering so do we say our thoughts are in pain, our emotions are in pain or our feelings are in pain? No, we always say, "Why did you hurt me?" If your loved one grabs your arm and leaves finger imprints in your flesh, you say, "That hurts!" But really, it is painful. Should you make the observation that pain causes hurt? When your heart is broken, it is not really broken, like a piece of dropped china on the kitchen floor, it is hurt. No-one physically grabbed your heart and broke it into pieces. But, in your mind it feels physically unable to function as a whole. When your heart begins to ache, it is hurting. The obvious feeling is unhappiness as a result of your partner's words or actions that have stepped outside of your expectations of the relationship. Therefore, your pain is a hurt as a consequence of your emotions. This is part of some couples lives. Step back and give them a chance to experience their pain and hurt and not take advantage of each other's vulnerability possibly leaving one to be more hurt. The same is in any loving relationship: at some point one becomes vulnerable because of the pain and hurt. Do not allow them to suffer too long. Remember, you love them. Having a partner suffer pain that has turned into hurt is not a form of intimacy, but a destruction of the same.

End of life living Lesson—When does the pain turn into hurt?

CHAPTER THREE

12 noon, Sunday, November 22, 2007— Saturday, November 28, 2007

Jill had finally fallen asleep in the early morning. When she awoke she had no feelings and no pleasant things like her coffee and morning bubble bath. She was truly empty of thought except "How can it be a wonderful life?" She had only to find the answer. But the "how" was hurting her head; the pressure was once again inside, like a fist trying to open from the inside of her head through her brain. Jill knew subconsciously that there were no answers and that left her with nothing.

Before the rest of the planned events unfolded, Jill called school and booked the day off sick for Monday, November 23rd, so no one would come looking for her. As far as Jill knew this weekend John would not be coming home until it was time to leave for his work. That meant she did not expect him until Monday morning at around 8 a.m. History repeats itself and as many a weekend before, they had had arguments over the phone. John would stay away until Jill went to school. For John that meant getting up at 4 a.m. in the morning and driving in heavy traffic to reach the city. He always took an argument deep into his understanding of a relationship and, in his head; it always blew into a tornado. Whatever happened to a belief in forgiving and forgetting? Is it your downfall to forgive to quickly? It certainly lessens the pain and is not meant to make you feel like the bigger person. You just want peace in your life. Why bother to continue an argument? It is best to "forgive and forget." But, it is not so simple.

It was early Sunday afternoon when Jill placed a small folding dinner table, the kind you would see someone alone eating a tin foil dinner from, by the sofa. Many years ago, her mother gave her a beautiful burgundy leather-bound Bible with her name engraved on the cover. She placed this across her chest and let it lay still on her lower chest. She placed on the table, pictures of John and herself, her mom, Lori and herself smiling and having a nice day. That was the killer picture for her, smiling like life was treating her like a queen. As well, she placed the wooden cross she had bought from a monastery during their trip back to John's home in Europe on the table so she might see Jesus and Mary. She went to the car and got the rosary that she had recently placed over her rear view mirror, the one that she kissed every time she got into the car. Then she went upstairs to retrieve her little wooden cross on a leather string, her silver cross from a purchase with John, a very happy memory on their last holiday in Europe, and she hung them all around her neck. She held closely and tightly to the crosses because it felt as if her life was moving into them and a deepening sadness for her life hovered around her. Jill settled onto the sofa. She had several bottles of sleeping pills opened on the table with a large glass of water. She said so many prayers to God to please forgive her and not send her to Purgatory or Hell, but to accept her into Heaven. Her parched and sticky lips were moving with each word of prayer as she asked repeatedly for forgiveness for taking her own life. She tried to look at her pictures but her eyes were blurred with the warmest tears. She stopped for a mere second to realize how warm the wetness felt on her face. She removed her left hand from the Bible and passed the warm tears across her mouth for ease of praying more and more. Her whispers became louder, and she could hear her prayers as if they were coming from an altar at the front of a church. It became a chant that took away the fears and seemed to lift her into another dimension or a parallel universe. Now there was calm and peace that reduced the trembling of her body. Coldness was releasing from her feelings. She felt as if her soul was digging into her inner body, the casing of life that had housed her soul for fifty-five years. There was a presence of pressure sucking inward from within as she spoke harshly in her mind, "I must let my soul return to the power of the universe." She made sure she put on clean clothes and went to the bathroom, because when you die everything is released. She still wanted to keep some dignity. How foolish of her—she had allowed all her dignity to diminish in the last two years. Silly to think she had any dignity left to bare it to some stranger picking up her remains. Now an overwhelming feeling of sadness had her clinching her Bible and rubbing a cross between her left thumb and first finger. It became so hot it started to emulate comfort, like standing in sunshine. There was no thought of anyone left, not even the effect this would have on her mother. She knew suicide would not only be removing her bodily presence but literally killing her mother as well. Her mother and she had always had a special bond because Jill had been born with asthma and had become her mother's cross to bear. Her mother had been badly afflicted with asthma and bronchitis until the day Jill was born. As strange as it seems, it left her and Jill inherited the sickness. She had never forgiven herself for her well-being and the feeling that Jill's illness that should have been hers. By killing herself, Jill had no doubt that her mother would die of heartache and guilt. She had no sense of caring, no ideas of anything and was so, so empty. It was a slow beginning. She saw her arm in slow motion reaching for the pills and water. She took two sleeping pills to start, because she knew these would calm her down, sleeping pills was her first choice. She lay there with the lights dimmed enough just so she could still see the pictures. She felt such sadness. It cannot be put into words. Then she took a third pill and within fifteen to thirty minutes she felt okay. Not even a yawn or sleepy *per se*, just quieter in her mind and heart. It was very easy to continue with another pill and minutes later another pill. She thought she was at twelve pills and she was deciding in her mind when she would take a group of pills. She truly believed she was accepting the fate she had chosen. Calmness and ease blanketed her . . . and in walks John. His entrance was totally unexpected and her mind is racing. She cannot let John see what she is doing. She needed a great lie in seconds because this would give John an opportunity to have her committed to a psychiatric ward in a hospital. Once there, heavily medicated, Jill would be seen as the only reason why the relationship had failed.

John's threat of a lawsuit came from his never-ending fulminations that he let his ex-wife free without suing her for money. She had doubled her salary, made investments, scored a huge pension plan, and all of this had accumulated while they were married. But he had let everything go to have shared custody with his girls. He could not stand to be without them. He never missed a child support payment simply because he loved them so much. But he never got love in return. It was very sad to watch his tears. He felt their love was the only love he had, forgetting Jill's of course. That was mentioned too many times, finally leaving Jill to feel like the caboose in John's life.

Well, if you could only be there and see, you would know why she needed to check out. John's first words were, "Remove yourself from the sofa, that is my bed. Go upstairs, I am tired and you are in my bed." She is thinking with a light head, "What the f***! Can you not see what is going on here buddy?" Then John leaves, goes to the car, gets his bags and takes some upstairs and some to the living room. He stoops over her and says, "What is this?" pointing to the top the table full of pictures. Then he snatches the chains around her neck and meanly says, "What is this for? Are you religious or something?" As he walks away he starts with, "What did you take?" and repeats it three times. Jill really did not feel that bad. She found it hard to believe that she was not groggier. So, on purpose, she made herself seem groggy, just to see John's reaction. "Pooh . . . get up and go to bed," he says. He moves his little table away from the sofa and starts to make up his nest, as Jill, now for real, staggers up the stairs. So she goes to bed a failure.

At around 3 a.m., Monday morning, Jill looked over at the clock on her bureau. She hears his voice and sees John's head above her about six inches from her face. That's the closest he has been to her in months. "Are you asleep? Did you take something?" But you must understand none of this was in a caring voice, not like he wanted to help, but almost to protect himself. Jill said that she had taken two or three sleeping pills that were all. John knows she has had trouble sleeping because sometimes he says to her," Oh why don't you just take a sleeping pill and go to bed?" in a fun-making way. That phrase was never fun to Jill: just a reminder of John's lack of caring for her. Again, John's disbelief, or simply uncaring emotion towards his partner, was expressed in a harsh tone. So Jill says to John, "I feel cold, my skin is cold." "Oh," he said with his hand in a furious motion swaying outward in a half circle away from Jill; he stares for a brief second. This time, Jill thought, she was going to get held in John's arms. But no, no arms, no warmth of his body against hers like she had wanted and needed over the last two years. John says nothing, just leaves the bedroom and that was that for the night.

Jill reached out to her friend Lori. Lori and her husbands crossed this path several times—they just went further with physical actions against each other. Because of two loveless marriages, Lori tried to leave her life and often wished she had done so. Her saving grace was her two sons from the first marriage. Then as Jill went into recovery mode, the two women talked about Lori's husbands and Jill's partner and tried to understand where they went wrong. Their first mistake was choosing the men as a life partners. Seemingly all three were straight, heterosexual men, but one of Lori's was definitely questionable. Jill's guy was a player from his first sexual encounter and Jill still wasn't sure if that included males as well as females. The similarity between Lori's husbands and Jill's partner was their disregard for another person's love for them. Seeking answers through stories traded between them and days of arguing points, they finally agreed on one commonality. Lori and Jill are scared to love a man because most times they seem confused about how to show love and tenderness. Loving is being weak. All three men see the woman as the weaker sex. John saw Jill not as a woman, but as a weaker sex—someone he could push around and overpower. Perfect for John because Jill saw him admire himself too many times in the mirror and the reflection fed his great needy ego.

That week was unexceptional, no different than the past months with two people just co-existing in the same dwelling. Jill could never see inside John's heart or discern any indication that his feelings might be hurt, upset, disappointed, willing to ask for change or ready to take flight. John was just there as filling a space at that time. She does understand why now, what she could not even logically understand then—it was the drugs. That will be explained later. When they were together that week, it was a process, a connection of pieces of things that they had done together in the past. Each evening would start with Jill home alone and eating dinner alone. She stopped waiting for John to come home, because there was no set time anymore. For him it was "I leave and come as I please!" So, Jill held a place on the sofa, always hugging a pillow and watching *Judge Judy* and the continuous half-hour mindless TV programs. She did not need any mental stimulation. Her mind was already overcrowded with thoughts of John and what she could do to fix them once again. Somewhere between 6:30 and 8:00

p.m. John arrived each evening. No smiles when he enters. It was always the same. Max (his perfect male cat) got the niceness, the kisses on the face and the gentle caress of his hand. Jill sat there waiting for her turn to be caressed, but the turn never came. Each day she just became sadder and sadder.

We are all important. No labels should be used, like "just a housewife." Some housewives are discarded in the evenings and sit in panic, their minds trying to discover where love has gone. The housewife today has dual roles to be independent as a career woman and also as a wife. I wonder how many career women come home and still get the same treatment, "You are still just a housewife." Does a woman who meets a previously married man and finds herself dealing with his unusual baggage wonder that if they had they met first, what would life be like if the baggage had never been accumulated? Yes, each situation is different but more likely than not, that person has been changed. Jill wished so much she had met John before he had met Mary or Cheryl—like most of us would in hand-me-down relationships. Sorry, but the clothing has already been worn, the partner, male or female, had already been tainted with different views from their earlier relationships.

Jill has a standing appointment with a GP every Wednesday for allergy shots, one of which was so she could be around cats. Funny how she even manipulated her inner body to accommodate John's wants and needs, like having a cat. Born an asthmatic, it was pure stupidity to live with a cat. The unfortunate part of her life is John never saw himself from the outside, how he chose to do nothing and eventually had nothing for himself, importantly in the process of losing Jill. This Wednesday Jill told her doctor that she was depressed but had no intention of telling him what she had tried to do the previous Sunday. Would you think she would have told him? Jill wanted more sleeping pills and asked for a new prescription. Remember, she had used up her extra reserves and needed to replenish what she might need in the very near future. Jill knew in her heart she was not yet done with herself.

Each evening, like a CD put on continuous play, the week went slowly through its process. Usually from 8 p.m. onwards Jill sat in the big wing-backed chair to the left of John, sort of behind his line of vision. She would always look over at him, with Max the cat wrapped into his left arm on the sofa while he lay on his side, eyes shut and absolutely no conversation. Jill's face felt so long and drooping and without any emotion. Was it anger she was feeling? She didn't even know what her feelings were anymore. She didn't really watch television. She only played the thoughts of her loneliness over and over in her head. Have you ever felt pure, daunting loneliness? It is cruel and, in your mind, there is no escape. The everyday shopping Jill would do on her way home to buy fresh treats for John had stopped. She kept wondering why the fresh pre-cut pineapple was not being eaten anymore. The favorite turkey slices and cheese were getting green with mold. Until now, it never occurred to her that John had stopped taking in any of the pleasures Jill wanted to give him. Now she is discovering that this is a very common occurrence when a partner wants out of a relationship. They stop receiving pleasures and gifts because of their feelings of guilt. In their mind, they know they do not deserve these gifts from you anymore. Should we look at this as, "Thank you to them for withdrawing during our recovery?"

Jill has a very few things to thank John for. She certainly knows that both Lori's husbands did not deserve one thank you. Both were distrusting of Lori and abusive of her overwhelming kindness. Lori had every right to punch a hole in the wall. Quite out of character, but very much a symbol of what each husband deserved.

What bothered Jill most, while watching John lying there, was his still body language. Today all of this makes sense to her, but the person Jill was then seemed closed off to understanding anything. Remembering now, she is saddened that she did not throw herself onto him and hold him tightly. Maybe if she had done that, John would have remembered how much Jill used to mean to him, how much he used to love her and call her Honey! John always lay with his head on a forty-five degree angle, pillows tucked high. You would think one's neck would be contorted out of place, but it was his way of sleeping. Because he was on his left side, his right arm would rest long and stretched out over his torso. That was fine, but it was the hand that gave it all away. It was always cuffed together, not relaxed. Jill would stare at his hand and thought, "This is not normal." Quite true, it was not. It was a sign of uneasiness, decisions to be made, stress, and maybe of not wanting to be where you are at that moment.

Every night Jill would make the offering of, "Would you like something, maybe something sweet or a drink?" John's answers got shorter with less tone in his voice. He didn't want to be bothered. Jill was a nuisance and this scene of family centered evenings was not what he wanted. Watching the clock to reach 10 p.m., her time to go to bed because as a teacher she found she needed to lie down nine hours an evening to survive. Jill went up the stairs, looking back at John. No kiss anymore, a grunt of a good night and into the pills she went willingly. Jill was up to four Ativans of two milligrams each a night in order to go to sleep and still she would wake up in the middle of the night. Brushing her teeth or any hygiene before going to bed had stopped. She just did not care. No one cared about her, so why should she care about herself! Sometimes, lying in bed she could smell her own body odor. Even that would keep her awake because inside she knew she was failing herself.

Saturday, November 28 finally arrived and the week's cycle of uneasiness was broken. Needless to say, Jill woke up and was very hesitant to go downstairs. She was never quite sure what she would find that would cause her more pain. Usually the blue light was still lit on the DVD player, which meant John had watched porn half the night after Jill went to bed or there would an empty beer bottle resting near the sofa, in arm's reach. Of course Jill would have asked about what she saw around him in the living room in the morning but only asked that question once long ago. She learned that there is only so much verbal badgering one person can take without feeling abandoned by God's interception.

As the saying goes, off to the market Jill treads, just to get away. To make her stay even longer away from the house, she called his niece to go shopping, for nothing. She also called John to tell him she would be longer and to let his niece say Hello to him on the phone. On purpose, because if she didn't do that, John would assume she was out playing around. He never gave her any trust.

Do you know what it feels like not to be trusted? Everything you do, you try to justify and prove that you are telling the truth.

Within the hour John called her on her cell. "Oh Jill, I just got a call from work and they need me this afternoon to be on-call and now I have to go. I will or should be back before dinner." What could Jill do but believe that was what was happening? And yes, that was what she believed again.

Jill pulled into the driveway behind his car. It was dinner time and still daylight. She was surprised to see his car home but pleased. The

Live in the Present and Learn Valuable Life Lessons to Improve Any Relationship

thing is, until they interacted when in each other's presence, Jill was always pleased to see John. She always wanted to be near him and feel him near. Every moment of every day she lived in a dream that they were a family and happy to live life as one. And every day, she would be put down, destroyed like a Canadian ice breaker crushing through the heavy ice off Greenland to make passage for another new ship to sail. She didn't understand then that John was making a passage way to bring in new life and replace her.

Outside on the front veranda John fiddled with Jill's new GPS in hand and says it is a good time to install it while there is still daylight. Jill agreed, and was very happy to see his big smile again. He got in the car on the driver's side. It would be easier for him because the power outlet, etc. was near the steering column. Jill jumped happily into the passenger seat to watch, thinking they were doing something together. You should have seen her face, elated with joy. You still do not realize how much she loves John. With a huge lump now residing in her throat, she remembered what had happened and was not surprised. The usual, she asked him how work was and where did he have to go. John happily said, "Out to the west of the city and that traffic was bad again today." Prodding as she had learned to do and wished she could have stopped this action, she went on to say how great now that John had some overtime money. His reply was in short and quick words, "No, there was no overtime for today." Puzzled, Jill did not say another word. Then John leaned towards Jill to reach the dangling cord from the GPS, and then Jill knew. There was that odor, and the closer John got, it was all over his face, neck, and even sweaty shirt. John wasn't at work, but at play. A few days ago, in snoop mode, Jill found chats in the cache of the second computer she bought for the house for John. This lady was discussing a possible meeting and raunchy sex for the weekend with none other than John. The happy smile and giddy approach to the task of installing his GPS was not real but came from the inducement of a small pill ingested earlier for his previous party. For numerous times Jill was still blinded by a few pleasant words that started this conversation today. She hurt inside when she thought of the number of couples who endure this type of lifestyle. For her it was easy to see John cheating in their relationship. The stories, over a beer, that John told her of his ex being at home and he supposedly on a business trip while in fact he was out cheating, made it all believable to Jill. Inside, you could see John had quite the laugh when one story entailed his missing wallet that a barmaid hooker, who he was charming, lifted his wallet. He had to call his ex and claim the wallet was lost and please would she wire money to pay his bills and a trip home. It was quite an amusing story to hear him tell it with a smile on his face and almost laughing. Except for his X, who never believed his stories even though he seemed to become good at telling them? Is it true, once a cheater always a cheater? I tend to see it is true.

While sitting in that front seat, can you even imagine where Jill's heart went at that moment? That front passenger seat became a prison cell with the door shut, window closed, and John within inches of her. This became a typical outcome of the day for them. John accuses her of cheating as soon as she leaves the house to do their chores that John never participated in because John used this time as his opportunity to cheat. Jill is literally running out of descriptors to tell us how she felt. Jill did not say anything about her observation and even now it hurts. No, even now it is painful. Sometimes Jill thinks she is not a woman because she never took the chance to truly stand up to John. This was yet another opportunity to make him aware that what was happening was only going to cause Jill to retaliate by doing the same. She had to get out of the car. Because it was a sunny day and the car was black, it was quite warm inside sitting in the black leather seats. What does all that do to someone who is struggling to wire a piece of equipment, it makes them sweat! The now pungent odor of another woman's smell on her partner was unbearable. And to make it worse, John was talking nicely to her, smiling, and making normal conversation. Why does Jill get what she needs as closeness from the one she loves by him cheating with another woman? Because of his guilt after cheating, John always gives Jill the attention she desires.

Jill felt like the housewife who, after eleven years of an okay marriage, finally gets her recognition when suddenly she is surprised by a very oversized bouquet of flowers arriving from her husband while he mouths the words, "I missed you today and thought only of you!" With a huge smile and a kiss on his cheek, she goes away to arrange her guilt-ridden gift in a vase and begins to water them with tears from her swollen eyes because her intuition about the cheating is now confirmed. Jill held back her tears as well and instead became nauseated and felt a rush go through her face. She had to leave even though for once she was being close in conversation with John. A familiar reaction for her was yet another lump in her throat that was so choking she could not speak. It was like lack of hydration which was her excuse to run and get a glass of water. She jumped from the car.

John tends to chase and conquer women these days leaving a loving partner at home, with no guilt. For Jill it was and still is all about real loving contact. It is not part of who they are as a couple to take on a dominant character role to embellish the weaker partner, as most believe this is what a couple would do in a rocky relationship. There is more dominance in a heterosexual relationship most of the times when the marriage begins to break down. Definitely this was true in John's own marriage with Cheryl. The dog with his tail between his legs was a daily routine for him. Cheryl made him so afraid of her walking out on him that he would have done anything. Funny, Cheryl walked one day even still.

Life living lesson: Are we having the act of sex or truly making love to each other? Does one or both as a couple forget intimacy?

We need to talk about "the act of sex" and "making love" to develop a healthy, deeper relationship with the person you are intimate. We have gone from marriage for life, to common law co-habitants, long term relations (LTR), a commitment to be together in some form, casual sex, friends with benefits, bi-curious not bisexual and uninhibited sexual actions in the performance of your sexual desires.

A male having sex has quite an impact on his health. The question though, "As a couple, any couple, is it okay for the male or female to have self pleasure on their own by themselves without the help or stimulation of their partner." Let's call it self-satisfaction/pleasure. And as the male or female of action, do you keep this information hidden from your partner? Always, there will be something that will give away your secret. And do you apologize for the extras you need to feel sexually complete? If you do, the other partner feels that as a couple you shouldn't need self-satisfaction. Even though having sex is limited, there is not much love-making, you question, "Am I enough for you and our relationship?" What is your response? Are you feeling it is okay? You probably have a higher libido, different urges to satisfy. You can always say, "At least I kept it at home and did not go out for someone else to satisfy my needs." Do you think there is going to be a positive reaction to your personal one-on-one? This is not going to happen! The biggest issue is that your partner will feel that they are not enough for you, and they will feel a bit betrayed, like they have failed in the relationship, or that you have deserted the relationship especially in time of need for more intimacy. Your partner may say, "There is no problem here because I was only thinking of you, dear." When you satisfy your sexual need and keep it hidden from your partner so as not to hurt them because your libido is stronger, can the problem be simply solved? Or is it even a problem if one partner needs to pleasure themselves? Talk about what are each other's needs as completion of sexual gratification.

It is not common to find two people with the exact same libido and the same feelings of satisfaction when you have sex. One issue I will call "the mistake" is the time after sex. You need to lie beside each other in some form of closeness, even holding each other's hand, sharing the same pillow or a genuine kiss somewhere on the other's body. Form a sense of intimacy. Secure your bond that keeps both partners feeling loved as who they are, and not that it was just sex and off to the shower.

Sexual excitement and the finale orgasm release hormones that overpower your pain threshold. Jill has a hyper mobile disk problem, meaning a disc can move anytime, in any direction it chooses. The result is she experiences back pain almost 24/7. But, during sex, no matter what position she is thrown in, she does not notice any pain. Try explaining that to a partner who has trouble believing you ever have any pain, and their belief is that it is only in your head. As a result, there is no winning with this one.

You can make and feel very secure if not all body parts are responding. But sex for a guy, you cannot fake. Sex is all about the erection and its longevity. Should you worry if your partner during sex begins to go limp? Is that an indication of lack of interest, boredom or it may be the wrong timing for one partner. Not everybody is always on the same page of desire. Remember, there are a lot of factors involved in a man having an erection. As said earlier, stress in it self. You may have had a hard day that plays on your thoughts. I am not saying thought is predominant, meaning you have to think sex for it to be good or great! It certainly helps if you are relaxed and committed to the enjoyment of your partner, even in casual sex. As an example, it has been three years into your relationship and your partner is seldom physically aroused, not responding to your emitted efforts of arousal. Should you worry that something is wrong? Could it be you or him? If you see your sexual relationship still just as sex without loving attachment or intimacy, where do you begin to place ownership in talking and solving what may be an obvious problem? I like to place this issue on its owner, the one with the obvious physical lack of intimacy. However if they are not a communicator, you have a bigger problem with them being unable to open up and discuss an issue. It will only get worse; you will only become tense and over-think, causing further dissention between your partner and yourself. Over-thinking this problem leads to analyzing every little movement and spoken word. Please do not analyze anything in your relationship. Use open communication with calm and explanations until you both leave the conversation with the knowledge needed for understanding each other for who you are as a person.

What is your style of sex? Is it pure lust, non-attachment from one to the next (the one-night stander), quick and move on, or a loving Sunday afternoon forgetting the present? Is your loved one definitely afraid of commitment to one person? This one you have to be careful of when you have this knowledge and you want them to be yours only; most often you cannot teach an old dog a new trick. In this case, when they do come home late too often, your first thoughts are of whom were they spending time with?

Some of the above are simply sexless emotions. That is a little coldhearted. Is that what you have been receiving in the bedroom? If this is your partner, take off the horse blinders you are wearing. Wake up and run for advice from those who know you both, or find partnership therapy. And if you feel like the sexual part of your relationship is forced upon you, rough play with only their pleasure, again it is you who has to change the situation. If every time you are together and in your mind there is confusion regarding, "Did we just have sex or did we make love?" it is a terrible place to be. Ask yourself if it is playing tricks on you, over-analyzing again. Then go for the heart, their heart, checking if there are things done by them that show love to you. These issues will not go away unless you approach and discuss them and be honest. Rely on your respect you should have developed for each other to help you get through these conversations.

More often than not, gay men have casual sex while in a drunken stupor or high on the drug flavor of the day. The next day brings the lack of memory, was it good sex? Did we play safe? Should I worry? I am confused as to why we still knowingly put ourselves in this situation. You need always to have safe sex. Does that mean no sex? Knowing that will not happen, be smart and educate yourself. If you are too embarrassed to seek information from local clinics there is always the internet, which is probably more up-to-date. Casual sex is more difficult for a woman. Attachment is easily formed and days later, day dreaming of what could be overtakes her mind.

Sex with someone new is always a turn-on, even if it is very quick sex. There are no barriers like being on the same level, liking the same dinner menu or type of friends or better yet, meet any relatives. However, because there is no connection, sex has a very good chance of being terrible? It is probably totally selfish definitely for one partner, leaving one without total satisfaction. Drop and roll. You can feel very lonely and empty; you do not get the hugs you need; and forget about a meaningful conversation.

Passion in sex, does it only have to be with a committed partner or can you throw passion in to one-nighters, a quickie or with a casual encounter? Passion is part of the sexual act that emits strong devotion to the person you desire and is filled with a warmth and deep emotion. Usually, if your passion resides in one of the above and not in a full loving relationship, then when you finally meet the one, can you give and feel the right passion with this new love? Will you have commitment issues partly due to your own confusion of passion used so casually and so often with many different sexual partners? Passion goes hand-in-hand with being committed. Statistics show that passion in a new relationship should last without question continuously for the first year plus.

You cannot believe how good your sex life fits into your expectations of a partnership if you hold onto the passion. Better yet, each time is practice time, like the football coach starting a new season. Sorry, there are no lessons for you on how to perform or feel passion. It comes from within because of the excitement and enthusiasm you have for your sexual partner which one hopes is the relationship partner. The sex will keep getting better and feel great because the right touch is recognized by your partner.

Turn the Discovery Channel on and see yourselves experiencing life. The penguins are having the time of their lives, jumping from ice patty to ice patty through the chilling waters for a swim. Be playful and know your partner's limits. Never play the game of, "I will hold off for a couple of days and then it will be volcanic." That may work in the beginning of a relationship. Holding off after the first year has quite a different interpretation. The first appears as not being that you are not interested in your partner. At the same time, your partner wonders if they are already unappealing. The spinoff is like looking for a job in the business sector. Do you know how many roads you can take there? Hundreds! The same if you play with another's emotions about sex. The mind plays dirty tricks, and usually not in your favor. You may think you are being mischievous, but your partner sees it as a peculiarity of your behavior. Your trick very quickly looks like deception and becomes harmful to the relationship.

Sex can leave you with multiple scars. I mean emotionally and/or medically. If there is enough chemistry for the two to connect sexually, one for sure will feel an emotion of attachment. This might be expressed as the need to exchange emails, Face book, Twitter, whatever falls into play for you after your first meet. Be partly aware that the other person may want to simply move on to the other person. And, the first words from a cheater during sex are "Do not leave any marks on me." It is at times like this I would love to bruise away, especially where it is impossible to be bruised by accident. Once I met a man cheating on his wife with men who immediately said, "No markings." Apparently, never wearing a t-shirt to bed with his wife before, he now was compelled to do so for a week while sleeping with his wife. His wife never bothered to ask any questions about this, and then the t-shirt disappeared again. The question is, why would a partner ignore such an obvious clue? She did not want to go there to confront the issue, but kept her eyes closed, hoping what she knew would all go away. This will not go away, but instead will get worse.

That is the physical scar, but do not exclude the mental, emotional/feelings scars. Oh, you find yourself needing to tell the friends, co-workers about the latest tawdry sex encounter! That could mean you are placing too much of an emotional attachment to one-nighters; or maybe you lack self-esteem and confidence in your sex appeal. Maybe your tales are a way of self-improvement, your own therapy to build up those lacking issues in your character. Keep your casuals where they belong. Most times you are judged as having no conscience and thinking with your privates. The worst outcome is you feel an attachment to this person which you need to put it in the right perspective, we were together sexually and for now that is the only connection.

No matter. Emotionally, one of you will want a repeat of sex, now confused with little scraps of love. Beware—most likely the other does not, and you are in a place too many times with too many casuals that can bring you pain. How many times do you think someone needs to recover from casual encounter sex? Too many! Actually there should be none. If you are choosing casual players, you need to adopt the mindset that needs to be attached to this scenario. If this is you, learn your lesson, free sex is just that, and you cannot be emotionally involved. If it is too hot in the kitchen for you, then get out of the kitchen.

The casual sex partner has everything on your list that you need: visible chemistry. But the sex is bad and you are faking/pretending it is the wow factor. You do this because at first the other person seemed to represent a part of you. Everyone would like to make out with themselves, it is a fantasy most people imagine but never admit. Do not continue in a rut of boredom, neither one of you deserves that treatment. Pointer: do not call out the sex partners name during sex if it is lousy. Calling out a name means you are really into it and do not stop. If it is bad, finish it quickly and say it was too much for me, sorry next time. Immediately they grab your clothes for you, offer no shower, while standing with your clothes in their hands waiting for you to get dressed. A message is here for you to observe. Smile and leave. Do not bother asking for a phone number. In their eyes, you are lousy at sex or there's a realization they are not as appealing as you first thought.

If you find that sex was great at once and now you are bored with the same person, a huge message abounds for you to learn. How do you think we came up with casual sex? For now, you are not a lover, the forever twenty-fifth anniversary partner. You are more of a player in your own game of sex and emotional attachment than you may realize. You have not lost your niche in personal sexual pleasure, passion and making love with your partner. For some this is all they want, but for the person who wants to find it all and cannot, it becomes a yearning, a deep emptiness. For most this gradually evolves as each anniversary passes. But is the male or female at risk of feeling empty sexually. Let's talk about the controller in sex, the one that takes control or believes he has the power and authority to control every move or action during your love making. He thinks he is running a business and every "I" must be dotted and everything accountable. This is not a partner for anyone. He even wishes to control your orgasm making it timed with his and that is not an easy accomplishment. If it does not happen, he has made you feel like a failure.

The safest sex is no sex. If you are the constant worrier about STIs or STDs then you will never enjoy sex unless it is with a committed partner and there is full trust. Casual sex will drive you into stress mode every time you walk away. Educate yourself fully from a reliable source until you feel comfortable with sex. HIV cannot live very long outside the body, so you really cannot get it through casual contact; such as shaking hands, hugging, giving blood, using hot tubs, public toilets, doorknobs or water fountains. And the only thing you can get from mosquitoes is west Nile virus, not HIV. Very simple, always practice safer sex and do not share needles and syringes. A very good friend of John's was one of these people. Every three months he would panic and run for a HIV test. Finally, he said I wish I were positive then I would not have to worry anymore. The next time we spoke, he was exactly that, leaving me to believe that it had been done on purpose. But ignorance here has left him having to be even more careful during sex if he has any conscience at all not to infect another person.

Casual sex has brought us new terms, like, "friends with benefits," "bi-curious," and "bi-sexual." The friend with benefits is a nicer way to say it. Bi-curious is the buzz for younger people who are experiencing sex with the same sexual orientation. I hear many young girls are now bi-curious and have no qualms discussing it openly. I do not believe again any term will take away a possible attachment with the other person involved. The risk is no different for stirring up emotions.

After an evening of memorable sex and we wake up feeling empty it is because there was no intimacy shared. The sex did not satisfy the inner need of affection and our own belief that all we wanted was sex is not true. It becomes two self-centered people gratifying self-satisfaction. You can have instant hot chocolate by pouring hot water on chocolate powder, but genuine love and intimacy cannot be instant. Why then do we sacrifice our emotions, mental, social and spiritual selves for the physical attachment? And especially men, our problem is that we want instant gratification, the need to defeat the urge. I believe as men what we really want is not sex. What we really want is intimacy, afraid as most of us can be, and as men we may think of this as being only part of a couple's relationship. Intimacy means total life sharing, a closeness, for sharing our life with someone completely.

Marshall Hodge wrote a book called *Your Fear of Love*. If you have problems with understanding love you should read this book. In it he says, "We long for moments of expressions of love, closeness and tenderness, but frequently, at the critical point, we often draw back. We are afraid of closeness. We are afraid of love." I will talk about hurt and pain in our lives and to be truly in love you have pain. The closer you come to someone, the greater potential there is for pain. We all build walls around our hearts to protect us from anyone settling in, taking up residence. Once in as a renter and it is winter time and you hurt the landlord by not paying the rent, he cannot evict you because of the laws. Can you evict someone you care about from your heart? But tearing down the walls of your heart leaves you lonely sometimes and confused in finding intimacy and love. There is a line to begin in tearing down your wall. Keep it straight and not cracked, for cracks never repair to look the same. You need to find that line and allow people to cross it. Share your space, share your life.

Yes, you now are in love. Two anonymous quotes: "True love burns the brightest, but the brightest flames leave the deepest scars." And "It is impossible to fall out of love. Love is such a powerful emotion, that once it envelops you it does not depart."

True love is eternal. If you think that you were once in love, but fell out of it, then it wasn't love you were in. There are no "exit" signs in love; there is only an "on ramp." God describes love in great detail in the Bible, especially in the Book of First Corinthians, chapter 13: verses 4-7. God's message is so simple: "Patience, kindness, non self-seeking, truthful, a protector, and trusting, always hoping for your good. Love is patient. Love is kind. Love is not jealous or boastful; it is not arrogant or rude. Love does not insist on its own way; it is not irritable or resentful; it does not rejoice at wrong but rejoices in the right. Love bears all things, believes all things, hopes all things, and endures all things. Love never ends." First Corinthians 13:14

Is the feeling of being in love a sickness? If you have the 'flu and your stomach hurts and you have a headache, all you do is focus and dwell on your symptoms. If you cannot stop thinking about him wherever you are, with friends or working, then you better consider that you may be falling in love. Actions as a result of your symptoms, love-sickness, a little nervous, daydreaming of the possibilities and unfocused in thought could lead to a minor depression. Can this be you falling in love? You need to find out whether he has the same mutual feelings and you are officially in love. Now you can live with your doors of life open. Allow your behavior freely to show intense feelings of affection and emotions.

Love has many forms, and I trust you can find all of these combined in your relationship, like a perfectly made black forest cake. You need passion, the sexual desire; emotional intimacy, sharing your emotions and feelings openly; commitment, both desiring for this relationship to work; reciprocation, mutual love for each other; attachment, you can each satisfy each other's basic needs; and finally affection, you appreciate having each other in your life. Love therefore can be defined as a mixture of various emotions and experiences related to a sense of both parties' strong affection to be complete as one. Not lust, but love!

In the gay culture I can quite assuredly say those who immediately fall in love have it confused with lust. The two are very similar from a hormonal viewpoint. Men unfortunately use their heads too often for sex and not their hearts, hence lust overpowers their behavior. Lust becomes blinding in the sense that sex becomes dangerous. Once a man starts to think only with his testosterone, then the idea of safe sex and caution may be tossed aside. His brain is focused on self-satisfaction. But to build a lasting relationship and to share your lives living together, you need love. There is a very simple answer for everyone in the complicated confusions of life.

Here are some memorable quotes on love:

> *"True love doesn't come to you it has to be inside you."* (Julia Roberts).
> **Roberts, Julia:Thinkexist. Retrieved February 2012, from http://thinkexist.com/quotation/true-love-doesn-t-come-to-you-it-has-to-be-inside/383469.html**

> *"Grow old with me; the best is yet to be."* (Robert Browning). Browing, Robert: Bing. Retrieved February 2012 from http://www.bing.com/search?q=%E2%80%9CGrow+old+with+me%3B+the+best+is+yet+to+be.%E2%80%9D+%28Robert+Browning%29.&src=IE-SearchBox&Form=IE8SRC

> *"The way to love anything is to realize it might be lost."* (G.K. Chesterton).
> **Chestron, G. K. Thinkexist. Retrieved February 2012 from http://thinkexist.com/search/searchquotation.asp?search=%93Grow+old+with+**

me%3B+the+best+is+yet+to+be.%94+%28Robert+Browning%29.+

*"What a grand thing, to be loved! What a grander thing still, to love!"(*Victor Hugo).
Hugo, Victor Hugo, V. Thinkexist. Retrieved February 2012 from http://thinkexist.com/search/searchquotation.asp?search=%93What+a+grand+thing%2C+to+be+loved%21+What+a+grander+thing+still%2C+to+love%21%94%28Victor+Hugo%29

Is love more powerful than sex? Love is a deep emotion, therefore it is more powerful. Love is an ineffable feeling of affection and solicitude toward a person, such as the recognition of others' attractive qualities. It is the true desire to be one with that other person. You have the need to attach and embrace that person, hold them and caress them softly. Watch out for the romantic love where you feel an emotional high. The saying, love is blind, represents romantic love. It is more of an infatuation that can last for years but will fail when each become critical of one another, become easily irritated at things that did not bother them before, lack patience with each other, and detach mentally at first by not caring about the other's wants and feelings. "Romantic love is one of the most powerful of all human experiences, it is definitely more powerful than the sex drive, and rejected men in societies around the world sometimes kill themselves or someone else", says a study by Helen Fisher, an anthropologist at Rutgers University.

What is the difference between having sex and making love? Date night, a night on the prowl and making love or having sex. Prom night and the final goodbye to high school lead most young people into promiscuity.

Unfortunately, some men clue in to their sex partner's desire that they need to hear the word love before having sex and that word becomes used very freely. For you that need love, remember, the beginning is just sex. It is quite possible to make love and not think of it as having sex. Sex can be the ultimate act of love because when you love someone so much you can share all your fantasies and complete trust. And it is possible to be making love and not have sex; simply by giving that look, a teasing, a naughty smile or a pleasurable touch. It just has to be the right two people.

Is there any point in making love? Most men confuse love, commitment, and sex, or assume they are all one. There are many ways to express love, and you do not need to have sex. Plus, having sex with someone does not mean you love them, either. Therefore, sexual relationships work best when both are very clear about what they are looking for at this moment. Having sex in a committed relationship can make anyone—especially women—feel closer, like best friends and drop the ego barrier. Back to friends with benefits, having sex in a non-committed relationship can be just simply fun and improve your friendship. But with all this said, it is very important that you like, respect and trust the person you are with and that you yourself feel liked, respected and trusted by them.

What about those who are addicted to love? Unless they are in a love affair their neediness is left unsatisfied. Love-addicted people have a belief of personal unworthiness, which results in choosing the wrong partner, usually one that fears intimacy. Romance and relationship addicts lack their own sense of spirituality and look for their identity in the one they chose to love. This addictive behavior causes them to avoid accepting their personal responsibility for failure, giving them a lack of intimacy with their partner. If this is you, read Anne Wison Schaef's *Escape from Intimacy, Untangling the Love Addictions: Sex Romance, Relationships*. This book describes how the role of "love" addictions is the belief of personal unworthiness.

Does the love of your life create pain in your life? And why do you have this need to accept pain? You obviously care more for him and his happiness then for yourself. You will do everything just to hear the word, "Honey." And do you know when that word is spoken it may truly mean, "I love you!" but do not second guess. You do realize that you cannot change your partner; the spots of a leopard will always remain the same. The best way for you is the need to accept that your relationship is all love. Real love, a pure love, is not about any pain or hurt. It is about a continued partnership of interrelating between the two of you on all your issues, caring and nurturing.

We need to see "having sex" and "making love" make a healthy, deep relationship with the person with whom you are intimate.

End of life Living lesson: Are we having just the act of sex or truly making love to each other? Does one or both as a couple forget Intimacy?

Life living lesson: From birth, our brain is a library of our life. There is no eraser for our memory!

Our mind is the true origin of consciousness within ourselves, and we have the freedom to make our perceptions real. If our thoughts are overpowering our life experiences at that moment, maybe the workings of the brain are out of order, and in medical science, the hypothesis of consciousness and space-time explain consciousness in describing a "a space of conscious elements."

Each one of us creates the meaning of our life; life is not determined by the God in any religion, or by an earthly authority like a partner. One is absolutely free with their mind. As an individual, you should see your life as being full of action, freedom, and decisions. In your relationship you need to see your purpose, your personality that is given the purpose of a human being to live life, therefore fulfillment of your life. It is your ability and responsibility to lead an ethical life of personal fulfillment, self-interest and a common good for you and your partner. Your happiness is based on you and how you interlink with your partner and the social relationships around you.

At many times, like my own, there is too much partnership turmoil bubbling in your brain and you ask, "What is the meaning of my life with this person?" There are many therapeutic responses to this question. For example Viktor Frankl argues for "Dereflection," which largely translates as ceasing to endlessly reflect on the self, instead of engaging in life. On the whole, the therapeutic response is that the question of meaning of life evaporates if one is fully engaged in life. The question then morphs into more specific worries such as "What delusions am I under?" "What is blocking my ability to enjoy things?" "Why do I neglect loved ones?

From my personal perspective, I see my mind as a library that creates the meaning of life for me and affects all those who interact with me, continuously or not. The three questions above have very daunting memories from my first encounters and still haunt me. If you fit one of these, it means your free will to have a one hundred percent loving relationship will be constantly challenged and this will impact on your partner. Giving it serious thought, one day in a library, I realized my mind is a fully stacked library with empty rooms down the pathways.

The definition of a library is a collection of sources, resources, and services, and the structure in which it is housed; it is organized for use and maintained sometimes by a private individual. My mind is a collection of useful material for my common good (sense) and definitely maintained by myself. However, sometimes I have no control over what is shelved in there, or even the source. Remember, you cannot control your partner, and some actions or words get curve balled into your memory banks by them and are there to stay.

Using the analogy that your mind is a library, we can see that all memories and thoughts are arranged in there. With no library classification system our mind churns through its shelves of memories. We have created hidden rooms in our minds to store needed reference agenda when required. Every present particle of every moment, we collect and circulate in our mind and reference it into a storage location. Even when we bring a memory forward in thought, we then have to re-shelve that material in its rightful place, done as if put in the correct library classification order.

Our mind keeps us informed of what is available for use as a machine, part in a machine or recollection as needed to tell a story. Our memory banks are made up of raw data absorbed and pieced together in our mind to become information and stored as knowledge. Most of us have common sense and are able to function this way accessing knowledge at the split second required. But then there is the term "scatter brain." Not sure why, but this person is inept in categorizing information. Their resources of thought are scattered everywhere and quite easily seem lost at times in a conversation, particularly in an argument. This is the perfect mate for a partner who loves to give verbal abuse and be in control. Someone who is unable to think as fast as they do and left speechless and non-argumentative, allows them to have exactly what they desire. In Buddhism it is taught that one makes decisions with your heart and absorbs data only with the brain. I have been trying to rationalize this and have come to the solution that this is true. That is why it is so difficult for me to make any decision. And those of you with great minds, you do not argue back because of the emotional hurt, actually sickening. Start to take back your life.

A lot of verbal abuse for me originated from my stories. Should we speak of all our past to our new partner? Unfortunately, unless you are good at it, selective conversation can be easily detected. When your partner says, "Come on now, tell it all. Why are you holding out on me?" say nothing. Are you lying by not divulging all your past, laying out the manuscript as if on display at a museum for all to read? My advice is, get that thought out of your mind. Doing this is easier than the argument that will come from that information later on in your relationship. Those partners, who like to abuse, relish that freedom of information you pile on them like a stack of fire wood ready to burn. By opening up all of your past you turn your previous unwelcomed experiences into new ones, providing them with more power because they have your weaknesses on tap. Keep past memories stacked on a cobwebbed shelf. Set your brain-mind into sections and subsections of memory. I actually visualize closing and locking a door in a long hallway of information that need not to be repeated. I see file boxes pulled down, placing pictures inside like a memory box carefully placed in the family shelving. I take photographic pictures by staring at what I want to remember, blink my eyes slowly and open, focusing that memory stored in my mind. It works, try it on for yourself. There is a sad side to this process and that is the pictures I have of emotional fights; memories of watching from the window my partner sitting in the backyard, calm and peaceful. At this very moment I cannot help but sit here and cry like a baby. Because I see those pictures and it hurts. Oh dear God, I miss him now, please help me.

Sometimes it is not so easy to retrieve complete information from our mind. If it was a hurtful argument, we tend to bury details because the memory is too painful. The mind accepts all information from around you from various senses: seeing, smelling, touching, hearing and taste. Any one of these can trigger a thought that was long buried, especially unwanted situations you were in with your partner. Too often this has happened to me, and it is amazing how you activate a dream, new reasoning and experience emotions all over again. All of your memory functioning is coordinated, controlled and regulated by your brain. Do you have control over your brain? You do have some control over what place you will physically be in acquiring data and therefore some control over the information that unconsciously packs itself in your mind. Be happy and be present, and the future will unfold as it is meant to be.

To love, does the quality of your mind, personality and intelligence matter? To have a productive argument, you need intelligence and common sense. Different people will react to the same experience differently. Hence, you and a partner can experience the same event, but show totally different reactions. Will that start an argument? Most likely! It is in our nature, our genes to react a certain way, for example, to death. If you do not show the emotion of crying and your partner is a basket case, he wonders what stone you are made from. And it is very hard to have another person understand, especially if the educational level and cultural norms are different. These factors will play havoc on one's mind and leave us full of questions about the one we love.

How much understanding do you expect? I see myself sitting in the doctor's office listening to a small child crying after yet another needle to protect him against diseases. Quick, someone give me a needle! Protect me please from the diseases of society: the hate, the torment, the never-understanding of my loved one's questioning. A small child's cry begins to turn into a whining. Definitely not sure of why he even began to cry, followed by what sounds like choking. When do you begin to realize why you are crying? When do you begin to know yourself, your thoughts and that others need to understand you?

End of Life living lesson: From birth, our brain is a library of our life. There is no eraser for our memory!

SECTION TWO

CHAPTER FOUR

Sunday, November 29, 2007, 11:30 p.m.

This is an outline explaining all the notes keyed on Jill's computer up to Sunday, November 29, 2007.

Sunday was the ultimate argument. John was in a rage and nothing would stop him from hurting Jill. The drugs had taken over his mind; his lack of co-operation for any relationship indicated again that there was no love for Jill, no relationship.

On December 1st Jill, in the stupor of knowing this was the end that she did not want to accept, began to note down her thoughts to try and understand—a form of self-therapy. She felt she needed to write because all was perched and hanging by a little branch. Jill believed these writings were a way to release the heaviness in her mind and to seek solutions to this challenging relationship. This form of therapy can help anyone. Sometimes it provides answers because you can see much clearer.

However, if Jill had not made these notes, what happened that night could have been avoided. John managed to read these private thoughts and this pushed him even further making him even less willing to understand what Jill needed from him as a partner. Jill knew John was reading her computer. Maybe Jill wanted an end. After all, she saw no way out.

Do we do things subconsciously to prevent danger, pain and hurt? The article on Pain and Hurt may help you answer this question for yourself. For Jill, it was a way to help the end speed forward.

After Jill went to bed, it did not take long for John to snoop around whatever information he could retrieve from Jill's computer, as he did every night. Jill saved her thoughts to a memory USB. But John transferred them over into the hard drive and kept the USB. Maybe if John had not read Jill's notes they would still be together today, but in what form? Most likely someone would have been physically hurt. Jill's thoughts and desperation to speak out are claimed by John to be the root cause for their end.

Does scribbling on a note pad of the pros and cons to seek the answer to an important decision actually jump off the page? If so, is it necessarily the right answer or did your eye just catch that line as you asked the question to yourself? The real answers are in your heart. They say most decisions are made from the heart. So "Stick to your guns," as they advised a long time ago.

These notes were all found on the C Drive—Second computer in the dining room downstairs. They are the notes that "Bottled Capped John's Decision"—all Sunday, November 29th. They were found on Tuesday, December 1st, 2007 after he was taken away.

Note 1, Folder 1-Monday, November 16, 2007
Note 2, Folder 2-Wednesday, November 18, 2007
Note 3, Folder 3-Sunday, November 29, 2007

Note 1—Folder 1 created November 16, 2007, notes.

Read by John after she went to bed that evening.

Have to place some thoughts on paper before I drive myself insane with them. Jill was trying to help herself.

Today again, without any guilt or remorse, John stands before me saying that he is the "white angel" and I am to blame for all of what is wrong. There is no-one to help me. I want to get help but not even my doctor sees my pleas for my worsening health caused by our relationship. It has left me with one of my worst days at school around the students and staff. The day was spent with a very long face reflecting empty beliefs and no help just depression.

Last evening, when he returned from his weekend away at his actual home, John returns and enters the doorway with tons of kisses for his cat, Max, holding his head so gently cupped between his hands. Soft spoken words of love are shared with Max followed by kisses, then John gently caresses Max before he walks away, heading up the stairs. Yes, I was on the phone about three feet away sitting on the sofa when you entered the house and Max was perched on the arm of the sofa to see his Daddy. We have a lot to learn from our pets or further abroad, the animal kingdom. Maybe I should have been perched there as well and see what attention I would have received. Well, I was not sitting by the door because I knew it would be another stroke of pain to add to my depression. I was speaking with Lori, who is very aware of all my disgust in every part of my life. I want to continue talking but I decided to end the conversation. Afraid of what is next, I yell up the stairs three times "Hello!" Down the stairs he advanced angrily and he starts in, "You have no commitment to me and us." Joanne, his accountant, has returned his taxes for 2005 and he now owes $2,800, and it is all because of me. He filed as common-law spouse without discussing it with me. He went and did it and now he wants to claim one third of this house as his office. First, I cannot believe he would owe that much money just because he could not claim this house. I tried to explain, he has made not one red penny of payments towards any expenses in this house. So, I feel it is illegal to claim it as his office. "Well, Jill you are not so legal." His face is blackened, another new image that has evolved, and scares me into "fight or flight." The obvious, I take flight in the form of being quiet with something very strange happening inside my whole body. When anxious or experiencing a fright, everyone gets an instant feeling of heaviness in the chest. However, for me it has become lightning bolts that start in the left side of my brain and moves slowly through my heart, not my chest, and continues into my stomach. This truly is a weird feeling for anyone and very difficult for a doctor to understand. I get the response from specialists and with many shakes of their heads, "Jill, I do not know why you have pains in your head!" John without hesitation, very belligerently says, "Look at all the medical claims you put through on my insurance." Now, get it straight. I cannot think as fast as him as to why that did not sound right. Today, in my predominate state of thinking about John's lack of love, I realized why I feel I am right. He pays for me as a dependent as well me paying for him as a dependent on the insurances. That makes it right and not illegal. There are no more evenings, none of the companionship that I desperately need from him, yes, from him. Even with the way he treats me, I want a hug filled with passion and warmth. My mind is so weakened. Please, please hug me and stop being this way to me. Can you not see? Open your eyes as to how much I love you! Again, he repeats as always, "All I have is my daughters and you, honey". With such disregard for me and lack of wanting me in any form, why would he call me "honey"? Oh, dear God, please never let another man call me "Honey". I will cringe and with a motionless expression begin to cry. That new person I will meet one day, rightfully so, will think what a mess this woman is and will run, far.

So now I set up my computer desk to show if someone has been snooping around it, looking for evidence that I am unfaithful or even doing drugs, as I am accused of every week. A user of substance often projects their actions onto someone else, usually the one they love. This way they feel guiltless or they give themselves a true reason to do drugs. Oh yes, I made a huge mistake telling John I found his playmates links and substance abusers chat files on the upstairs computer. He is now very busy erasing all history daily on that computer. I owned both computers and even his daughters when visiting here asked why I allow her dad to take over everything. They are certainly too young to understand and I never communicated with them anything negative about their dad. I regret that decision now. It probably also has something to do with Cheryl and being unable to take what he felt belonged to him. When I asked him about all the things on my desk that have been physically moved, now knowing for sure he was searching my computer, his quick thinking response is that the cats must have done it. He is so good with the words, and our cats are so smart to be computer literate. Guess we should have even toilet trained them since they are so capable of learning difficult maneuvers.

John is definitely doing another street drug called G around the house. I have found many an empty vial on the desk upstairs in the mesh pen holder case. I am sure he placed them inside, exposed on the edge just so it was easy for me to see. Why I ask, wait! In the kitchen, two empty vials in a coffee cup. Second drawer down where the extra utensils are located, two more vials are placed just so by the corn cob holders. I threw not only the G vials but the corn cob holders in the garbage. Just get anything in relation to this nightmare out of sight. Yes, he never cooks or does dishes and is unable to make this into a home. My dream is to have a home and not only a house. He definitely left his drugs there for me to find. Like then, I allowed it to happen only to keep the peace and have a person with me to replace loneliness.

I was emotionally trapped. I chose to feel uncertain about myself on my own and caused myself to be psychologically unable to make rational decisions, like asking John to get out of this home. What happened was this attached to my emotions and left me dysfunctional, depressed, anxious and very angry. I still had belief in Gods' intervention to help me. After all, I have been sticking to my morals and ethics as a good person. Why did I not look deep inside myself at this moment and stand up for myself? I have no answers. All I thought of was how angry he made me but in fact I was making myself angry. As my family had shown me when I was divorced, they desired the approval from society that their daughter's conduct was out of principles and the divorce was caused by an unloving husband. I often wondered, as I did all the time with John, how much my family truly love me. I needed John's love more than anyone now, but I forgot to love myself.

I told him years ago when I discovered his drugs to keep it away from the home. I am a teacher and that reasoning is simple. Lori believes that first; it is definitely done on purpose to drive me crazy and second; maybe to push him out so that he has a reason to come after me legally for removing him from the home. That is something he could not do with Cheryl and he constantly reminds me of that situation. John is definitely showing signs of drug use again. A lot of the time his pupils are huge! If I say anything, then all hell breaks loose. His famous line now is that I am a trouble maker. Then as Lori notices, he has a disgusting odor, the smell of the excretion of drug sweats. Smells a bit like a horse after not being taken care of. Lately with a little more strength in my voice, I remind him of the language and unloving phrases he says to me but he denies everything. "I did not say that."

I reminded John that my health is suffering at a more intense level. If he would only give in a little to me and realize he needs to give me recognition for wanting to help and change our relationship for the better. If I could only have this emotionally, I would feel better physically. It feels, John, like you are killing me on purpose. You cannot deny any of this because when I look into the mirror I see the sorrow and pain. I hurt deep inside and am drawn further into being a different person. I tried often to smile for you, John, and to say things to make you smile. I am almost certain you held back just to give me deeper pain. John, you are displaying cruelty to another person and this time it is someone who really loves you. I am not your Cheryl.

John, my darling, when are you going to realize I am offering you the world? I am a great woman. Not like the party girls. Not the one who cares for nothing good or for the moment because they hold no responsibility even for themselves? To John, "How do I make this all go away?" Why do I feel so much suffering and pain? I cannot see it in your face, in your voice—just anger. That is not telling me you want us to be as we were in the earlier years. John, I am losing you. I wish you could see me now. Please kiss me. Make me feel loved. Why cannot I have your love without anything else that is negatively attached? In other words, John, can you give me pure love? Innocent love! I know with all that has happened, you are still here in my life because I can lock up the past and move into the light of freedom to love without question. But, now I look at your face and it is so full of gloom. Where is that smile from the corner of your mouth? I used to love to hear you laugh, but when was that laughter? I can't remember. Oh my God, I cannot remember. John, I cannot write anymore. Please, please anyone who reads this one day when I am gone, know that I am so hurt and in so much pain for lack of love and understanding from John. Please, John, leave the drugs alone and love life. Such a beautiful life I can offer and hold to, to make all your dreams come true. Even the sailboat you wish to have. Why, why do I love you so much and you hate me so much with the same intensity?"

I have lost my reason for this folder. I am supposed to be listing the ugly from you so I may relax my emotions and lay no blame. I have to stop. My head is pounding and I am unable to swallow.

Note 1—Folder 1 created on Monday, November 16, 2007, end.

Note 2—Folder 2 created, November 18, 2007, notes.

Wednesday evening and I have to write this to you . . . unbelievable!

You do know who "you" refers to. It is obviously Jill, me, speaking out loud, hoping I could hear the words and therefore make some sense of why am I getting so physically ill.

Thinking about this all week makes me determined that I have to tell you John. Tell you how easy it is not to be able to collect your thoughts and how stupid people are, especially those who themselves have dealt with depression. On Sunday evening I was very depressed about my whole life. Even as I write this now, the front of my head inside is starting to pain and I feel dizzy. I thought you would not arrive until Monday morning to go to work, like you have done in the past, due to a fight. I have to say again, to the tenant who lives in the basement apartment below it must be like sitting in a cheap theatre watching a movie full of sounds of action above his head, extremely aware of the fights John has directed at me, not with me. You know the tenant will tell you how you start crap and will not let up, and how I sound unbelievably lost. David is his name, and he has quite a story of his own to tell one day. He was once very successful and now at forty-eight has lived the last eight years with John and me. David just could not take it living in the house as a roommate. He used to rent the back bedroom and sort of shared the house with us. Wow, John, you showed resentment at the loss of space because of David living with us! It even showed me a part of you I had not realized, a lack of self-confidence. Yet another issue I need to explain to myself first and then try to have your understanding. By the way, doing your own laundry is a new thing because this was the beginning of my saying "No" to doing everything for you. David would yell through his bedroom wall which was next to our laundry room, "Why don't you just leave?" I always did your pants and dirty underwear that were filled with sex that someone else had played with. Now, trying to regain some self-respect, I refuse to do your laundry. David would come near the basement door to the laundry room and just yell at John, "What are you doing here?" Funny, John, you must get it or I really do not understand. You just smile like it is a crazy man downstairs. But for real, David is a very smart man because he hears what is going on and how I am mentally beaten, beaten so badly that I do not believe there is a return for me. I am too far gone.

Note 2—Folder 2 created November 18, 2007, end.

Note 3—Folder 3 created November 29, 2007, notes.

This brings me back to late Sunday afternoon, 3 p.m. or 4 p.m. I wrote a suicide note to Lori and put it in a sealed envelope with her phone number on it. The note was placed in the mail box by me and I called David. "David, tomorrow evening, when do you get home?" "Around 9:30 p.m. I will be at home, Jill." "Okay, there is a note in the mailbox for a friend, her name is on it. Tomorrow can you call her in the evening and tell her there is a note for her in the mailbox on the veranda." David says, "Sure, Jill." "Ok, thank you, David." Now, tell me. Does he not wonder, knowing how he hears I am so upset, what am I planning because he hears our fights? Numerous times David told me that he is worried for me. Why doesn't he call me and ask if I am okay? And, why didn't he question a note left by me in the mail box asking him to call my friend to pick it up? Alarm sirens like Pearl Harbor attack sirens should be going off in his head. There are no memories in the present or my past to stop me now.

   I just cried for the first time in maybe two years. I watched myself in the mirror to see if I am in self-pity mode but decided I am not. I am truly fed up with the bullshit of my life and the last part filled with John's hatred has capped it off for me. How can he be so distastefully ignorant to me over nothing if he would compare me to his wrongful habits? I just remembered today that only a few months ago I found two used syringes in his briefcase. These injections are called Tri-Mix used for patients who have difficulty getting an erection. This injection is used as part of the treatment of Erectile Dysfunction. John definitely has no problem in that part of his life but wanted it for purely recreational purposes, meaning it keeps you erect for at least three hours longer. Imagine what a performer you are in the eyes of those focused on sexual desire. This is offered to any male with ED problems. This is definitely better than Viagra and other methods of a longer lasting sexual pill. When I confront him, knowing what the result will be, he yells, "That is nothing. Screw you for going through my stuff. How dare you look into my personal belongings?" So now I am the bad one. I let it go. Ten minutes of belligerent behavior but now I am living weeks of blame for nothing compared to his shortcomings and he cannot let it go. Daily he keeps on shouting at me about his belongings. Right after that, one week later I find two more used syringes in his eye glass case. Again

I ask, and this time his response is, "Oh those are old from my house. Remember? We took them from there a long time ago." Sorry everyone, he is lying. I was suffering from such head pain that I thought of another mini-stroke may be imminent. Alone and in fear of something worse happening to me, I lay down on the sofa to relax. What an enigma for me to say "relax." My mind is worse than ever before, flash cards filled with images of scenes with people I do and do not know. I hover over sights of people interacting while at the same time I hear conversations but I never see myself as a participator. This could truly be a bi-polar creation from the stress in my life. And yet I continue because I want to help John be his old self as when we first met.

How pathetic, I am seeing this obvious cheating plus lying with my eyes. Is it okay? Back to this Sunday afternoon, I recognize what quality of life I am living, empty of heart and soul, my facial features once bright and full of love only for John. I have decided on this day, November 29, 2007, to finally take care of me. God, you must open your hand because this soul has outlived this host. After crying as deeply as I could and reaching within myself I decided no matter what I do in life, this will not change. I am not a person to show openly true emotions. I do not laugh out loud at really funny comedy. Hence, for me to use the term crying does not tell you how or what state I was in at that moment. To understand, you all must have seen the little girl crying in mom's buggy at the store with huge, huge tears running like tiny waterfalls and dripping on a now wet shirt that causes each new tear to almost splash as it resides among the other tears. That was me: a person I never knew existed. I now knew something was definitely wrong with my thinking and behavior. My dear loving mother, still alive at eighty-two years old has never missed telling me that for my fifty-five years of life, "Jill you will always be unhappy. You will never be happy Jill because you always want too much and only the best." Well, excuse me mother for wanting to do well. So, even with the thought of John going, which now I am certain will happen, I cannot see myself ever with another person. I tried to picture another person in the car with me or on the sofa by me. I can't do it. And if I do, it will only turn out the same. Oh, you say you do not know that. Yes, I do. I am committed to choosing the wrong people to love. And mother, what is wrong with reaching out for pure happiness, a fulfillment and embodiment of pure love?

P.S. You know every time I found signs of John's drugs and cheating, like I explained above, it just came to me from something telling me. I did not have to search for even five minutes. I was led to everything by something in my head. John does not believe that, of course, he sees me searching like a mad hatter through his life looking for his wrongful doings. Not true, really, I was shown, pulled toward whatever I found.

File 3—Folder 3 created late afternoon, November 29, 2007, end.

Live in the Present and Learn Valuable Life Lessons to Improve Any Relationship

Life living lesson: Who says it really is a lie?

A lie, a fib, or is it a condemnation of the pure truth? We all do it to save our pride, to protect our ego or our sense of responsibility to the other individual. Some people actually believe it is their responsibility to lie to save an argument or possible worse scenarios. They are the knights in shining armor. Therefore they feel no guilt. Why should one feel guilty when they are being noble? Who knows their real reasons, the thoughts that meander through the other person's mind? You would like to say that the person lying does not even realize their character is in question.

A lie is the untruth, an actual intent to deceive another, especially someone you love. Whereas as a fib can be called a trivial lie that curtails the actual truth. Should we call these our "White Lies"? White lies are usually thought out only to let a small part of the information escape, really thinking "I am protecting myself from giving the truth"—a guaranteed argument to follow. But in actuality, you are still hurting the other person, sometimes even more so when they encounter the real truth. Then they know that you purposely deceived them and their honor. Yet a fib if not considered a white lie is not seen as an actual lie, it is usually forgiven because it is not intended to deceive you. Most fibs begin in childhood and continue into adulthood. They are regarded as being insignificant, small and of no consequence. You need to decide if a lie is equal to or less than a condemnation. A condemnation violates your human rights. It is always an expression of disapproval stating your well-being as wrong. It represents evil, an expression of strong disapproval and the power to inflict all wrongs onto you, as a recipient.

Liar, liar, pants on fire! A common childhood phrase used anywhere where a group of kids are playing and they gang up on one child whom they all believe has lied to them, whether the lie was of importance or inconsequential. We have the liar at the office around the water cooler. Everyone knows his stories are unbelievable, yet no-one will approach him and call his game. Is it the same reason why a partner, the loved one at the end of a liar's lies rarely says "You are not telling the truth?" Are we protecting them, their feelings or our own? If we were all straightforward with no deceptions, how boring life would be without any mystery! Did I just call a lie a mystery? If you do nothing about the lies, then they are mysteries—theirs and not yours.

If you feel they are deceiving you about their true actions or concealing the true answer, how do you approach their actions? To say that you do not believe them and that they are lying, you will only start an argument. How do you prove it is a lie? Are you supposed to keep notes, a diary of all the things they said to you, of all the actions that happened, have them initial these at the end of the each and every day as facts, so you may recall them later to prove a point? Does it become a log book of your life? Well, this is not the way to a lasting relationship and a loving union. Go with it. Believe in your sixth sense. Once again, you basically feel that you are being told a lie. Remember, love or friendship is not pure! Now, you have to trust yourself. Do not let anger build up inside. Do not create something totally different in your mind from the frustration of not being able to call a lie a lie. But you feel you need to argue. All of this is not fair to you. Turn it around and make it *their* problem or issue. Discovering infidelity, or deception by a loved one, creates a lot of uncertainty. After all, it is *their* lie.

> *"The truth is rarely pure and never simple."* (Oscar Wilde)
> **Wilde, Oscar:Thinkexist. Retrieved February 2012 from http://thinkexist.com/quotes/Oscar_Wilde/**

A lie has two separate sides to its ugly head. Is what you are hearing a deception or simple deceit? The act or practice of deceiving is deception. Lovers can lie as well as they can appear distant. How do you define distance between two lovers? Is it created through a series of lies, or does it depend upon how your relationship evolved from the beginning? Unfortunately, being distant is not the same for everyone. If you chose as a partner someone who is different than you in the action of being distant, you will always question their actions. Am I getting a lie, deceit or deception this time? An attempt to or deceive to deceive is very complicated, and detecting it is almost impossible. Most of deceit and lies that your loving partner tell go undetected because you just think that would never happen to me, to us.

All of these forms of communicating with you through lies or fibs and not the truth can be exaggerations or an understatement of the aspects of the truth. I believe the white lie, the small lies we detect are a way of concealing, covering up the monster yet to be unleashed. You never reach out your hand to pet a monster; somehow you do with your better half. The worse mind shaking and head turning is the liar who constantly contradicts himself and looks you in the eyes and says, "What are you talking about? Get your hearings checked or your eyes covered in glasses." Hurtful to the core and you in all these scenarios are not alone.

Deception is pre-meditated, just as a murderer plans out his actions to kill another individual and bring upon them their demise by his intent. Deception is the hardest to believe and understand. It causes the other's feelings to digress into self-betrayal and expectations of them as a whole. The population as a whole does not expect this or participate in this form of behavior. So take comfort, when you move on, it will be to a better person and place. If you think about your day, you yourself have deceived someone and not a thought was given by you as to the consequences. But to have a relational partner significantly deceive you is a violation of the rules of love.

What could be a motive for a lover to deceive you in such a way to compromise your relationship, even destroy what they have and probably cherish? Avoidance behavior, the intent not to face reality will place worry and hurt onto your partner. One huge part of this is self-deception, using deception to protect their own self-image and not be attacked with criticism or embarrassment. The only words to describe this person are truly not a nice individual. How did you become involved with them? The only true protection you have against their deception is as the listener—you have to keep in your memory bank what is being said. Does the story remain constant and believable? Guess what! The story does eventually leak like the old plastic shopping bag carrying water. The male and female perception of a deceiving partner is not the same. Then how do same-sex relationships place significance? Women are appalled by this behavior and men see it as natural, maybe even macho to tell their friends. Lying for women is in the most despicable category. All lying, no matter how small, is significant, and they will become very emotional in the outcome. I personally believe the woman is the stronger sex, but why then are they so innocent of betrayal and emotional cheating? Well truth be told, women judge what they hear from their partner as more truth than lies. And the well-played out untruth is hidden, camouflaged by times and events you already think to be true. It's very difficult to beat a true deception, a well-played out hand previously planned—the card shark with the ace up his sleeve waiting for the right moment to drop it on the table!

Deceit is of the moment, a quickly thought-up response to avoid an immediate negative confrontation. A lie can be a hidden secret shared only with oneself. Deceit takes a breath and becomes alive and accessible to your partner. The problem is, to whom do you tell your secrets? And at what moment should you share? Your revealed secrets can become your lie, but not your deceit. At the time of deception you are acting falsely and being purposely dishonest. Deceit is any collusion, false representation, or underhand practice used to defraud someone that you love. The Bible defines deceit as telling a lie to someone to get something as well as an action or activity that suppresses the truth. The only good thing about deceit is its temporary, and a person will be free from that deceit once they know the truth. Deceit originated when Satan deceived Adam and Eve in the Garden of Eden about the eating the fruit of the tree. Psalm 72:14 tells us that God will redeem our soul from deceit. And self-deceit is getting caught up in "little white lies" when you forget about being good and kind to others. Jeremiah 9:6 tells us that self-deceit leads us to rejecting God.

> *"After people have repeated a phrase a great number of times, they begin to realize it has meaning and may even be true."*
> (H. G. Wells)
> **Wells, H.G.: Thinkexist. Retrieved February 2012 from http://thinkexist.com/search/searchquotation.asp?search=%93After+people+have+repeated+a+phrase+a+great+number+of+times%2C+they+begin+to+realize+it+has+meaning+and+may+even+be+true.%94+%28H.+G.+Wells%29&q**

So the advice is to live your live in harmony for now and be prepared somewhere in your heart that the closeness you dreamed of having is broken. We cannot prepare for this event. Your reaction simply comes from your heart and not from the power of your intelligence. For you, the receiver, you not only get the lies but you experience anxiety, stress, and then the uncertainty that maybe most of your lives were a little fake. If your loved one is able to lie about something trivial, well, what about something enormous? It came easily the first time.

You may believe the way to detection is trough their body language. After all, you know them best. Most importantly, those who lie have been doing it a long time, way before they met you. They are good at it especially if it is not in your nature to lie, you will be even harder pressed to detect their lies. Research says that people lie all the time to those they love most. I can think of only one good reason for that happening. We feel the ones who love us most will be the most forgiving, so why not lie? Keep in mind that lying is a skill and skills can be learned very early in life. Don't you remember being a kid in the playground and telling mommy that Jake ate your candy bar when in fact you did and you are aiming for a second candy bar? That one worked with the tears, so let's move it up a notch and create even bigger lies until we are adults. As a child it was planned, but as an adult it becomes natural, and that hurts.

Guilt happens to be an emotion, and most often we express our emotions openly and quickly. If the person truly loves you and is guilty of a lie or deception, then believe that they too are suffering. You look closely and there is frustration in their body language and speech. Most times they cannot help themselves and could feel depressed. After all, it is according to society and religious teaching that this goes against all morals. But still, how can that person look you straight in the eyes and lie? I asked that question only once because I knew the truth. There was no remorse, no moral standard, and no blink of the eye. This person does not know how to stop and refuses to correct themselves. Do they see themselves as heroes? These are moments in your life that cannot be erased; no amount of flowers, diamonds, or passionate love making can change that moment. And research shows that the guilty person, by washing their hands or taking a shower, is relieved of their guilt. Are you going to worry every time your partner comes home from work and he immediately takes a shower? Well, I never did until I picked up his clothes to hang them up while he was in the shower. Evidence again and more evidence, jumped all over me. Now I am the victim once again. At this moment I felt that I was good at detecting the deception, and that made me secure in my regular thoughts. A victim yet in control of the pattern of lies and a mixed-up affair; leading to the simple fact that I really did not want the truth because it hurts. Only look for the truth if you are prepared to handle it. Am I or you invading their privacy by entering the bathroom and picking up their clothes? Are we like a surveillance camera getting caught up in detecting?

The most common reasons for a lie are the continued questions from a weary partner, not sure of their relationship; their expectations of a partnership are never met, or simply the liar cannot deal with divulging the truth because they do not know how to react to their own guilt. Lying takes much more mental effort then telling the truth. You have to have a note pad in your head to keep all facts straight all the time. The more you do this, the more your intuitive partner will become the analytical freak. And this happens because the liar has a tendency to tell the same lies or similar lies over and over. Actually by doing this, he begins to believe his own lie and it is so natural now to speak that lie. Could it be so far-fetched to say, the words I love you, may be a lie, a repetitive lie that even he believes he loves you. Do you want that kind of love? Do you deserve that kind of love?

> *"Ask me no questions and I'll tell you no lies."* (Oliver Goldsmith)
> **Goldsmith, Oliver:Thinkexist. Retrieved February 2012 from http://thinkexist.com/search/searchquotation.asp?search=%93Ask+me+no+questions+and+I%27ll+tell+you+no+lies.%22+%28Oliver+Goldsmith%29**

If you seem like a never-ending interrogator," Why did it take you so long to get home today?" What choice is left for the guy but to fumble and look guilty even though you're not in the wrong? Where is the privacy and control of their relationship? And as a result, partners often fight back by lying. Deception is useful when trying to win back a sense of freedom and independence. Lying can be considered as an indirect way of getting a partner to "let it be." The reaction in my partnership was aggressive, a raised voice and making a huge scene. This was a great way to stop me from trying to put ownership of the lie where it belonged.

Lying, deception and secrets that your partner keeps are not unfamiliar to how the rest of the populace lives. You have to decide what is important to you. Accepting that what you have is what you get or arguing your way to a truth. It is not right to live this way, "Is it God's way?" No. Spiritually, can your heart be at peace and find complete happiness in a restless soul? That definitely will not happen, but I want to be in love just like you want to be in love and for it all to be perfect.

End of Life living lesson: Who says it really is a lie?

Josh R. Himmelman

Life living lesson: Can verbal abuse vs. physical abuse be more significant in a relationship?

Trust me, as a recipient of abuse—it is a serious problem, whether social or cultural, between two partners where love should dominate. It finally came to me my own self-worth was at risk, but I did not have the tools to help myself. Now I know there are community abuse resources, such as shelters for abused women. That's great, but I never found a shelter for abused women, especially because of the stigma. And of course there is the internet, seeking legal advice, mental health professionals, or hitting the bookstore for printed resources.

An abusive relationship means one partner is getting mistreated. It does not go back and forth. There is a dominance associated with abuse; always one person is more dominant then the other. Yes, it can be two very manly men living together, full of testosterone, but one will be dominant. It is violence and we know, animals act violently but are unconscious of their actions. Humans are able to understand how things should be, so to act abusively is intentional and wrong.

Still sounds not too devastating to you? Well you are wrong. For me it was both the psychological and physical consequences of my abuse. Now I have to learn the buzz word and its meaning, as a post-abusive person, "abuse sequel." As I said, give me a bruise, like a man-to-man. I have and there is no therapy to erase the effects left on me. This did not just happen at the end of our relationship—it started at about two years into the relationship. I knew I was better than an "idiot." That was the first word used against me. I will never forget. And to heal I needed to remove it from physical use, because the next day I used that ugly word, with that ugly tone of voice to become a password on the internet. Do not know why I did that, and I do not know why it is still my password. It is just one of those negative things as it is until you let go. That means another piece of what was a relationship is now gone. Holding on is not healthy.

As with spousal abuse, domestic abuse at home is when one partner in the intimate relationship tries to dominate and control the other person. And yes, this is also physical violence also called domestic violence. There is no fairness in this player, the abuser. He will use fear, guilt, shame, and intimidation to wear you down. Usually the first fear is that I am going to leave you and it is your fault, you take the blame. If you have a feeling of fear around your partner and afraid to voice any opinion or thought, afraid he will blow up at you, then you are in an abusive, unhealthy relationship.

Do you know how many times I told him to "Please, just hit me" Hit me so I bruise, feel it, take care of it and then eventually it goes away. There are no remnants of that fight that screws up of something again that made no sense. There are ointments to cure, to take away the pain. There are bandages to apply pressure if it is sprained and heals correctly. Even just a touch of a warm hand over a bruise helps with the discomfort. But, verbal abuse and healing are not the same. I know that this abuse was used to control me and manipulate as a victim. He was always putting me down as a teacher, wanting to insult my integrity. His abuse was sexual (lack of having sex with me and making me ask), emotional (liked to see me cry, with a big soft heart), and the famous verbal abuse, (I could never respond as quickly as him and his words would confuse me to a point of speechlessness). The sad part, these not only happened at home but in public.

Once home, in my own bed alone, no dignity left, I just lost another little piece of who I am and who I want to be in life. I would lie there wondering if I am crazy, emotionally helpless and trying to understand if I deserve to be mistreated and hurt. And I realize he is controlling who I see, where I go. I have fewer friends and the whole experience was completely about possessiveness and jealousy.

As you read above, I trust you asked yourself questions about yourself, be a self-learner from now on of "Who am I"? If you have not understood it as yet, never been told to or explained to why, you truly must love yourself first before someone can love you as a whole person. I heard this so many times from family and friends and just passed it off as fluff. I never loved myself, inside or outside. Still today, no one understands why I see myself so unlovable.

We are our own worse critics. Again, the popular phrase you need to adopt is to "love yourself." You need to explain to yourself what that phrase means to you and not what someone tells you it means. We are all guilty of self-criticism, harsh judgment of ourselves. We can do enough damage to our own self-esteem even without a loving partner taking his turn. Criticism is the most popular verbal abuse. Criticism can be either positive or negative, depending on our own understanding of what is being criticized. I believe and I want you to believe that there is no such thing as negative criticism. When you are getting criticism, look to see if it is constructive. It should only be directed at something you do, not at yourself. That would be an attack as an individual. After all, did your partner not fall in love with who you are? Take the emotions out of the comments both as the giver and the receiver. Put your ego aside, and hopefully your partner is only trying to improve something that may be seen by many as a fault. Throw the comments aside and say, "Thank you for being helpful." Learning to accept suggestions that are intended to improve you as a person in your lives together is a great feat for you as a person. Your partner will feel more at ease being able to discuss issues openly.

It is not easy to say the right thing using the right words to make a comment acceptable. Try and listen carefully, intently and ask questions without hurt feelings. If you still do not understand, ask for an example of your behavior. This will open your eyes to your lives as he sees it going. Maybe you are blinded by your own perception of your relationship and are oblivious to your own behavior, which could be destructive.

Always remember, this is coming from a person who fell in love with you and loves you now. Look at the source of the criticism and see it as loving help, not hurt. There is a goal here to make life better for all. It is a use of language to improve your lives and is coming from a person you respect. Best of all, he is giving an opportunity for more personal growth.

Unfortunately, here comes the ugly side of criticism, narcissism, and emotional abuse. You are treated very differently in public than at home or in private. They do not care about your feelings, the fact that you may have an illness, or simply upset yourself about something important to you. Into your inner self sneaks the feeling of being hurt and if done often enough can cause you to be depressed. The worst for you is when you try to break out of this treatment and your outside supporters consisting of friends and family do not believe you have a problem in your relationship. Your partner is so good at hiding his true self in public, so good at lies and manipulating people for his attention, that others feel there must be something wrong with your thoughts.

If your partner, like mine, often creates fights and you are left in wonderment, think very hard. You will be caught up in being told it is your fault and you are making the relationship unhappy. I have too often found that the fight initiated by him is a cover up for guilt and lies. Maybe you can remember an argument where you brought up an issue like, "Why are you arriving home so late?" and the response immediately is, "Are you trying to cause a fight?" A perfect shut down, put down to keep you at bay. Talk about a stress inducer. When you feel put down, do you see enjoyment in his expression? Does he not realize that newer problems are created for you as a couple? Is there an attempt to make amends because of guilt or feeling of doing a wrong? I questioned myself then and more so now, how could I have loved a liar? My answer for me and most likely for you is simple, we ignore the truth because of its hurt.

If out of a fight comes physical abuse, a force of his hand or an object that injures you, then it is battering or an assault, which is a crime. You can call the police but then you are making a conscious decision to end your relationship then and there. The same applies to forced sex by your intimate partner of which you do have consensual sex. This again is an act of aggression and violence.

Abuse in a relationship takes many forms besides verbal. Physical abuse; slapping, shoving, physically restraining, isolation; controlling contacts with friends and family and monitoring phone calls, threats and intimidation; threatening to harm you; sexual abuse, forcing sex or specific acts or criticizing your performance in bed; and destroying property; breaking furniture, trashing your clothes or important possessions you treasure.

If you are looking for a way to arouse anger in your partner, keep up not responding to his behavior of verbal abuse. There will be consequences, if not immediate, definitely in your future. It is part of our human code to protect ourselves even if it is a loved one hurting you. If you find yourself constantly hurting your partner, question yourself, if there is a hidden agenda within yourself? Maybe you have feelings left over from past hurts that were not resolved. You just may be falling out of love and are not equipped to communicating or are afraid of their reaction. So the best for you is to try and drive them away, make it their issue. Devious as it may be, a lot of relationships begin breaking down with the above intentions of one partner.

A heated argument encompasses what should have been direct answers and reasonable behavior. It turns into a battle of who can come up with the most hurtful one-liner. Arguments are typically non-productive and highly stress-arousing. While in the midst of an argument, we are not rational, reasonable or sensible. Making your partner feel inferior when you are angry does not solve the problem. A bad situation has just now turned into a worse situation. One of you needs to keep your cool and be objective.

You are the one who instigates an argument, verbal abuse. And you are surprised that your partner does not argue back, there is no sparring off. Be aware of her emotional hidden stress, because indirectly she will find opportunities to release this. You ask for help the next day and suddenly they are staying late at work. Or you come home and the usual dinner is not prepared. With these kinds of feelings and reactions from your partner, it is going to take a lot longer to heal the relationship. Getting angry in itself causes even more stress within. Anger is an emotion that many of us have been taught to disapprove of. It's just not nice, especially with your loved one. Just getting angry enough to verbally abuse our partner makes us recognize how uncontrolled we have become or how irrational we are behaving. In a lot of arguments, anger feeds more anger. This makes it easy to heat up our emotional thermometer and be even more irrational.

It is true and simple: there are reasons why a loving partner sometimes takes the brunt of verbal abuse. It is easy to choose a loved one to get angry with because we believe they are the first to forgive. Not any more, people. The coined word "next" came about for a reason. In all types of relationships, next has become a simple expression put to use like making a slice of toast in the toaster. Push down hard and in time it will pop and release. Unfortunately, your loved one is the most available and at times receptive. And you always hope they will understand, but not if it is a lie.

It is important that you realize who is at fault and you are not responsible. If you live in a pink bubble, believing that soon this will all stop and we can fly through the universe happily after, not so. You have to decide what to do, and it really seems unfair that he has put you in this position. Begin by telling a trusted friend and ask them to help you find professional help that understands his issues. It is important the counselor understands pertinent issues of abuse in order for you to be comfortable and focused instead of explaining every fraction of detail. Tell a friend you are achieving an important alliance that can give you courage and confidence. The best beginning is just to have someone who will listen to you and understand. Get out into your community centers and see that there are others like you and to expect relationships that are mutually respectful and free from fear and any form of abuse. There are numerous local papers and speaking forums in the community that address these issues as well. Seek them out and attend.

I am not a commodity to be owned, and to abuse me is socially wrong, wrong in religion, ethically wrong, and does not comply with the unwritten rules of a relationship. I have the innate right and worth as a human being to be equal under the guidance and eyes of God. Keep a positive state of mind. Repeat to yourself, "I love myself and every experience is a new learning for me." At first, I did not believe in thinking this could ever help me love myself, but without conscious thought, when I say those words in my mind, I find myself smiling.

End of Life living lesson on Can verbal abuse vs. physical abuse be more significant in a relationship?

CHAPTER FIVE

Sunday, November 29, 2007, 11:30 p.m.

Jill heard some general walking noises and doors opening downstairs. Especially the back door opened and she is thinking, now what? She walks through the upstairs hall to the bathroom window in the back of the house and she sees him fast-paced scouring the yard. Looking up at the house and walking from end to end. She was confused so she went downstairs to see if she could help. Down the stairs she came and asked what gives. "Oh, I hear that noise again like someone is hitting the back of the house with something." Jill shook her head and said just go to bed, which was the sofa in the living room.

To explain, the living room sofa became John's place to stay at night. Jill never could, at that time, figure out why he chose to sleep on a sofa. She has her answers now. Once she was lying in bed and hearing the person she loved so much downstairs, she yelled "Please come to bed with me, I miss us!" John did! Crawling in on the side, clinging to the edge like a new born bird in the nest, he managed to lie down. Not five minutes later his foot stretched out and touched Jill's leg. With an obvious shock reaction he whipped his foot back. Jill's voice trembling, asked, "Why are you pulling away from me like I am poison?" No response. Within minutes he left the bed and only ever appeared in the bedroom two more times.

It is so hurtful to have someone you love so much to obviously pull away from your love and you do not know for what reason.

Another time, Jill just went to bed and he came up and stood in the doorway. His right hand and arm were perched up in the top corner of the doorway, bent knee touching the same side and butt pushed back into the other side of the door casing. Jill felt like he was a stranger to her as very few words were exchanged. The memory still makes Jill very emotional, seeing the man she wants to hug and hold so much in her arms, in their bed, just standing there like she is nothing to him. It all lasted about five minutes. Jill cried and cried quietly so she would not be yelled at from downstairs with some incoherent comment that would make no sense to anyone. The only other time John showed up in the bedroom was November 29th.

So up the staircase she walked slowly, no answers about why John was outside and no energy to lift her legs anymore, she went back to bed. Within minutes she heard John's car starting up in the driveway. Jill was exhausted from the confusion she was living in but had to see what was up now. He had moved his car out from behind Jill's. Jill waited and back into the house he came. Going down the stairs with suppressed wonderment, Jill stepped into a nasty one-line comment by John. "I can't handle this stress anymore!" His "stress" was the second computer Jill had bought and placed in the dining room to do her school work. She had a great office upstairs which John, during the early years, helped to put together for her, his "Honey" as John called her. However, it had become John's domain. Like the vicious dog in the backyard, that room was off limits to any intruder, even sometimes to its owner. Hence, Jill had to find more money and buy that second computer placed in a little corner of the dining room. Even John's 14-year-old daughter said to her, "Jill you let my dad have everything. Why would you do that for him?" Jill didn't answer because how would she explain a crazy love between two people? Lately John fought so much with her that the only avenue of release for her was to write about their fights as you read and save them on a USB. Little did she know that John had set up her computer to send every key stroke she did to the C drive, where he could access what Jill was doing. And she thought using a USB would be the only record of what she was keying in. So, every time Jill left the house, John raided her computer and saw what Jill could not say to John face-to-face. And, yes, there was a written note from yesterday about how badly she was being treated which you just read. After the backyard confusion, he went on my computer, switched the cars and then went upstairs. Jill did not actually hear him packing. She was still not in the loop, just lying in bed with ears pricked up like a cat waiting to hear John's next movement. She is thinking, "HE MUST HAVE BEEN ON MY COMPUTER AFTER THE BACK YARD DASH!"

With switching the cars, she was sure he was off to do one of his outings, telling Jill he was going out to a night club for fun, while Jill lay upstairs, tired like always. A famous line would be, "Don't cause trouble, woman!" John could never see who caused the trouble. At this point Jill came down to stand on the bottom step of the staircase in the foyer and saw him with the door open. He wasn't showing any signs of struggling, quite organized with his work briefcase and other bags in his hands navigating out the door. This was a familiar sight. Many times he would threaten to leave but never went through the door. Some discussion would take place and NEVER was there a solution to what seemed to be wrong.

Jill hates that word "wrong." Right or wrong—exactly what do they mean? Is it a math test, an x or a check mark? Proud of the check mark and so disappointed by the x, almost like saying, "You failed at this part of the test." Has life's meaning to share with someone become a test? Then that would mean all of our marriage vows or personal words on scrolls unwrapped, are all a test of your lives together. This time, without hesitation, John looks from the side of his face saying, "I am leaving you! I will be back later for Max." Max is his male cat that was adored much more than Jill. When he would talk to his cat, it made her jealous, how sad. There was no Max around this time, only John, and it all seemed to be unreal, like watching a rerun of the past when John made threats. Jill, in some sort of trance, watched, as in slow motion, the back of John's figure walked away. Please, she just wanted to see his face one more time, knowing this may be the last and as of today it was the last chance to see his face. Left with the ex-partner syndrome everyday lurking within her thoughts, she still finds it very hard to move forward.

Dear God. She knew she would not see him again. In the past weeks, he was making so many threats to ruin her life. A week ago Jill asked John if he loved her and the response was "I am fond of you," with a big smile on his face, "but I love my drugs more." Did she continue that conversation and ask what does he mean or ask just anything? No, she did not. Ms Co-dependent, Jill could not let go; she still believed she could fix everything. A day later she asked "What is it you would like to do, leave or what?" He did respond and quoted, "I am not ready yet!" Yeah, you guessed correctly. Jill did not pursue the conversation. This time Jill's inner and outer self was in sync, it was really happening. The only man she had ever, ever loved in spite of all the shit was leaving her. But she did not step out the door to try and stop him. In her chest she held a pain for not seeing his face. She told herself that if he looked her in the eye, he could not have done it. She walked to the glass screen door in bewilderment. She didn't chase after him like twenty times before when he would leave for sex or whatever, she never did know. She has this terrible memory stuck in her brain of just the back of her partner leaving, no discussion, no reasoning. The answers are all in his mind and she has nothing. She is left here bewildered with nothing to hold on to and with no-one to call. Alone and cries for help sound in the emptiness with not even an echo. If a tree in an empty forest falls, is it heard by anyone? She is now that tree! She was not allowed to make friends while with John, he saw them as trouble makers. She would talk with them but not be capable of being a true friend. He was so wrong. Now left with all the physical illnesses she developed during this turmoil, she has all her glands shutting down and is weak from stress. No hug good-bye or I am sorry. Nothing! Empty so much so, she sat on the bottom stair and thought I wanted to say so much. Please! Please!

Jill is not sure of any time from this moment on. But within hours this is what took place that night. Jill believes she experienced pure pain. She has had many painful days of actual physical pain that started in 1988 with a herniated disk which happened because she worked a full-time job as a teacher, worked twice a week, three hours each evening as a continuing education teacher and then came home to work on renovations on the home. She grew up on a farm with family with a European background and was always told, "What doesn't kill you will only make you stronger!" Therefore, extreme work ethics were so ingrained within her that to see a healthy young bum on the street panhandling made her sick and disgusted. But then, she had to realize there may be a good reason but it had better be a very good reason. She has always been proud to say "What I have accomplished has come from these two hands." Many times, especially men like John, who from envy, quite often quizzed her about her ambition, not to admire her but rather to make her defensive about her ambition. Those comments are the ones that got her two hands thrown in the air in disgust and a short story about her background coming from a poor family and a poor neighborhood. As far as I know, she was the only one to get out. Her parents sent her off to university with a bag of potatoes and turnips. She bought wieners and beans to compliment her gourmet fare. She never went hungry and never placed any accountability on her parents to be financially there for her. Her first Christmas in university, her parents' gift to her, the one and only gift under the tree was a card size white envelope with a crisp fifty dollar bill inside. It meant so much to her because it cost them a great deal of physical work in the woods cutting trees and selling strawberries to get that fifty dollars. That fifty dollar bill never got spent. It remained with her for years, always visible when she opened the top bureau draw, a reminder of just how simple life can be so rewarding and bring peace and to your heart. Unfortunately, about ten years later her town house got broken into and, yes, that fifty dollar bill was gone and it was all she could repeat to the police. The whole place was ram-sacked and truly valuable things were gone. But the most valuable was her parents' fifty dollar bill. She still thinks of that Christmas and how proud they were to present her with their trophy of hard labor.

The other pain close to this evening, again out of so many I could mention and you would say, "No way man!" happened in the mid-1990s. With a hyper mobile back causing disks to literally turn sideways as if commanded by a captain to do so, Jill could wake up in the morning, lying still opening her eyes and seeing the sunshine casting a shadow on the bedroom wall from the venetian blinds and think, "Wow what a great day!" One of those days was a Sunday morning and she turned to step out of bed, only to find her right leg about three quarters of an inch shorter and excruciatingly painful. The first time it happened, she thought she was having a heart attack because it touches the nerves behind the lungs and sensors feel like it is your heart.

PS. Did you know the symptoms of a heart attack for a woman is quite different than the symptoms for a man? Needless to say, she always made her pain, her own. It was one of the first things she discussed with John when they met. At that time her back was pure hell, so imagine having sex. She looked at John and said, "Help me, please. The pain is too much!" She tried to stand and her whole right side was contorted, shoulder wanted to meet the hip bone, not meant to happen, trust me.

John was as always was not convinced. Help her get dressed, she thought not. The stair case, she was on my own. She could only show tears in the corners of her eyes because she was not allowed to show weakness. She said, "Please find a doctor, a chiropractor that will come in on a Sunday and treat me." John did get out the yellow pages, without much enthusiasm, and thank God after two calls found the voicemail of a doctor that would come to his office on Sunday for an extra fee of one hundred dollars. She would have paid anything. It would have been nice if John offered to help, but no. And guess where the doctor was located but in the heart of their village. Down we go; the doctor arrives and works on Jill for over an hour. He sort of quizzed her on her partner's role in the back rehabilitation. She didn't answer. He knew! Without a nod of his head, the door of the treatment room opens and he yells, John get in here. You need to know you have a very sick woman here and what she says as pain and what I feel in her muscular skeletal frame, I cannot imagine how much pain she feels. The same story unfolded in the car on their way home, disbelief from John and an accusation that she is looking for sympathy now from strangers. She sat quietly and multi flashed many reasons why he would be this way but no flash seemed to supply an answer. It was like watching the slot machine after yanking the handle anticipating that promising big win with a one dollar bet. I will win and today I will have just a little more to live life. That is all she wanted from John was a little compassion so she could live this day. You know the pain would not have seemed nearly as bad if he would have put his hand on her leg on the way home or just said "Honey, how I can help?" She made lunch and dinner that day. Plus she ironed the work clothes for them both for Monday, first day of the new work week. She never got to wear hers though. She was left alone to her empty thoughts for days lying in bed and yes, driving herself for additional treatments to get better, literally holding on the roof of the car to help herself slide in behind the steering wheel. The thoughts of crying came to mind but who would she be crying for? Herself? It has become obvious that she is not worth crying over.

Those were painful moments, moments of first emotional and secondly physical. Now she is thrown in to what she cannot endure, the third form, hurt, emotionally deeper than pain. Of course pain and hurt have many origins but for her, these moments of non-belief of the severity of her pain and more importantly the lack of love and closeness from John represent in my mind unworthiness of herself to be loved.

Jill was retrieved from her thoughts by the movement of John throughout the house. It felt like coming to after having a nightmare. But Jill knew she did not leave the nightmare under the bedroom sheets but was about to meet it head on, alive, in the home.

11:30 pm, Sunday, November 29, 2007 or about that time, John has left her!

It started with Jill sitting curled over in pain, large tears soaking her t-shirt and thinking, she needed to say this to John but she will never ever have a chance. Every time Jill personally read her recollection of love for John, she would choke on her tears flowing inward down her throat and building a damn behind her voice box, leaving her unable to speak.

Jill wrote this letter some time ago trying to get the courage to pass it on to John. There was a large desk in the front hallway where Jill had hidden this letter to John, hoping he would find it and read Jill's true thoughts. Jill retrieved the letter and posted herself on the bottom stair of the staircase firmly seated as not to fall over from her weakness. Her letter began:

To my Dearest:

For the most part of my feelings, I feel quite sick, disappointed and very uncertain. Sick because of how we relate (talk) to each other about what has become our way of being every time we are together on the cell phone and yes, even our text messaging.

Disappointed because I thought I could find the perfect peace and happiness with my John. The dreams, of growing old and sitting by the riverside sharing one beer with no conversation because we know the years have passed and life was kind, are now beyond even a faded wish.

Now I am uncertain, because I still do not know if I could handle any future relationship. This is becoming more obvious each day, every day. I am frustrated and a little disconcerted, even a little thing seems to corrupt us with misleading impressions about the honesty of each other regarding something that was not even there to begin with. This makes me very angry because of our promises to always communicate have failed.

It is constant, that no matter what I say or what advice I would like to give, it is going to sound like I am saying to you, "I am right and you are wrong". So, most importantly, it is not so much about who is right and who is wrong. For me, it is about what I can accept and cannot accept in my life. You, I would say, must have the same (similar) thoughts. But, how am I to know when you simply cannot finish a discussion through to a solution? You certainly can open up a mouse trap, lure me in and snap the conversation ends. I look around in wonderment, like the poor mouse who is hanging onto life, what have I gotten myself into. Can I escape? Is this the end? What about my future plans of a family, happiness and where is my belief in God now to provide the answers?

The more I say to you that I want peace in my life and happy times, the more often it is the contrary. The unhappiness appears when I display even just a smile of contentment. You send words like a bloating blow fish across the room, a chilling darkness, to destroy my vibrations of the peace emanating from the corners of my mouth, displayed with my lips in a straight form that quickly turns downward. The mirror does not lie; the sadness is reflected. I am afraid to stare for very long because the souls within the mirror will absorb me. Will these souls be kind to me? Do I deserve to be loved in an afterlife? The contortions of life will engulf my whole being, leaving an empty shell like a summer's road kill baking in the intense heat.

Hurtful things to me (hurtful to me, an individual and not hurtful to anyone else), once the hurt has been done, it is difficult for me to forget. Why in my mother's good name did our families teach us as children, "forgive and forget"? Who coined that little phrase, just to confuse the hurt ones in their decision making? A "sorry" goes a long way but then I speak from the experience of multiple discussions with young people—a source of untainted processed information. They do not realize yet that their parents' thoughts will be their own knowledge. Too many declarations of "sorry" from the same person lose their meaning and their seriousness. A hurtful thing for me was when you said, "I made you the way you are now, full of attitude, possessiveness and mistrust regarding me." A card is given, then more cards, turning into a gift. Then more gifts, then tearful words all to say you are sorry, become overwhelming. Eventually, the person receiving all of these wants to say, "Take it back!" and I did not make you who you are.

Where are the moments when we first met, when all was understood? There was no looking in the conversation for a hidden message then. No asking multiple questions to make the other person account for every minute of where they were and what they were doing. First meetings were full of respect for the other person. There were many ideas and contributions to the conversation. Discussions of self-esteem were understood and the importance of looking good were a reflection of one's character, not meant as a means to attract a glance from the person across the dining room and you emitting sexual overtones. Now, the utterance, "I would like to look better" is taken as, "I want to shop the market, look for a pick-up, casual sex, and a tease." What ever. But, it's oh so wrong of you to now disrespect my love for you and my wanting to be appealing to you. How jaded you have become to think your partner is strutting beside you only to leave a distance between each other's stance so another can slide in between.

Hurts are so unexplainable. One would think that after a tense discussion in a restaurant where everyone knows me much more than you, you could understand the embarrassment for us both. Well, then why do you continue to intensify situations with verbal language and thrusting body language? And worst of it all, this is in front of people who respect me. Are your intentions to try and change their opinion of me because I am standing out in the crowd just the way you met me and now you need to be the bull with the biggest nose ring?

So many avenues of arguments, a living room scene, another disaster in a restaurant, a chattering obvious fight as seen through the windshield of our car and yet you lie in my lap and I massage your back, you are so beautiful to me. It reminds me of how I was so scared to let myself love you because I would lose. I always knew I would lose. That is how I have seen my life so far, as one having truly loved someone and then losing them. It seems since I told you I love you, things began to fall apart, beyond even my own personal space. My personal space used to be the outreach of my arms swinging in circular motion but with John my personal space developed to be nothing. There was no space for me to be a person with ideas and dreams of forgiveness. Therefore, when I stretched out my arms, you were untouchable because I am closed like a morning tulip waiting for the sunshine to expose itself. There are no petals left on the stem like there are no arms left on me to open and give or receive love. John was and is the only true love of my life that stretches far beyond all the horrific dealings we endured. And why would I allow this separation filled with misguided hurtful slurs to happen over our years of being together?

Please do not blame your story on "your other relationships" because this should be seen only ever a first relationship. Where are the ideals of the not-so-distant past? Solve your problems. Fight for your love and recognize your differences as making you unique. Probably the reason why we even first noticed each other and more so the reason we fell in love. After all these years of being together, do not blame your distance on material financial matters or the now maturing daughter from your marriage. The saying "opposites attract" started somewhere and it is so true in life but I do not think so in the animal kingdom. This probably leaves much room for heated discussions. It was always said to me, "How could you know about love? You do not have a child." Then there is the placement of you in his life. Who really comes first in your partner's every inch of being? If our relationship were the Titanic, I would be the only one left standing on the deck as she grinds her way into the black jaws of hell. Do I have to understand? Of course I do. It is his daughters, family blood. I grew up on a small farm and unfortunately or fortunately have many a wise tale or sayings to tell. Blood is thicker than water. Okay, maybe it is, but whose blood is truly full of love and compassion? Who will really be there when you fall down the stairs and break a knee? If nothing else, I wish you could have only settled your finances of family support and separated your previous life from your new life with a partner. Why must you see these issues as disappointments? You should see your new life, me, as the good side of your life, your lover and protector, the happy side, the smile you can receive when you walk through the door after a disappointing day. Instead, you use the famous, "You do not understand!" Excuse me! Look at what I do for a living. Every day when I walk the halls of my school, I am inundated with questions mostly for advice. I have students call me on a weekend for advice and help with them with their own personal decisions. They do this because they see the respect I have for them as individuals and they recognize me as human. I eat and I cry. So, then why can you not look at my advice to you at home as being valuable when so many young people look to me for similar advice? How can I be right for them but not right for you?

I have always had the answer to these questions and you never, ever believed in me. Eleven years of disbelief turns one's fullness of life into brittle eggshells that when passed around each and every shell is so full of cracks that when we try to connect we begin to break, just like our conversations—we must touch and speak softly. First, during the early years I never had a sexual relationship like I did with you. Second, you are the most handsome person I ever held in my arms, held in my eyes, like the pixels of a digital picture printed on my lenses. Third, I know you have a caring love as you say. I do believe you. But, I feel ripped off because I want all of the above and it is not there for me. I got short-changed; the buck I invested got no returns. There are no gains to reinvest but instead a lesser amount from Day One, leaving too little to patch a broken heart! I got the one who wants to control my inner thoughts because he believes they are misdirected. I am left with no personal space, no freedom to explore friendships and as each month goes by the walls move closer together as I fight for the love I deserve. The truly sad part is that these walls are not padded, as you pound away on them for attention or bang your head against them for a thought of how to get him to see. You bruise physically and bleed noticeably but not as before when everything was hidden inside.

The worst problem, John, is that you see what you want to see. That is, you believe in only you and only in what you do. Well, SO SHOULD I BUT I FIND MYSELF JUST PLAINLY, SIMPLY DEPENDENT ON YOU FOR SOME RECOGNITION OF LOVE. I believe in me but not enough. I am afraid, so afraid of speaking and that is the main reason why every argument goes unsettled. But I do not understand why you settle for this way of having a relationship. Is it because in this format you believe to have overpowering control and I am your passive non-conventional partner? I want to believe in me and what I know we need to do but I cannot seem to put anything to work for us as a couple. It is to a point now that I want someone to reach in with a handful of answers like the man betting on several horses in one race where sticking between each finger is a slip of paper of hope. I just want to take normal breaths of air, not anxiety attacks. I've been there before simple air, clear and fresh pockets settling in my inner left-over soul. But beyond that, what can I have? There is an empty shell forming, six feet and two inches tall, which soon will crumble leaving thousands of small pieces that will not fit together to form a whole. That is my physical body I see, like in church when the priest says, "Take this bread and break it." Well, that is to make you feel new again and full of hope. There is no hope here. End of letter!

Moving with trembling legs, Jill moved off the stairs.

Jill is not an uneducated woman in book smarts and has a very high IQ of common sense smarts. That tells me she should not answer to anyone right now and everyone has to accept that fact. And guess what? She will be lonely and compared to everyone around her, who is fighting, arguing, walking out on a conversation, unhappy with their lives, even she does not know why people are so estranged from each other. Does John know why?

Have they gone too far? Did they lose everything and become shadows to each other's thoughts, emotions and ways of doing things? It scares Jill that her chest of emotions sinks more deeply and maybe is unrecoverable. It scares her not to be at PEACE!

Jill believes John does not know that everything they did for each other was from the heart, for caring and love. A caring touch, a love that cannot be forgotten, that is what Jill felt after reading her letter that was meant for John.

Numb, she does not know how or what number she called. Jill has no memory except of sitting on the staircase after John left but all of a sudden she was speaking to two police officers in the foyer. There was one male and one female with their notepads to hand write what she has to say. She was bewildered as to why they were in her house. So, she asked why they were there. Their response was simple, "You called for the police, mam."

Then the obvious happened. The general questions of name and what happened. Jill said that her partner, John, had just left her and she was sure this time it was for real and she was afraid of what he might do to himself. They did not understand what that statement meant. They didn't know that John had a recent past of drug use as another possible solution to his problems.

They knew nothing of last week or of the last eleven years. How do the police make a judgment when called to a domestic dispute? They will take notes, which they did and offer, in his case, a number to call police headquarters the next day to speak with their in-house counselor. As a comfort, someone from the station would call her in the morning to see how she was doing. Well, that sure covered it all and she was definitely feeling better now knowing all these phone calls on her behalf would happen. What about this moment which they must have seen was hurting right now and was inhibiting her judgment. Why did the police close their note pads and say good night? She was all alone, obviously incoherent in speech and mannerisms. She remembers having much difficulty giving them any information such as his house phone number. When they walked out through the screen door, she remembers seeing her reflection in the pane of glass in the door. She looked so pathetic; tears were sitting on her cheek bones and her eyes stared, not a blinking. She didn't want to blink because when her eyes would open, then she would be certain John would have disappeared and for sure she was alone. Couldn't they see? She needed someone with her! She was a danger to herself! Not knowing what time it was, she picked up the phone and called Lori.

Lori answered the phone only to hear yet again a grown woman crying profusely. Jill had only a few words, "John has left me!" In the past, Lori always heard John and Jill had had a fight and Jill thought they had broken up and John had gone to his house. Not this time, Lori knew that it was different. Not unlike before, Lori knew Jill would have a problem with recovering, if she would ever recover. As much as she did not like John, for the many things he had done to her, she still held a regard for him in Jill's life and this time she was worried about Jill. She did not fool around with words. Everything was said with gentleness and understanding, even if it did not make sense. Their conversation was short and to the point. "Jill you must call a locksmith and change the locks now. I will be over as early as I can in the morning." Taking Lori's advice, she searched for her glasses without emotion; she just needed to focus on one thing at a time now.

The locksmith was actually very easy to find at 3:30 a.m. When there was a lot of money involved, anyone will make themselves available. Jill tried to be a strong woman; whatever that was when you had been torn apart. The locksmith spoke very little and it was obvious he has done this many times before. The locksmith was respectful in not asking questions or giving any words of wisdom. He knew his role in this confusion and that was to change the locks and leave. Once he was gone, Jill turned on all the remaining lights in the house. Like a deer in the headlights of a car, she glared at the stairwell and like a zombie she went up the stairs only to fall into a familiar empty bed fully clothed. Even if she left only the kitchen light on, she would still notice it with her eyes closed. The problem of being a non-sleeper for years made her sensitive to every little display of life in conjunction with any noise and helped to keep her awake. But this evening, nothing would make her sleep and the warmth of all the lights illuminating the home seems to create a blanket of comfort. Another experience from John, totally nonresponsive to Jill's love and leaving Jill knowing with her common sense that Jill would know this was the end. Years ago she had promised John, if he did not stop using drugs and ruining their and his family's lives, the only way for her would be to end her own life.

It was early morning because she hears her neighbor leaving on his morning Tim Horton coffee run for he and his wife. This was one of his neighbor's pleasant aspects of being retired.

What will you have when you retire? Will there be someone, your appreciating loving 'other' waiting for you to give them a pleasant morning smile while passing over a simple cup of coffee. A cup of coffee—is it a simple representation of his commitment and love? Jill smells no coffee brewing and quickly realized that she will never smell John's coffee brewing again. Normally when she awoke, her back was very tight and painful. The first thing to do was to run a hot bath, jump in and soon relax all her muscles. Sometimes there would be a cup of coffee dropped off, nestling on the edge of the tub for her. A smile and a thank you would be exchanged. Not today and no bath today. All the pain she felt she believed she deserved . . . and more. The next place she found herself was in the living room sitting on the sofa, John's bed of two years as you recall. She began to hold the pillows tightly and smell them looking for any remains of the life that just walked out the front door. Jill believed but did not understand that this was final.

Monday, November 30, 2007

Police notes

Monday, November 30, 2007—2 a.m.

Jill received a police phone call after the initial police visit to determine what had happened. The officer started with, "Jill how are you doing? This is Detective Constable Charles with 66 Division of the Police Family Section. I am just calling about the incident when two police officers were called to your home this morning near 2 a.m. I am just kind of doing a follow-up on it; if you could call me tomorrow I would appreciate it very much. Thank you and try to have a good sleep." Jill sort of repeated what the officer had said and promised to call back to see if they could provide any type of counseling. Not only did the Constable call but Head Quarters was on the line as well. Jill was not sure why she got all that attention. In her head she imagined that the police might already know John was into drugs and might have been caught before. Jill would definitely believe this to be true, after all John did not tell her anything anymore. As well, as much as Jill wanted to tell the police the night before the main reasons for this domestic dispute was drugs, she did not do so. But, it was quite possible the police had seen two people before in this situation and drugs usually were the reason. Maybe they were hoping Jill would let go and tell them the truth.

The constable called John and went on to say, "Are you doing okay?

Jill just got off the phone with me, no issues with her. The police made it very clear, very clear to John to get his belongings. John was actively very polite to him, but said," Ah, I want to get my stuff and make an arrangement with Jill to do this calmly." John promised he would be very, very civil and the police cautioned him about no threats to Jill or anything. John told them he would like to come down after one week. The Constable told John, take some time to calm down and then set something up with Jill as far as getting your items. The constable advised him to call the police when he was ready so they may be present when he arrived and saw Jill. The constable gave John a non-emergency number to call when he was ready. Once again, he was told if he showed up, Jill had a right to remove him from the property, the constable counseled John every way but Sunday. Jill was told that if John showed up without the police he was not to hesitate to call 911. He said good day Jill and gave her a hotline number if she felt distraught and needed to talk with someone.

How quickly someone can land in jail by saying the wrong words because of emotions running high. One should guard their emotions and feelings and say very little when at that moment you are willing to say anything.

The police said to Jill that it was obvious that John cared for her but that she realized that the relationship had ended and that Jill seemed a little distraught at that moment. Jill would tell you this day was a blur of obscure events but that would be a lie. She started to meticulously plan her day. The hours to come were very clear to her. The phone rang; she answered thinking it was Lori to report on her arrival time. But it wasn't, it was John. In a distant voice he reported that he has been contacted by the police and told to stay away until matters cooled down. As in the past, John never saw these arguments as needing cooling down because Jill would just accept his behavior, take some ulcer medication and make dinner or whatever needed to be done. John saw everything done by him as being right and there should be no disappointments or complaints. This was definitely not the way Jill was reared; however, for John it was culturally very much accepted as a normal part of a marriage and a relationship. After all, he and Cheryl had many fights, and eventually he was removed by the police on their recommendation.

Jill tried the hotline number that was given to her that morning. She did not care about showing her emotions anymore and broke down crying to the officer on the other end of the phone line.

Josh R. Himmelman

Life living lesson: Being afraid cripples your decision-making process.

The fact is that being afraid cripples your process of making an appropriate decision at that moment in time. But being afraid is just one of several options. In this emotional mode, does your brain send a message or do your hurt feelings send a message to the brain, "I have a broken heart"? After a trauma, is your heart ever the same either with your partner or in life in general? What do you need to mend your heart? What do you use as glue to hold the pieces together, to hold all of you together? Do not let yourself become a train wreck out of worry because there will be always an answer. Guaranteed there are many cracks to be found, especially if you do not find and use the decision-making process that works for you. Some friends will offer condolences, whatever they are worth, and others will stay away because they either feel there is nothing they can do or it is not their business. You don't need such friends. How about you being a friend to yourself and showing that you are not so easily won over?

All too often the one who is suffering goes on a quest to find another love. Loris' friend is such a person. She candidly will admit, once bitten never shy, just keep on trying. The reason for her and others are: not to be alone and to find that soul mate, true love. Even with all the hurts, she is a true romantic. Too bad that has not rubbed off on either Lori or John. It is most often too bad because in these times in such a rush you will choose a person very similar to the one that needed to go. Fear not because eventually one will be the right person for you. And where is the time to heal, will your final decision be an action to fix the broken parts all to be done without worrying what will your future be for you.

During the process of worry, you may be moving about in an unconscious demeanor. My mothers' famous line to all her nine children was, "Do not fix what is not broken." With that thought in mind you may wonder was my relationship truly broken. Search your broken heart. If it is in pieces then you need to fix it most likely without the other half. Take time. No matter the hurts involved. Begin a repair process, if the process has you worried, you will never mend and have the normal life you know and deserve.

Have comfort because we all worry about something at different parts of our lives which can turn out to be our best part of life. Even though you are now alone, you can defeat worry. Always remember, if they left or you decided not to remain together, were they your true love? Do you need that person? Why not rely on one hundred per cent of yourself? If it is true love you need not to ask any negative questions because this will leave you in worry about how much hurt will they cause you today. Just take a bite of the largest piece of hurt and let them go at once. You are risking your own health and physical and mental well-being for someone who does not care for you. Sure, your partner is gone. Identify exactly what is hurting you. It may be obvious or it may be a subtle problem however it goes down. Being afraid is in our control and only we can do something to change our lives.

The process itself of being afraid and worried about what went wrong and realizing you cannot do anything about the future can leave you in a state of numbness. Unless you step outside your comfort zone and do things you thought you would never do will you begin to heal. For most it is hard to believe but relationship problems cause us to not only worry about ourselves, but mostly our health, finances, career and the big one, our future. I call this the "box theory". You have four sides, not all necessarily the same length; and only two every meet at once. When they meet, this is the opportunity to say one problem is fixed and I am ready to move down the side to the next problem. If you are not ready, the whole box can collapse and this is your life, collapsed and destroyed for the moment possible resulting in severe depression and requiring mental help. The sides most often do not match in length because our problems are not all of the same intensity. You travel around the corner and see yourself coming closer to your future. As each problem is solved, you will have less worry and more freedom for your own self-expression. However, you do have the choice to stay stuck to one side like sticking to fly paper that would mean neither moving forward or backward. No lesson has been learned and there is no sunlight on the horizon to say you are winning. Finally, to reach the corner of the fourth and last side, the last decision, your worries are less and the intensity should decrease because you had plenty of practice to win. This is the point where you see where you once began and recognize that now you are at the turning point. Throughout the sides of the box you kept seeing your future, sometimes well and other times badly but now you begin the stages of recovery. You are no longer afraid, because you have met your demons, your enemies. When you follow the box the beginning is the end and you cannot redraw the box over again. To do so, you will revisit the exact same darkness you were in before with the same reasons. Those decisions have been answered. It symbolizes an end to your pain and hurt. A full recovery is yours if you choose. There are no more bumps in the road. You crossed the finish line, worn and exhausted, but you get up on your feet and walk through the crowd smiling and strong.

We are talking about today's world. In the past the first point of direction would be to seek advice from a friend to help you break out into an unfamiliar world and for them to help you with the reasons for the partnership split. In a life of so many with so many experiences, you shy away from others because each believes that their magic bullet worked for them alone. You may also be afraid that you will be viewed with less respect for having made your decision. The most common advice is to forget and move on.

Being afraid to face your issues in a relationship and sitting in wonderment is a huge time waster. Try to get yourself up, shake of the misery and grief. You will find yourself happier for doing something positive and being on your own. Your mind needs to be at peace, but it can only do that with positive action for yourself.

End of Life Living Lesson: Being afraid cripples your decision-making process.

Life living lesson: Do not get angry

Anyone can and does get angry. But how do we know if we are angry with the right person? And how angry should we get? Sometimes we get angry for the wrong reason. It really is not worth the trouble to be angry at any level. So many times I heard my mother say, "Turn the other cheek." What she was really saying, try forgiveness and let go of any resentment for that person. Maybe one day all will be free of resentments and losses.

"Good to forgive; best to forget." (Robert Browning).
Browning, Robert: Bing. Retrieved February 2012 from http://www.bing.com/search?q=%E2%80%9CGood+to+forgive%3B+best+to+forget.%E2%80%9D+%28Robert+Browning%29.&src=IE-SearchBox&Form=IE8SRC

When we get angry with someone, this is always supported by an incident. The worst is when the other person gets angry with you for being angry, the, "What's wrong?" When we use the term "wrong, "we need to understand that every individual right vs. wrong at some level will not be the same for everyone. You may say that communication helps and that heated blow out do not help. With talking comes listening. Or else the message causing you to be angry is lost with a bigger blow out and "In your face".

The intensity of anyone's anger depends upon whom or what set it off. Is it for the wrong reason? Again, some people just get very angry about not being able to see what's wrong. You cannot change their anger but remember they can change their own self-concept and retrain how to react to a situation.

What value does one put on being angry? Does it make you feel better? Feel in control? Does it shut the other person down or lead you closer to a mini stroke or possibly a heart attack? Is it all worth the trouble? You become unsettled, even sometimes confused to a point where you cannot think of the right words to react with, or you even become speechless.

For some, their value of daily life is having a tiff somewhere along their day. It gives them a sort of euphoria. This is not too strange because the opposite is also true . . . Smiles all day when approaching strangers, we could say is valuable to life. The type of clothing, the wardrobe you buy, the choice of clothing in the morning can certainly depict your personality for the day. Happy, open and receptive to others or black, frowning and intolerant will be the character for the day. Check the local transit and watch the passengers. You will see this.

If one is very angry, they are in a state of extreme passionate displeasure. Passionate is the key. Anything done from passion has a stronger feeling and emotion attached.

The uncontrollable anger turns into a rage. Now we moved on to fierce and violent actions that go far beyond an expression of anger. Anger into a rage or is it rage into anger? Everyone whether they are carrying anger inside or externally, the fender bender on their car brings anger first and rage is determined by the following: emerging intensity from the situation. Maybe you are the one that always causes your partner to violate the conversation with rage. It could be a habit you possess, a regular practice that is very hard to give up. Those habits could be what set your partner steaming, especially if they have already had a bad day. If you are the brunt of your partner's anger, you have two options: leave or start building a tolerance to their anger. To do this you must separate the behavior from the partner you know to be basically good. Consider alternatives to achieve more success with their wrong behavior. You must choose an alternative, even if it means a time out, for example, going out to a restaurant together in public for a meal.

With anger come more actions to interpret. Look at their facial and body language, gestures that are not them; their use of language that can go as far as to swear, which might be abnormal; the dreaded high-pitched voice using a tone that you know you cannot mistake for their anger; and back to how they dress and their overall appearance. Color of clothing expresses emotions.

Even—Steven, a kid's game, not even sure where it originated. But it places a strong meaning here never to try to get even. You will most likely be the one worse hurt. As much as you want it to be 50-50, nothing appears in life in total equality. Getting even will not make you equal. Sometimes it can make you less than before because it shows a part of your character that is undesirable by loved ones, family and your surrounding society.

Not all is bliss day to day, and eventually one partner will have a bad day outside the home. Why then does this anger come home to choose a loved one to dump on, be angry with? At home there is someone available, your partner, your children, the family pet. They are all safe to let go on because after all, they love you and will not hurt you, unlike at the office. When it is all over, you are still loved, not rejected, and best yet they are more likely to understand. You build a home together not only from love but to be with each other. One comment: the individual who quickly and unconditionally forgives you is the family pet. Maybe we should make our partners the family pet.

Out of your anger comes fire, but the flames can turn on us, creating problems and stress for us. We are not all that evil, and we feel guilty or wrong about being angry especially with two people, our mothers and our spouses. Remember, as sadistic as it sounds, everyone can be replaced but our mother. Being a good person, showing our anger leaves us dissatisfied with ourselves and then feeling even more angry and stressed. And when we decide to make amends, we bring on more strained emotions and never settle into a calmer state early enough.

The anger engendered may not stop with your partner, it can pass on to further family members, and eventually your partner will create a hidden agenda against you for putting them in such an embarrassing state. Focusing on how to retaliate is a huge time waster. If you are wasting that much time on one incident, then check your reasons. There is something underlying the surface from before that which both of you hasn't cleared. Hence this argument is really about a past unresolved problem. Now the issue has shifted from the partner who is arguing with the partner at home who is now giving the brunt of the anger back trying to resolve issues attached to their existing stress from the previous argument.

In the middle of an argument, being angry becomes who can shout the loudest. No-one is rational. I call it "bombing the emotions" with words. It is a bad situation made worse. A possible solution is to listen and understand the message before you respond. If you do not do this, the expressed anger will feed on itself and emotions will rage higher. I believe the worst situation is if your partner will not argue back. This time you can be certain there will be retaliation. Each will find it difficult to communicate for a very long time. If one partner sees the anger as negative, or if a request or a suggestion is made to them, they experience emotional rejection. These indirect effects are often hidden but powerful. Much anger in a relationship causes chronic stress for at least one of the partners and that partner may never recover.

End of life living Lesson: Do not get angry.

CHAPTER SIX

Monday, November 30, 2007
Life living lesson: Friendship.

Why should we be concerned about friendship when discussing relationships? You want an awesome relationship, and then your partner is also your best friend. If you neglect a friend, what usually happens if there is not a strong enough bond between the both of you? Ask yourself, "Have I lost many friendships and it appears I am going to now lose my partner?" Could there be a connection between how you treat your friends and how you treat a partner? Research has shown the most neglected social relationship is our friendships. Looking at today's views on living, I can only see relationships as becoming the same, neglected.

When Jill first met Lori back in the spring of 1994, Jill was her adult class teacher. Jill had no need to be looking to make a new friend. From teaching Lori a bond developed in the connection of friendship, respect and honor. Jill gave Lori a letter with a card on her birthday. Now as I read the letter to myself, I knew I had to share this with you exactly as it was written and the idea of having friendship in your relationship. This was Jill then, but not the Jill today, who is very saddened and needing to reacquire the real Jill.

A card to Lori for her birthday from Jill:

This year I know when your birthday is, therefore I am able to wish you the happiness you deserve.

Would like to take the time to say thank you for your friendship and trust that you will always have for you a wealth of friends like yourself to be there for you.

Josh R. Himmelman

Kindness is one of the first thoughts that come to mind when I think of you. It is certainly a special trait that you give to all, even those who do not deserve such kindness.

They say flattery is only as good as its source and should be directed at something about the person that is not the obvious. I have chosen to flatter you about your laughter. It becomes you a great deal. It is a part of yourself you seem to ignore or believe not to exist. Your laughter is cheerful for others to hear and see. It becomes you. You have the physical characteristics that make others expect laughter from you. Be more aware of the wonderful sound of your own laughter and from this notice the good, warm feeling created by you, within you, and then, notice the warm glow on those near you.

The decisions we make in life first affects ourselves whether it be conscious or not. It then filters out to the people we believe the decision was first meant for. One could say we are terminally selfish, but after all, who but ourselves is responsible for this spiritual, physical, emotional machine, self. It is all so complex. That we first should be taught not to be afraid of our own thoughts, emotions, and physical actions and see our individuality as a continuous challenge. Most feel they are in a constant pursuit of happiness. There is not happiness for all, and each has their own form that happiness will take. I cannot tell you to be happy; I cannot show you how to be happy. I cannot give you happiness. If I knew the formula for your individuality that equals happiness, I would give it to you today as your birthday present. But this formula is as rare as a precious gem. You must mine this gem and then refine and polish it. I believe the search through the muck has been done now. Your stage in life at present is to refine your gem and start polishing.

My present to you today is to tell you of all the wonderful days there are to come. As well, I can see these days are willing to burst from within. You must see them; pull back the protective cover you have manufactured though your life, like the cover over the bird of paradise and let the explosion of color burst as a big as no limits allowed. Be proud of your accomplishments and thrust for the food of life, happiness.

Having even one friend is like finding the lost treasure off Chester Basin, Nova Scotia. It is a gift and a reward with the attachment of a true friend having no expectations from you. If we are speaking of a married couple, married by a person of God, we are taking two souls and creating one soul for eternal life. We looked at all the markers of true friendship when we discussed relationships; trustworthiness, honesty, loyalty and if need be, you love them so much but cannot keep them, then you let them go. The most beautiful creation of love is after you selflessly let someone go with all your love and they return to you, then you know it was meant to be. How powerful that connection now exists and the completeness of peace and happiness just is.

There is still nothing more Jill would ask for, even after all you have read than to have John call her and start over as friends. That new friendship with John, like many friendships that just happen, would be very hard to explain to everyone. Being a teacher Jill knows for a fact this is nothing we can teach in school or provide in a book to read. Friendship just evolves, like a partnership into a marriage. Yes there are so many factors involved. But if two people match because of who they are, nothing will stand in the way of friendship.

Not sure if it is a sad fact, but as we travel through life we not only make friends but we lose them as well. Could that be why we fail in a partnership or our marriage because we are no longer friends? The word "friend" itself is ambiguous. Does it mean an acquaintance, a friend, just a friend, good friends, or best friends? The only uncommon word here is acquaintance: a person one knows but who is not a close friend. This person does not give us trust, loyalty—you do not share your secrets with an acquaintance. Of all three, honesty is very significant and defines the absence of lying. Truth is the strongest bond that can exist between two people, and lack of honesty only provides a place for worry and questioning your friend's advice as being truthful.

I have often posed the question in group discussions, "How many best friends do you have?" It always puts a smile on my face to watch the reflection after this discussion and to see each wondering, who is a best friend? Happily I will say, young people seem to have at the most two best friends. Wow, I do consider them to be very learned today. As adults we believe we have so many best friends we can count on, yet when we're in trouble they are not there for us. Think of your partner and how many times they were there for you. Have you made emergency visits to the hospital alone, gone to a funeral alone, went to your elderly aunt who needed help alone or just spend a lot of evenings and Saturdays alone? Would your best friend make special arrangements to be with you for some of those, and not your partner? Here is your answer. Envy, changing needs, unresolved conflicts, negligence, and lack of intimacy, a lack of openness or common misunderstandings are destroying that best friend who was your best partner. If this is happening to you, the answer from them is almost never there. And what you get as an answer will never be a satisfactory reason.

Where have things gone wrong in friendships, especially the friend you need when you and your partner are in conflict? All of the types of friends you may have are all connected to you as an emotion. In a marriage or a committed partnership there is a ritual moment with a pledge of loyalty, but not so in a friendship. Do you see your relationship as having benefits that satisfy a need? Again in comparison, relationships and friendships exist on being beneficial to both parties. Once that does not exist for one party, the union begins to break apart. Sounds superficial but this has merit and truth. Both are idealized by each person involved but can exist only if the expectations are the same from each. An agreement on what each will contribute to the relationship, as in a friendship, may seem abusive or manipulative but will work as long as there is an understanding by both parties. Again, what is wrong with marrying your best friend, being a partner with your true friend and knowing each other's weaknesses and deficiencies?

If we are talking just friends, yes, we do use our friends for a purpose. We have different types of friendships for different things we do; and even in different periods of our lives we choose different friends. We have friends at work; at the gym; old or familiar friends; and distant friends. They all have different bonds with you, and most often you could never have them all together in one place. Think of the recent wedding ceremony you were at and the place settings at the tables. Certain friends are seated together for a reason. And most likely they are not seated with family.

Now think of your partner whether in a commitment or a marriage. Do you feel unable to take that person with you to certain events? Is it because you are afraid of what they may say or do? Are you a part of each other's lives one hundred per cent? Is all of this necessary? It is very hard work to maintain a loving relationship, more so in a partnership. Maybe that is why some people choose to be alone. They want the easy road ahead through life. Why bother with the extra work. As we get older, it is not only more difficult to make a friend but also more difficult to find a loving relationship. Lori is Jill's best friend. Ask yourself who your best friend is and tell them so. They may not feel the same, but after all, it is a friendship not a partnership. And even bigger, if you believe your partner is your best friend, make it known.

End of Life living lesson: Friendship

Tearfully Jill got out of bed to be with Lori who rushed over to be her support and fell asleep on the living room sofa, the sofa that was once John's bed. Jill wanted to see John lying there and when she realized that would not be anymore, her physical body went into shock and began to tremble like a fig tree in a cool breeze. No part remained still. Lori tried to hold her but it was not what she wanted. Then she tried to make sense of something with Lori by just rambling with run-on sentences, short of any grammar and very confusing for poor Lori.

Play the Game John, but who is the biggest loser this time? A sleepless night and daylight is here but not for her. She is as dark as the elderly Greek lady who just buried her husband of fifty years. Lori as kindly as she can be is trying to help but Jill is sputtering on with Lori's response seemingly to her as an empty expression. She does not know how to follow her words, stop her tears and make sense of her sentences. She is trying to tell Lori the story she thinks she understands about John. She is so confused. Poor Lori is in a state of her fourth espresso and it was only nine a.m.

John had been accusing her of playing a game of emotions. He accused her of living during the day in some level of secrecy. Jill knows herself not to be this type of person and was always frustrated with his comments. John knew there was no secret side to her character. But the more John would push her, the more she needed to play the game as well.

To act secretly can be part of one's nature or it can be brought out and directed by an outside force, usually someone you care about, a friend or someone you love. Why then would anyone want to act this way to another person and intentionally cause them to feel harassed, hurt by you or frustrated with a situation? This happens because in the first place, that behavior of theirs should not exist.

John should not listen in on her conversations with others, then question her about who they are or what she is doing later, who was on the phone. John would even go to the phone after she left the room and check the call display. This pushed Jill further into a pattern of provocation; she would lead John on for being so distrusting. Now it appeared there were huge secrets not to be told. Was it Jill's fault or John's fault? Should she have had to deal with this or should she have ignored John's behavior? Well, she believes to have any kind of interaction between them, it cannot be ignored. This always brought about another argument to see who was seeing things right. And Jill ended up with being accused of never being able to take the blame.

She learned from John we all see what we want to see. We all lie to ourselves at some level, whether through tiny or enormous lies. We do what we feel is best for ourselves. Again, another part of what we are all about. A lie becomes a part of a big protection of everything we are or even want to be. It was obvious in John's mind; it was easy to say words, hurtful words, by telling Jill this is for her, being selfish. Jill was challenging him to look in the mirror at his image and tell a lie. "Look at your reflection of yourself and that is what others see around you when you lie." John spoke back to her like she was a mirror and Jill's face became his reflection. Therefore, he found it very easy to lie to her. Oh, and the mixed emotions that John would stir in her. Jill could not determine which was the stronger. Never did Jill use body language to express herself until John managed to confuse her thoughts so badly that she would shake her head in wonderment, clinch her fist to remain still, throw herself into a chair or walk chasing John as he was bellowing something else to hurt her feelings. The worse from John would be when he slammed the doors throughout the house. Because it was Jill's house, she took it as a slam against her own body. To Lori she said, "I feel as all the world is a mirror and I have to wake up and pay attention to that reflection." See myself? And yes, others will react accordingly to the reflection I create just like the reflections John created. Beware of your lies, others know. A lie is never a secret!

Waiting for something to happen, especially a loving touch or words of comfort is never fun. It is the old tea kettle story, standing and watching the kettle for it to boil to make a cup of tea you are so deserving. Today, Jill waited broken and defeated for trying to love and help a person, a living human being. This day her only thought raveling through her head and speech out loud like an old beggar lady repeating herself, Jill repeated one hundred times; "I do not understand, why? Her life is an unfinished game!"

A lot of times consciously or unconsciously we make waiting a game. Like a sweet mom who has dinner cooking in the kitchen and an apple pie steaming in the oven as a sweet for her sweethearts in life. Her little girl is waiting impatiently by the front door in a large foyer that seems cold to her waiting for daddy to arrive from work today. She is holding the crayon drawing of the family at a picnic, a bright sun in the sky and the hands of the family held together with big red hearts on her mommies and dads chest as they appear only to be looking at her. She hears nothing in the driveway as yet and thinks maybe he is not coming home. But a quick glance from mom sees a disappointed frown as the mantel clock strikes 6:00 p.m., an anxious little girl in anticipation of her dad's arrival. Mom overcompensates by making it a game. A game of hide and seek. Honey, find a hiding spot where dad will never know where to find you and you can scare him silly. Waiting depicted as a game! The results of your last blood test to tell you that you are finally cancer free and the waiting is over, the last game piece is played. While sitting in the living room in an overstuffed arm chair, daily with her knitting because it is so habitual that no thinking is required to knit. Always resting her head, sinking into the crest between the folds of the high back chair, provides the feeling of protection from hearing any horrific news of her sons possible death in a war over seas even he does not know the reasons for this war. The game is not over. The most important game piece is missing.

Can our whole life be a game? Game pieces moving around a board, some slowly and others very quickly. Does it depend upon skill or the mind that is so corrupt it will eat anything in its path? If you play using your emotions you stand a chance of being hurt. If you use only your intelligence some of the challenges that were meant to be, will not be and life becomes mundane and boring. The heart is where your decisions should come from, but how can you rely on a broken heart? If the game piece is broken, the game stops and so does your enthusiasm and lust to be alive.

John sees life as a game and has no remorse. This is his conscious act because life with Jill to him became a game, a cruel game. But with Jill, it is an innate form of choice and consequential behavior, knowing that life is not a game, and that people are not pawns. John needed no more sources of input to play his game. He had an arsenal of anger and jealousy. The thrill for him was the challenge and even more so the interaction with Jill to make her even more depressed; John was the bully in the game. The rules were in no order, only John's order. The pieces of love, honesty, trust, peace, harmony, respect seemed not to be played. Jill tried to move them about, but John would quickly brush them from the game. To John it was a thrill, and his game piece was selfishness.

"A game is a form of play with goals and structure." (Kevin Maroney).

Maroney, Kevin Bing. Retrieved February 2012 from http://www.bing.com/search?q=%E2%80%9CA+game+is+a+form+of+play+with+goals+and+structure.%E2%80%9D+%28Kevin+Maroney%29.&src=IE-SearchBox&Form=IE8SRC

The key rule of John's game was the psychological play to evoke Jill's mental stimulation to a point reaching the piece of no self-worth. John's game tools were tokens of love meant to bring other things in his favor. Jill was his pawn to move about for enjoyment. Hidden at home was a different set of rules then those out in the public. You could see no wrong with John outside, but the house tenant who lived in the basement could tell you a different story of John at home. Rules determine order and the responsibilities of the players and their goals. John had skill; he was the master of the forked tongue. His strategy was confusion and once he struck he would remove himself physically so as not to allow Jill to strike a play. But in reality, Jill wished not to play any kind of game but trust.

Today Jill resolved that her life should be spent mostly in bed, hurt and too emotional to attend work. Are we sure of why we begin our day by extraditing oneself from the embodiment of comfort, the bed? Is there ever a true reason to remove you from the warmth and complete body experience of calm? The extra pillows with different density of fillings are to be used for a purpose. The hugger, a big over-stuffed extra long pillow; some call them the body pillow. Can it be a replacement for a loved one gone? Do they alone, need the comfort simulating a missing part of their life, now replaced by a manufactured all foam, non allergenic five foot hugger? If the loved one was never meant to be there then the pillow represents freedom. When we see such a pillow being purchased, ninety per cent of the time it is a female making the purchase. The pillow looks at its new owner and wonders what place does this pillow represent in your life?

Reasons of course exist to begin a day. Though not today for her, feeling like no more days will exist. A lot of people reluctantly begin a day they do not want to participate in—its functions of living all laid out for them. There are so many things we can learn from our pets. Jill never learned, or was it innately there for her to stretch long until some release of energy fills her completely? Try a stretch and feel how your whole body seems to come alive. Jill began to wonder why her kitty cat always upon rising from a lazy posting watching the events unfold around her, would begin with a wonderful complete body stretch. You could see inch by inch how she became alive to move onward and into the next excursion. Literally from watching her she began consciously to stretch when she awoke. Wow what a difference a stretch! A release from one state into the next can make you want to change your present for a future. A totally different bodily expression when your feet touch the floor. We all have so much to learn from such a small existence with the brain size of what we believe incapable of providing any understanding of living, moment to moment. How did Jill's brain become less wise than that of her pet? This day more than ever before there was her cat's insistence to crawl up onto her chest with her eyes almost touching hers. She purred so loud it drowned her thoughts. Do not underestimate their unconditional love! A kitty can stretch anytime and "Strike a Pose". Within a few days from that day, Jill did not know it yet, but her cat would be her only friend at home.

Making it through this day, she wondered how Lori felt watching her best friend of many years escape into darkness, a place from whence she knew coming back would be almost impossible. She lost her common sense, her sound judgment based on the perception of her situation. The fact being, she was alone and rotting like the last apple in the orchard in the final frost of the year.

Common sense does not just come. You have to search for it even though it is naturally present within. However, using your common sense makes you biased in your decision and what is acceptable for you and maybe not for others.

> *Common sense is in spite of, not as the result of education.* (Victor Hugo).
> **Hugo, Victor: Bing. Retrieved February 2012 from http://www.bing.com/search?q=Common+sense+is+in+spite+of%2C+not+as+the+result+of+education.++++%28Victor+Hugo%29.&src=IE-SearchBox&Form=IE8SRC**

> *Nowadays most people die of a sort of creeping common sense, and discover when it is too late that the only things one never regrets are one's mistakes.* (Oscar Wilde).
>
> **Wilde, Oscar: Bing. Retrieved February 2012 from http://www.bing.com/search?q=Nowadays+most+people+die+of+a+sort+of+creeping+common+sense%2C+and+discover+when+it+is+too+late+that+the+only+things+one+never+regrets+are+one%E2%80%99s+mistakes.+%28Oscar+Wilde%29.&src=IE-SearchBox&Form=IE8SRC**

Where are her regrets today? Her whole life is a mistake. She is now to die with no living. She will not hear what most people will say, "Where is their common sense?" Common sense has nothing to do with what other people think or feel. What she considers to be factual and the only truth today as in any one's thinking can be very false. Why can a sheep sense a wolf, not just the color of its fur, the sound of its howl, its odor? It is because animals without rationality require common sense. Does this mean we are supposed to be equipped with noticeable common sense? If you recognize another as having common sense, you yourself must have the same trait. Does this prove that all people have this trait? And does it really matter to have common sense to live and understand our purpose of living? If we all understand everything, that would mean we are provided with completely appropriate knowledge to live any life, hence peace.

Lori tried to give Jill advice, the kind that in her state of mind it provided no rationality. Her recommendations were messages of action she needed to do to take care of her and the life she had worked so hard to acquire. Her advice was trying to define a path more appropriate to start taking at this moment. But Jill had nothing in her mind to work with, no mental capability even to go to the bathroom until she started to pee her pants. She did know she was angry at the distrust she felt from life and a feeling of deep displeasure. She had lost control of every part of herself and she knew any attempt to regain herself would be futile. When a group of friends joke around and calls one, "Mr. Negativity!" they do not realize the damage it is doing to their friend. Why are people so ignorant? There friend is now angry, just like Jill having negative emotional thoughts. Thoughts for her based on a feeling of fear of being alone disgusted with herself for allowing her life to have transgressed into nothingness; shame because she is so weak of mind and hostile towards John for causing this to her. Why did Jill deserve this to happen, to play out the game as a complete loser and become a creditor with many I.O.U.s owing to herself? That evening she was without sensibility. She knew that without thought, the actions resulting from so much defeat and anger would lead her into a path of very negative consequences. After recent events, Jill knew that she was capable of impulsive action with no rational thinking.

Jill needed help, more than she had ever expected. She was now haunted by the expectation of a lawsuit from John looking for pieces financially of JILL'S HARD WORK. John never acquired anything from Cheryl. He was blackmailed by part custody of his girls. In this relationship, there were no children, only financial gains for someone vindictive or illogical from drug abuse. To sue someone is to lack dignity or to covet what has already been paid for years. Payment for what, though; for being in a committed relationship where all is supposed to be equal? Were all problems communicated on a regular basis? No. Payment for lack of respect, dignity taken away, lack of honor, and no trust left.

It all weighed on Jill's mind so heavily that she began to look for protection. She thought that the first and best place to begin was with her physician. After all, they are sworn to an oath to care for a patient and their word is totally trusted in the eyes of the law. This idea made Jill feel both comfortable but also uncomfortable because she had to reveal even more weakness. The physician, without a question, began to draft a letter immediately with Jill.

There were several calls made that day from John to Jill's home. She only knew of the first call when Lori asked her if she wished to speak with John. So crippled by emotion of tears and shakes Jill asked Lori to speak with him. Jill did not want to know any detail of the conversation; Lori did not even ask if she wanted to know. It was obvious. Not known to Jill, John had called Lori's father that morning asking him to speak to his daughter to allow Jill to take the phone. Apparently, he told John, "I have no intention of being involved," and then John's kindness on the phone turned to what he was really all about. Lori's dad is elderly and this was all too much for him to understand especially since John was talking about Jill. Lori's dad immediately called her at Jill's home and gave a complete synopsis of the call. Lori was furious and John did call again only to be told neither his presence nor his calls were welcome anymore at Jill's home. This is when Lori took Jill to see her doctor. She was in need of help.

As stated by the doctor:

Monday, November 30, 2007

To Whom It May Concern:

I am a family physician certified by The College Of Family Physicians of Canada and licensed to practice by The College of Physicians and Surgeons of Ontario. Jill has been under my medical care since 1995. She has been seeing me regularly since this time for various health issues and I feel that I know her and her personal situation well.

Jill has been suffering from increasing symptoms of anxiety and depression since approximately 1997. Her situation appears to be directly related to difficulties she has been having in her relationship with her partner, John. During this period she consulted me on numerous occasions feeling threatened and fearful of living at home with her partner. She described very erratic and violent behavior from her common law spouse, John. Jill commented repeatedly about John's drug abuse and feeling coerced into taking drugs. Jill reported feeling extremely fearful of consuming drinks at home worried that they would contain drugs. She repeatedly expressed a desire to end this relationship with John, but feared violent repercussions. Jill described an acute deterioration in her domestic situation in the last two to three months. She appeared very anxious and emotionally unwell. She was having severe sleep dysfunction and I prescribed sleeping pills and an antidepressant medication on November 30, 2007. She continues to feel fearful of violent repercussions and has been severely traumatized emotionally by this.

Signed by: family physician.

The doctor gave Jill a number of prescriptions and instructions to Lori on how to give them to her. It was just her fear to finally be on medication for depression. She knew a lot about depression because she had studied in school and taught it as well to her students. It was not funny for her to realize one does not practice what they preach. Lori went to the drugstore for Jill. She could not be out in public. Her tears would not stop and would be in anyone's eyes a total screw up. Society does not like to see a grown woman so distraught.

There were no movies tonight to watch at Jill's house, no laughter and no eating popcorn. In fact Jill and Lori spoke very few words, Lori, simply because she could not. She was in a sense of shock. Lori did not speak because she did not know where to begin. To point out John was all wrong for her from the start or now was the time to learn to be alone and love yourself, this was not the time to tell Jill. Such was the obvious dimension with Jill and her lack of love for herself. She lost it all through the years living with John. Time not only heals but it changes things and people as well. Lori saw over the years the change in both, pushing each other into a loveless relationship. Jill was more in love with John and still is today. They say the length of time being together will be the amount of time it will take to heal. That is a long time and for Jill I believe it will take that long for her to remember who she is.

It did not take much convincing from Lori to send Jill off to bed. After a few hours of Lori lying on the sofa she no longer could take the sobbing from her bedroom. Kindly, Lori went upstairs and knocked on her door. Jill mumbled some words and Lori felt it was okay to go in. Shaking her head all she saw was a crippled-looking old woman, doubled together with a box of Kleenex on the bed. Jill did not even crawl under the covers. One can only believe that would have meant comfort and warmth to her, just not what was in her state of mind. Lori was actually afraid and has never helped anyone in this condition before, not even her own children when they would hurt themselves and have those big sobbing cries. She decided to lie on the bed behind Jill in a comforting position which meant trying to move close to her in a fetal position. When we hurt so badly, why is it we tend to revert back to the fetal position? Is it because we felt so safe in our mother's womb, held and protected. Needless to say it did not work. Jill had nothing left, no pride, and no substance to hold on to and was empty of everything except tears.

Loir was a very intelligent woman, especially after experiencing her own two break-ups and some therapy. Lori decided she must try something. She must see Jill turn the corner in the road or at least try. Lori asked Jill if she could talk to her and started to speak.

"There is a song, "Breaking up is hard to do." Ending a relationship is not what you really ever want to do. The fact is when a relationship has gone

irreparable someone has to make the move to end it. As in your case, Jill, the truth is that many relationships last beyond the expiry date only because it is hard to break up."

How does one end a relationship so no one gets hurt? The old throwing the clothes out the bedroom window never worked. Jill needs to be clear on why to terminate the partnership. It sometimes never happens but the relationship must end. Usually one will decide it must be their reason, but usually they are wrong. Jill needs to be honest with herself and the process will be easier. It also means to be honest with your partner as well. Nothing worse than no answer, no return of a phone call, text, or email; you are left dismissed and no true answers why they left. Should you know the reason, not necessarily? Love is blind.

Some agree to be in an open space like a restaurant surrounded by people as the way to be honest and break-up. At least composure is held together. But most think this is not the best way to do a break-up. After all, is this not the way a relationship begins with a presentation of the engagement ring in a fine restaurant?

> *"The best and most beautiful things in this world cannot be seen or even heard, but must be felt with the heart"*
> (Helen Keller)
> **Keller, Helen: Bing. Retrieved February 2012 from http://www.bing.com/search?q=%E2%80%9CThe+best+and+most+beautiful+things+in+this+world+cannot+be+seen+or+even+heard%2C+but+must+be+felt+with+the+heart%E2%80%9D%28Helen+Keller%29&src=IE-SearchBox&Form=IE8SRC**

"Listen, Jill, there was no increase in his aspiration around you and all he did was cause you to suffer, the only result was unhappiness. Jill, this is called functional happiness. You lack a feeling of joy or elation that a person should generate themselves through their own personal focus in dreams and the passion of life with John.

Jill, you'd said you try to go to a Buddhist temple to learn their teachings as well as the life's suffering that would focus on the acceptance of truth and no answers from John. You must open your mind and see this is what happened. Buddha does not focus on suffering but happiness.

Right now, Jill, you are displaying mental dysfunction and it scares me. It is a mental misalignment. Your thoughts do not satisfy anything you deserved in life. Keep this up Jill, and you will never be happy. There is only one way for you to understand. Change your thoughts, how you speak, and act. Place an effort to heal and concentrate on what is best for you and that will be your way out of the ignorance of this situation.

What you want most in life is "peace." To achieve this around John, change your mental state and detach from the passion of what you believe existed with John. Stop what you are thinking as your needs and wants to live with John. You can do this and then you will begin to be well. Search within yourself, dear Jill, for mental growth away from John. Make an effort; know what is all right and concentrate using all that knowledge and mental skills you have to achieve happiness. Please, Jill, you are an intelligent woman who has been crushed in a relationship, but only you can fix it now, you must!

In the effort to stop thinking negative thoughts eventually positive thought will begin to make you smile, at least inside. Stop this Jill, and see what you have. Smell the roses. Just try to keep your mind positively active. Stop craving John and what could have been. You are imprisoning yourself by regrets of the past and desire for the future that is lost. Right now I am sure John is not feeling any of these thoughts because he left not loving you. Do not let him win and tear you further down emotionally and physically.

Look around your home, Jill, it is all you created over the years and it made you happy while you were doing it. You put so much love in the home to satisfy others and not yourself. Find passion for your work and remember that it was done by you for you. You should concentrate on happiness for others, yes, for others as the person you are. But right now it should focus on you. You are trying to act like this was for you, but you know it was not. Now only your heart and thoughts are broken—nothing physical that is irreparable like a stroke. Use the above to start mending, and the glue will come only from the desire to be happy again. Face reality and the dysfunction of John. That is not your destiny. See a way out. Think your own positive consciousness and practice what I am telling you, Jill."

"Our greatest joy and our greatest pain come in our relationships with others." (Stephen R. Covey)

Covey, Stephen R. Bing. Retrieved February 2012 from http://www.bing.com/search?q=%E2%80%9COur+greatest+joy+and+our+greatest+pain+come

**+in+our+relationships+with+others.%E2%80%9D
+%28Stephen+R.+Covey%29&src=IE-SearchBox&-
Form=IE8SRC**

Without a word spoken, Jill, with suppressed thoughts, slowly turns over in bed. She could not say Thank you to Lori because her mind was now very confused and still wanted to fix everything. She lay in bed wishing John and she could get back together. As she reminded herself of the days at the beach, she started to remember the little arguments every time she tried to make the experience nice. Those thoughts did not make her happy and starting to realize that they would never change and then she would never be happy. The break up that happened this time again will most likely happen again and again. She thought of the time when they tried couples therapy, and what a disaster that was again, because John was selfish and non receptive.

Continuing to remember that life was more fights than something good and this final year, definitely it was not healthy. Jill wondered if she could call him and push him again to come back and do couples therapy again. In the past Jill did excessive texting, emails and phone calls out of desperation that pushed John even further away. It was definitely the wrong way of trying reconciliation. Jill lay in bed thinking this time she could beg and plead her way into John's heart. Soon though she realized that in John's state of mind this would only make him happier to see how badly she was hurting.

Digging into her common sense, Jill knew she must concentrate on what was going on now. Maybe she should back off; space was needed in a new break-up to begin to live life. But Jill saw no life. She longed to get back with someone who cared nothing about her. Jill wished that John would begin to remember the good times; memories shared and want to at least talk with her. But when an ex-partner such as John shows interest in starting over, to him it is just a game. Jill's feelings would be the pawn. John knows that Jill will never give up, and for him once again he gets all the attention and nothing is left for Jill. Another problem: if John were to come back it could also be only to pass time until he found a better prospect. Jill was beginning to realize there was no win-win situation. It was a win for John and a loss for her.

Jill lay there before finally falling asleep and remembered one comment from John about a year ago. They were in bed and John looked over and said, "You are nothing but an old woman!" knowing this would kill Jill's heart. How would one react to that statement? Jill said nothing, turned to her side and quietly cried. This was after thirty years and three relationships, Jill wondered why she was here and not happy? Yes, as in some relationships, one has a health problem—that was Jill with several health issues. That did not change her heart and feelings for John; as a matter of fact she always told John she would never make it his problem. That is exactly what Jill did.

This was a very difficult time for Lori, once a very calm woman, now experienced stress like most people today. Lori's idea of a rough day would be when she could not give something to someone, just from the heart. Jill loved Lori for this reason. Both together were very generous. The only problem was Jill expected a Thank you in return. A long time ago in university Jill was told by a professor to be successful, never do or give expecting a Thank you in return. That is not giving. Too bad Jill only remembered the phrase but never practiced it.

There are two different types of people and two different categories of stress. Chronic stress which is ongoing and continuous, as in Jill. Episodic stress is an occasional stress that happens from time to time, as experienced by Lori.

Jill was the typical chronic life individual allowing her personal life to be totally adjusted to John's life and adventures. This meant she was always in distress and negative stress. If you met Jill, she operates always with the on button pushed because she continues to be geared up. She never relaxed between one stress crisis and the next, eventually leaving her with less and less energy to work positively through the next upheaval from John. The terms that gave her away: her feelings of insecurity; anxious feelings; headaches; crying; muscle aches everywhere; and frustration and anger.

Lori, as I said, was thankfully the opposite of Jill and therefore recognizing she could always be there to try and help. She did experience a stress level called, episodic stress. It occurred occasionally from time to time. I believe you can guess when that would occur for Lori—only around Jill. Knowing this, Lori still came to her side, always a great attribute of a true friend. This did cause a disruption in her life, but she tried to keep its severity and duration only with Jill and not adapting it to her. The type of stress Lori would have is called Eustress, a short term interruption in Lori's life. As soon as Jill's challenges were stable,

Lori would relax quickly and return to normal, unlike Jill who could only experience chronic stress.

For both Lori and Jill stress was not only seen on the outside but very heavily on their internal selves. Lori was able to respond to and deal with Jill's external stress because of her own emotional well-being. However, there was none in return, no help given by Jill because externally and internally she was maladjusted: insomnia, fatigued, nervous, loss of enthusiasm or energy and mood changes. It was apparent that Jill's lack of helping herself and Lori; she needed to be medicated for mood disorder and/or cognitive behavior disorder therapy counseling.

Almost any emotional problem tends to drag other issues along. For Jill, the memory of an elephant, now experiences a heavy loss of memory. It went as far as experiencing losing what Lori's name was and why she was there. This was hurtful to Lori but again in true spirit, she understood her situation. The problem with Jill's mind: she was overwrought with too many memories and worries about how to fix so many issues with John. In studies it shows short-term memory can only take in five to nine pieces of information at a time. There is no wonder Jill always looked spacey and her eyes were sunken into her head. Her eyes were of wonder, moving rapidly, and the sadness was deep as you looked upon her face.

Lori knew as well her memory was weighing heavy because she found little notes everywhere in the house. Jill was very intelligent and knew written words help you visualize in your mind that mental list that was haunting her. Almost like a simple grocery shopping list not to forget anything. But Jill had too many personal notes therefore they were of no aid to her. Again, her biggest failures to herself were her internal distractions of chronic stress. Stress can cause memory paralysis and that anxiety kills her ability to think positively to see what she is doing to herself. To be honest at this point, no device such as pictures of John or a gift from him or even Lori's presence could help her now.

Is the emptiness of happiness the same as excruciating pain? If she could experience positive feelings and joy and feel no pain, then curling into a ball of emotions would not be fatal. We all want happiness and the good life; but Jill s' experiences had left her hopeless. Jill had forgotten that her happiness must come from within a place which was left blackened by sorrow.

> *"Happiness is the meaning and the purpose of life, the whole aim and end of human existence."* (Aristotle)
>
> **Aristotle: Bing. Retrieved February 2012 from http://www.bing.com/search?q=%E2%80%9CHappiness+is+the+meaning+and+the+purpose+of+life%2C+the+whole+aim+and+end+of+human+existence.%E2%80%9D+%28Aristotle%29&src=IE-SearchBox&Form=IE8SRC**

"Some cause happiness wherever they go; others, whenever they go."
(Oscar Wilde)
Wilde, Oscar: Bing. Retrieved February 2012 from http://www.bing.com/search?q=%E2%80%9CSome+cause+happiness+wherever+they+go%3B+others%2C+whenever+they+go.%E2%80%9D%28Oscar+Wilde%29&src=IE-SearchBox&Form=IE8SRC

Lori went back to the sofa, sleepless mainly because of the sobbing from Jill. She held on to Sweetie, Jill's cat and thought, "If only I could do this for Jill, cause her to feel happy again." She tried to help Jill see the positive side of this break-up; to see that she should be content because John was unbearable and hurtful. She wanted her to see that she was an intelligent woman and that she should be optimistic. "Start thinking happier thoughts and your attitude will improve towards life." Lori continued to list for Jill all the things she had to be optimistic about: a great career and education, a greater intuitive sense than others, her friendship; that she Jill should learn to forgive because it would help to heal her heart. "Remember it is your heart that is in pain." After all of Lori's help, Jill's comment was, "Slime slithers through the vulnerable heart!" Finally Lori put aside the conversation from upstairs and fell asleep. And so did Jill. She awoke to the smell of coffee brewing from the kitchen and for a moment thought it was John. Then she realized it was Lori and for a moment felt total resentment for Lori. She wanted it to be John.

CHAPTER SEVEN

Tuesday, December 1, 2007 A.M.—to—Thursday, December 31, 2007

It was still a work day for Lori, and she was already short-staffed. Jill did not mind because she wanted her out of the house. They had a coffee together and for these moments Jill was no longer crying but extremely unhappy. Her voice was low and hoarse from depression and lacked content; the conversation was about the weather, which was all.

Jill now realized that the first time she had tried to commit suicide was for recognition from John. She realized how much distress she was in with a great need for John's love. It was done purposefully and manipulated by a well-planned attack on John. She was now in a relationship with someone who supposedly loves her and is committed to her but not there for her. The partnership vows, spoken and unspoken, in the relationship, were all the opposite of their meaning in reality.

Jill was looking towards retirement soon and wanted to travel with John around the world. No matter that John several times showed discontent and ignorance of a retirement plan by Jill. John was younger and could not retire at the same time as Jill. He could not understand Jill's plan. All he could think of selfishly, "What about me?" Jill offered him a very successful life but John could never see this: a huge lack of visualization. John could never see beyond the moment. When two people do not see eye to eye on their lives together, it is a failure. In a great relationship, both parties work together and plan their finances, family, travel and retirement needs. There is no "This is yours and now this is mine." Separate planning means you will always be separate; it is not enough to bond you together, even if you are in love. You cannot live off love alone.

It was mid-morning and Lori still did not leave. She was so tired that it took a long time to get ready for work. Jill was impatiently waiting to carry out her plan—a plan, just to be accepted by God. With a glare in her eyes she began to wonder. She saw two love birds that mated for life. She started wondering why she should see this. As she looked closer, one bird was without wings, as if they had been ripped from the body. One could fly and the other was in pain, staring at the blue sky, missing flight with its partner. The love was there, yet separated by others' hatred of its beauty. The bird was still beautiful but lost without its partner. It wandered in circles and was dazed, as if it was about to fall down. There was no help and the flying bird flew over several times and then took flight high in the sky, disappearing into the white clouds. The bird on the ground came to rest in a seated position looking around her surroundings and then fell further into the dusty ground; dusty ground that existed with no life, no living grass or even water to drink for survival. It was close to the end, no love, no help and no perception of a continuation of flight except through death.

Seated on the sofa, Jill saw her soft blanket begin to move. Have you ever placed a soft blanket over an empty chair, ready to snuggle down and have a cup of hot chocolate? The blanket moved, she realized, because it was covering her feet. Jill placed the blanket over herself and the sofa where it fell peacefully, with no sound, no movement of air, even the silence had decided to fade away.

Jill felt nothing: any love for herself, no flashes of her past and no embarrassment of what she would leave for her family. Everything she seemed to do now was methodical, in slow motion, with no color, with no distinction of beauty or ugliness. There were no crosses to bare, no pictures in the room as reminders or rosaries to shed tears upon.

When you're in love you think you are at peace, and that nothing in your life matters except being more loved. You can still be loved but not at peace. If you pray daily, for a peaceful mind, your prayers should include all of the following: peace, health, happiness, and safety. Jill was empty of all—there was no need to pray.

Jill forgot about the relationship with herself. She was coherent enough to remember the amount of emptiness within an ugly world.

She had no intelligence and her chest sunk inward from deep sorrow for herself. To see her one would have said, "This is a terrible waste of a sweet woman."

It is so important to feel accepted or you are not happy and become unfocused about what to do to regain acceptance. Jill tried with such difficulty to learn and accept John's previous lifestyle. She did not learn; therefore, at least some of what she was doing now made sense. John's previous life and the way he lived were disrespectful of others'; everything had to be his way. Jill could remember once when visiting his aunt and she had brought out a tray of food for them to enjoy. Without thought, John pulled the whole tray in front of himself. Jill was actually pleased when his aunt who had just met Jill said, "John, how can you be so selfish?" Without any embarrassment or shame in any way, he shoved the tray part away towards Jill, still showing his selfishness and lack of acknowledgment of her. John wanted to be top dog everywhere, even with his own family. He felt he was the important one and should dominate all conversations, even two or three at a time. These memories were so painful to Jill; it made her chest hurt with anxiety.

Blinded by being so dependent on John, Jill had never judged him as negative and as dark towards her. She was still willing to be a part of his life. Jill, so co-dependent and in fear of loneliness, still saw her life as being worse without John. John's relationship with Jill had definitely been territorial. He controlled the whole home, the Saturday events, even how the car should be driven. This may seem insignificant but eleven years of the same was not a minor event. To be Jill meant, she got zero consideration from John even though she was another human being. John never thought first about Jill; he was so selfish that he was truly, "the man in no matter what place he would be."

Jill gave up asking questions and looking for who she was now as a person. A constant effort was made by Jill to do everything right to please John. John chose not to do anything regarding the home and loved seeing Jill's tears and her unhappiness. Jill kept trying to ask him to help, to show some love for the home and her.

Jill had no more tolerance left. She was at the point where John's habits and mannerisms really depressed her. Usually one's tolerance level changes constantly from good to bad in such a situation. Her frustration resulted from her whole life that seemed to be intolerable, wrong and unfair. It all pushed a gentle woman into complete rage and anger.

There was no reason to look for Jill's source of dismay; everyone knew it was John's influence over Jill. Even when John noticed Jill's deep depression and stress, he didn't stop putting her down. His best attack was to be a constant reminder to Jill how transparent his lack of love was for Jill. He saw Jill turn inwards with unacceptable and painful emotions, compelled to seek doctors' prescriptions as a mechanism of defense. In his present state, riddled in a street drug, John was killing the one thing he was so proud of years before and that was Jill. She knew in her heart that all this was not the real John but the John on heavy drugs, yet this did not heal Jill's feeling of loss of love.

I hear from so many today that peace is like a golden apple. The stresses of life, people feel like the old saying, "One step forward, and two steps backward". To feel at peace and to use any form of suicide, a man once told Jill, your soul lives on in eternity the way you die. Those who die in their sleep are truly at peace, as we say, what a peaceful death. I hope I leave this earth one day in the same way. But this man made it very clear, if you jump in front of a bus; you see that bus and hear your screams for a split second. Hence you go through eternity seeing that bus and screaming, a completely painful soul. Yet your destiny was to leave all hurts behind and now you created no peace for ever. Jill told her psychiatrist she believed the only way to accomplish peace from stress and depression was to have some way to extinguish her own existence, which had become very difficult now. The psychiatrist said the angels and those protecting her soul, her guardian angel that loved her would have the power to change her life and blackness, if she only could believe and accept.

It was now near noon and finally Lori looked back from the doorway at Jill, who was curled on the sofa, and with a smile said," I will be home as soon as I can. Please try to sleep at least an hour." Jill started immediately thinking of little phrases and seeing her life as nothing. She saw her life as "forced living", forced to breathe, to think and smile into emptiness. No walking, running or skipping with joy, no friends and no family it was all emptiness. Jill felt it was time to realize she disowns all that is beautiful. She went on to think that her emotions were a "façade of emotion." She had to learn about her emotions first and which ones she could trust and why right now there was a fight inside her between her emotions. She thought of all her living and deemed it be a waste of life. She was trying to eat and live healthily, for what? She realized she had no children and who would hold onto her legacy? What was present here for her today? She did not live in a present and the past seemed so empty. If she could see the future, and it pleased her, Jill would wonder how she could get to that place. She was so tired of therapy. Her mind was sick; no more drugs, no more specialists, no more shrinks, no more alternative counseling, no more books, maybe just the pills. Thinking of what a crazy old aunt used to tell her daily, "Life is a bowl of cherries but they left the pits in the cherries." It may be okay but she had more pits than cherries. John had eaten the best part. Some were too sweet and some were sour. Her days were never sweet. She had lived a lost life, or was it lost lives? When you have a break-up, do they take a part of you with them? And what part of you dies? Is all of this a prepayment for a better future? Lessons learned so as not to forget or repeat those lost lives? She had never wanted it all: just a small piece of overly sweet pecan pie with the nuts soft and rich. How does she end this for herself? Is she sacrificing anything and if so does it have a price? No end is without pain but pain can be beautiful if you have no expectations. Sirens howl to save lives. Where was her siren?

What, no guarantees, no warranty, no extra purchase of another three years in case of a breakdown and no extra charge for parts and labor? How much labor do you expect from Jill to work in a partnership? Is not a partnership like co-workers both having a common goal to achieve production and success at one thing, achieving an outcome with pride? Was Jill proud of John or plainly dependent on John? There is no pride in co-dependency. Therefore Jill has neither pride in herself nor has she received any pride from John.

Feeling empty with no pride in oneself was all very strange yet real for Jill. As soon as Lori left the house Jill sat at the computer and wrote a suicide note. As to what she wrote, she has zero recollection. It was just so simple and easy. After all, any one-time experience at anything makes the next journey easier and most likely more successful. Once again, Jill gently placed a small table by her side near the sofa and with great ease started collecting pills throughout the house and a couple of bottles of water. After all, she felt she deserved pure water this time. There was nothing in her mind like before except to gather all the pills she could find. Because she knew from the last time, taking an overdose of pills was very calming, especially after the first dozen or so—she would be very able to do it this time. No tears flowed; there were no warm expressions on her lips, no feeling of sorrow, no prayers to God and no anxiety. She had only peace, like warm air on a beautiful beach. She was glad this was an opportunity not to have her life on hold anymore but to let it fly away. As well, this time for sure, she knew she would be found after her death by Lori and not over-riddled by an odor and decline of flesh, a body now without a soul.

Jill never even looked at her beautiful home and thought she had forgotten the suicide note. When a note was found, there was information in scribbled pencil in between the keyed text. Only the police and the doctors knew what it said; therefore she did not even know who it was addressed to.

John was not on Jill's mind. There was only a sense of peace and finality of a tormented mind. She really felt glorious and that was all. Again, it was indescribable how calm Jill saw herself. This time right away she took a dozen sleeping pills because she knew it was what she needed to be at rest and to be able to proceed. As the last sip of water was washing down the pills, a shadow appeared quickly across the front window. It was a small bird that flew into the window and dropped downward. Old superstitions from home—this meant the imminent death of someone in the family. She was pleased. Jill actually smiled thinking it was a sign for her. She would be successful this time. She was so happy; she began to invade the pill bottles like a child for candy and made them disappear, swallowing handful after handful. She became quickly non-functional, not lucid of her surroundings. She tried to open her eyelids but it was as if they were glued together. She knew, no more stress, no more depression because it was euphoric now to lie so still with a mind free of thoughts without even trying.

Jill was well on her way to achieving her goal of suicide. She now was placed in the sofa as if placed in a coffin. If one could have been there, it probably would have looked very peaceful, just as she had wished. Well, was it a wish or a command over her life? This was all near 2 p.m. in the afternoon.

It's so strange that it could be unbelievable but has to be believed because it happened for real. Lori was at work trying to concentrate on her job but then it happened. Coldness came down across her shoulders;

a cool breath was mouthing by her head that made her hair move slightly from the ear, so as to be audible. Then a lovely woman's voice said, "Lori, Jill is in real trouble, you must save her. You are the only one now who can do this for her!" Lori dropped the papers from her hands and as they slid loudly across the floor she started to look for a phone. Her co-workers looked her in the face. "You look like you seen a ghost, are you okay?"

Lori recalls that for the next five minutes she had no clear idea of what she was about to do. She quoted, "I do not know any police division numbers, especially the one nearest Jill's home." She did not use 911 but moved her fingers across the phone number pad and dialed the division. Lori never told the police about the aberration, she knew they would think her not quite with it. Instead, she urged them to send a police car to Jill's home, "I think she has hurt herself because I cannot get her to answer the phone."

For Jill everything that was almost divine peacefulness became a blur of the front door smashing open and her trying to open her eyes. Jill was not aware that the police were outside looking in through her little lead glass front windows. They called back to the station for a description of Jill as given by Lori to confirm. She remembers one officer saying, "She is in bad shape!" She remembered the second police officer holding her suicide note, shaking his head and holding it above Jill's head asking why the pencil marks were there between the keyed notes. Jill also watched as he read the note and he studied each word while looking back and forth with the second officer who was making notes in his little pad. Then loudly, as if I were deaf they asked, "Where is you ID? Who are you? Are you Jill? Is this your home? Do you know a person named Lori?" Jill could not answer; she couldn't even move her body let alone her mouth to speak. Jill then remembers one officer yelling, "Get us some ID and go get your wallet. Where is it?" The other officer again repeated, "Go get your wallet." They demanded this of Jill, yelling and bullying Jill so much that with all her remaining strength she rose off the sofa first falling on her knees in a praying position. One officer took her arm and helped her to her feet. Jill crawled on hands and knees up the stairs to find her wallet which took some time. In the background were the voices of the two officers. Hanging onto the banister, like dangling on a rope over the side of a ship, Jill made it down the stairs.

By now as she approached the foyer floor and she saw an ambulance crew and a fire truck's red lights flashing. She fell to the floor and her next recollection was of being in a hospital bed in the emergency ward with Lori gently holding her cold hands. Tearfully she said, "I am here, Jill!"

Bewildered Jill asked, "What is going on? Why are you here Lori and not at work? Where am I?" Then she looked away from Lori, not in shame but in anger and dismay for Lori's involvement and interference. There were several nurses and one male doctor with clipboards staring at her, whispering amongst themselves and shaking their heads. They asked if she was able to sit up by Lori. Lori put her arms around Jill's shoulders and neck and said, "I will help you." Time passed but how much Jill does not know.

Lori and Jill started to speculate about how much trouble Jill was really going to be in. The second in command, a young woman, seemed to be telling the head psychiatrist what should be done for Jill. Without a doubt she wanted her admitted for observation and counseling in the psychiatric ward on the sixth floor. Lori just stopped talking and starred at Jill. Jill's eyes were welling up and her face was white with fear of the sixth floor. Everyone left, disappearing behind the white curtain that appeared to move in an angry wind. The voice began to elevate in tone and it was definitely a focus on Jill remaining. Shortly afterwards, the two doctors returned—the female doctor broke the news almost with pride. She had won her case to have Jill admitted.

Lori asked if she might accompany Jill to the sixth floor and keep some of her personal belongings. As they left the elevator, they were immediately confronted with heavy wired glass doors, a buzzer system. As they peered through the door, they could see a young patient with a runny nose dripping far down to his belly, losing his pants. It was at that point, as they entered through the doors, that Jill knew she had lost all her rights. Her freedom was no longer hers but was in the hands of these doctors and all the decisions were theirs to make. A clipboard was tossed into her hands and she was asked to provide a list of all medications she was presently taking. Needless to say, most pills have names that you cannot pronounce let alone spell. Finally a nurse said "Here, I will help you.", as she relieved Jill of her belt from her pants. Lori again asked if she could go to Jill's room and help her get comfortable. There seemed to be no problem except that look in a very staunch looking nurse's eye said "no" in an effort to discourage Lori. The nurse seemed to hide inside a cage affair where all the staff appeared to hide from fear of the inmates.

To the right of the cage was a huge white board with all the patients' names and associated doctors' names, plus some encryption for their reason to be there. As Jill passed by, her name was being entered with one of those boards with a heavy smelling red marker, the kind you get high on or a headache from. It looked to Jill that the nurse was high, probably from some extra meds lying around. To the right was a common room filled with something like furniture bolted and enclosed in metal brackets. On a huge table there was a phone book and one very large antique phone for all the patients to use. Even though it was approaching 11 p.m. the television was playing very loud but no-one was present watching. Through the other side of the common room was another large doorway that led to another hallway just like the one where Jill was standing. Jill was very observant and realized the shape was a horseshoe affair with no finish line to cross over. There was no place to run; and if you tried . . . she did not want to know the answer. As she looked left there was another white board but this time it had a clock on it indicating times to come and go. It was evident you must obtain permission for time to leave for a while. Then at that moment she heard an alarm sound and the doors behind her banged open. With a limping walk, a very rough looking man in pajamas, unshaven, tangled hair and smelling of cigarettes, started to push by to sign in on the board. He forgot his time and was quickly reminded by a passing nurse.

Fortunately or not, Jill's room was right behind the prison station. They both stood in the doorway and started to cry. At first sight it did not even compare to a gruesome movie scene. The room was about twenty by ten feet in size with two much stripped down beds: no headboard, no sides, just strapped on legs underneath. There was only one much overused pillow and only one sheet. You were not allowed two because then you might use then to hang yourself. Jill was used to a goose down duvet to snuggle under. Not tonight. The belt was already gone. Lori helped with Jill's clothes as a nurse stood by and swept up every piece. With a straight arm forward Jill was handed a hospital gown and that was it. Lori had such huge tears on her cheeks that Jill herself could not cry. Lori was crying enough for both of them. She went over to the side of the bed and showed Jill that the picture on the wall was screwed on fast and the side table had its draw removed. As they looked down the floor was stained and the table was screwed fast to the floor. The room was meant to have been white and have the appearance of peace, but it didn't now. Scared to lie down because then Lori would leave, Jill sat on the edge of the farm-style mattress that sank to the floor under Jill's weight.

A nurse entered with a cup full of pills and a small glass of water and told Jill to swallow them all at once. Lori was in shock when the nurse asked Jill to open her mouth to prove she has swallowed all her pills. Standard procedure but it felt so distrusting. Jill was told to lie down and Lori pulled the very thin overly-washed sheet close to her neck and kissed her on the forehead. Then she was gone.

Jill never sleeps with the lights on—not even with a night light burning anywhere in the house. No "lights out" policy here. It was like daylight all night long. And worse, on the hour a nurse would walk into the room and stand by your bed demanding to know your full name. Two things bothered Jill that evening. How could anyone who was really ill get well without sleep and how cold she felt as she asked for more covers but was jokingly told "no."

There was a second bed in the room next to a window ledge. Jill stared at every trophy in that space. There was no-one sleeping there and the bed had its sheet hanging over touching the floor with a dirty half-filled pillow lying in the center. On the window ledge lay an old toothbrush that was hard with toothpaste that had dried fast to the ledge and an empty plastic cup. During one of the night nurse calls, Jill asked if someone was supposed to be staying with her in the room. The nurse gruffly said, "She signed herself out two days ago and has not been found."

A sleepless night brought Jill to a morning breakfast call. Everyone was expected to be in the common room for a lovely treat of plastic spoons. No forks or knives. It was easy to figure out why. The phone rang and rang. Finally, Jill answered. Someone looking for the person in Room 607 kept yelling to go get them. So Jill, not familiar with the location of the rooms by number, went in search of Room 607. She kept on nicely knocking on the door but got no answer. She returned to the phone only to hear a dial tone. That person had now gone as well. She thought for a minute and realized where she was at this moment. It certainly fitted in with every other experience in this place. Nothing seemed normal to her because everything was structured on making the abnormal normal but everything *was* merely abnormal.

Jill's name was the fourth name on the list as an in-patient, so she expected to see three patrons for a lovely continental breakfast. It did not take long after the bellowing of the staff for everyone to be present. A tray especially made for each was given at a specific spot in the room. Only one person sat at the table and it was obvious she was anorexic and had to remain there until her food was eaten—quite a long haul. Jill did stay for the poor girl. Jill's tray was adorned with an over-cooked egg—cold of course, with half a slice of bread buttered, despite her preference for unbuttered, and a plastic cup of weak orange juice to drink. No morning coffee. After all, it would be a hot substance. Jill, with upward looking eyes, tried to see her roommates without staring. The girl at the table was being stood over and commanded to eat. If only the nurse would just hold her hand and with a comforting voice, suggest she have a bite of food.

Just like in the movies, an elderly woman dressed for Sunday church was moving about, fixing the magazines, checking everyone, and asking "How is your breakfast?" She then sat eating her toast like she was seated at the Park Avenue lobby overlooking Central Park. The fourth person was an elderly man sitting quietly, not staring and no strange bodily twitches. To Jill, he appeared to be just a nice granddad that may have recently lost his only love and was very sad. Unfortunately, there was no pill for sadness. Most believe sadness and depression are one and the same. Then you could believe there are no pills for depression; however, the drug companies seem to think that there are. Granddad, like Jill, did not belong. The room was like an empty 'fifties café except everything that was left was screwed to the floor.

What a great surprise when in walked Jill's doctor with papers in hand! This was the male doctor from the night before who had wanted to release her from the hospital. Now he was the head doctor today and he had a great smile for Jill. With a piece of paper in his hand for her to sign, and without the smile, he said he was very sorry he had kept Jill in the previous night but by law Jill now had to stay for two consecutive nights. On the good side, the piece of paper was a release for Jill to leave for the day but be back by nine in the evening. She must return or would be considered an escapee and the police would have a description in order to look for her. Jill would be in trouble for sure, worse than what she was in now. The doctor spoke softly to her and said, "Jill, I know you are just depressed because your partner of many years walked out on you and sometimes we do not think clearly during those times." The doctor was very understanding and told her that after tomorrow he proposed that Jill should leave and then check in on the fourth floor to make weekly appointments just to talk. He handed Jill a second piece of paper confirming what he just said and gave a gentle understanding smile.

Jill happily knocked on the window of the wire cage where they all looked like they were in fear of an uprising from all four of the inmates. They gave her an ominous stare like "Why are you bothering us." Jill questioned in her mind, where is the love in here?; where is the compassion and the understanding that we all have moments where the darkness covers our dreams and clouds our judgment. As she peered in through the wire reinforced glass, she noticed eight nurses, two for every patient. She wondered how they would react if they were to change places with the patients. They looked worse than the grand dame in the lunch room. At least she spoke softly, had a conversation with you and smiled. Standing there Jill held up the piece of paper from the doctor like it was the prize turkey from Scrooge. Finally, one came to the window and yelled, "What is that?" like they had never seen a release form before. What a way to antagonize a person! To make them seem violent! Why? Jill had to explain everything and still had to ask for her clothes. Then a nurse exited and in a controlling manner, said if she had her way Jill would be here for weeks with no papers. Jill's heart started to pound. She did not know what was possible. The more the nurse spoke, the more it was like a drill churning a hole in her chest. Jill's eyes looked like pieces of coal, like black despair.

Jill got her clothes and swept her way past the others immediately to the phone. She knew that Lori was at her house worrying and not knowing what to do. Lori was relieved because she told Jill she had tried to call there several times and they would not let her speak with her. Jill said to Lori, "I have some control of my life back at least for this day; come and get me." Lori had taken the rest of the week off. She was too distraught to work anyway. Since she had left the hospital, she lived in chronic guilt, not sleeping and smoking about two packs of cigarettes. All that consumed her mind was that it was her fault that she had had

Jill committed. In reality, it was the police who had her committed because she had given up all of her rights as a free woman by trying to take her own life. But Lori's feelings were not far from the truth about this relation with Jill because Jill blamed her for interfering. That meant indirectly that Lori did have her committed.

Jill stood at the steel reinforced door waiting for that release alarm to sound which meant she could push it open. As soon as it opened, she took extra large foot steps towards the elevator just in case someone changed their mind. When she reached the lobby, Lori was already there and they exchanged tight hugs. It was so tearful for both of them as sobbing; they sat for a minute on a fake leather sofa in the lobby. No one stared, it was common to see people crying and hugging in a hospital. As for the reason, no one cared either; it was just as it should be in a hospital lobby. They sat there five minutes, fifteen minutes, who knows.

Jill told Lori she was so sorry she called the police after John walked out the door. Tears just kept streaming as she used John's name. Lori did not understand or agree but let Jill be what she needed to be for now. She asked Lori for her cell phone, looked her in the eyes and said, "Sorry." She called John only to receive his voice message. Jill left a voice message not knowing if John would listen or not. "John, it is all a mistake. Please see our good sides and meet me today." Then Jill asked Lori if she would call John as well and tell him that Jill felt she had made a mistake. With hesitation, she did and she also received his voice mail.

Lori's normally angelic face turned and looked shameless. She had to tell Jill how John had called at the house and how she had tried to explain everything to him. His reaction was horrible—foul language and threats that Jill had better watch out because now she was in deep trouble with John. Lori said he had a smile in his voice, devious and almost a laugh. John had said, "Good for her. Let her get what she deserves." Lori was choking the words as she spoke with Jill. Then she nodded and smiled. "Let's go home, even if it is only for the day." Every minute of that day was spent like the last nickel at the county fair. They had breakfast, lunch and dinner out at their favorite restaurants. Jill slept for an hour due to the lack of sleep with the warden. It felt so good to Jill to lie in her own soft bed. Waking up meant it was time to leave for what Jill deemed to be a dysfunctional place for anyone.

Earlier than the time required, Jill and Lori arrive on the sixth floor. Lori was turned away at the buzzed in-and-out door, left only to wave goodbye. Later Lori said it was hell for her for what she believed she had done to Jill, her best friend. In reality, Jill had done this all to herself. Then out of character for Lori, she made a small scene pounding on the glass to get Jill's attention. She yelled, "I forgot to tell you, John wants to come by tonight for more business papers and his cat, Max." Not sure if Jill heard or even what Lori was supposed to do, she left hoping that is would be a calm event and part of the natural progression of a couple breaking up.

Jill did something she was very proud of and that was to smuggle her cell phone into the room and hide it under her pillow. While lying there, she could not take the cold anymore, so she got up and took the other pillow, as grungy as it was. She laid it over her chest to keep warm as well as a comfort like clutching a teddy bear. As she settled in, the rounds nurse came by and said, "Put that pillow back where you got it from." Jill pulling her head up and forward from the pillow pleaded to keep it because it was just too cold. In a slight disgust the nurse turned and left.

You had to be very coy and watchful in there to avoid getting into any trouble and incur the worst—an extended stay. Jill had her cell phone on vibrate so no-one could hear. Smart move with the phone because John started to ring Jill as the nurse exited the doorway.

It was John, no hello, no "How are you?" but a "Good for you, Jill; using up our tax dollars." In a louder voice he said, "Stay there. That is where you belong," demanding to know where Jill put Max's cage and toys. Jill tried to speak over him but John was the one acting as if he were demented. Without allowing Jill to say very much, he hung up the phone. It was a click again Jill would never forget. Even today when someone hangs up on the phone first, it is a haunting memory to Jill. Jill's mother used to do this to her if someone walked into her home when she was on the phone with Jill: she would just hang up on Jill. With her mother, Jill let it slide a number of times but could not take it any longer. Her mother's click felt like John not wanting to speak to her. Her mother's response was, "I cannot talk to two people at once." The ominous telephone click ignites two memories.

The cell phone rang a second time. It was Lori this time asking Jill to speak with John because he was so belligerent to her. He got on the phone and says to Jill, "Listen you son of a bitch, you called the cops on me, and now I am going to sue you!" and hung up again. Jill lying in a dreadful place and now threatened with the same news she had once had before was wrought with fear. She wanted to cry even though she was a grown woman but that was all she had to do was to show some negative emotions and her stay would certainly be extended.

After this second phone call Jill was caught by the nurse. She went from a smile to anger in about one second, like the start of the Indi five hundred car races. "How dare you bring a cell phone in here? And how did you pass it by when you were undressed and put to bed?" Jill would not answer because she felt she owed no explanation. The phone was in the nurse's cold hands before she knew it and it disappeared out the door.

The hospital stay was only to get worse that evening. The same head nurse just would not let up on Jill. Hourly she came to the door, flicked a flash light above her head while she leaned against the side of the door jamb like a state trooper on his car phone standing between his door and the car. "If I had my way, you would not be going home tomorrow. Girls like you end up here again and in worse shape. Then we are supposed to help you." There would always be the treat of many more weeks if she had the power to sign my forms. Jill believed she had a personal vendetta with the head male doctor and Jill was in between. No matter, she still put a fear in her that would make her never want to return there for any reason.

A sleepless night again, but this time because Jill knew early in the morning she was going to be released. Breakfast arrived like clockwork with one exception. There was a new patron under her name. Jill sat at the table with the phone just watching everyone appear slowly. Then the new guy arrives: a very young man, early thirties, unshaven, dark hair, dragging his slippers and wearing an opened hospital gown. He has such a forlorn face with grayness around his eyes and with an unkempt nose from crying. Jill wanted to get up and tie his gown together, how embarrassing for him. No one looked, no one cared so how would he begin to care? Jill just wanted to talk with him like a sister would and try to help. He sat down, leaned both elbows on each knee and rubbed his hair. There he sat. At the same time, the doctor arrived for Jill and with an inward smile she sees him signing all the release forms for good this time. He shook her hand and said, "Go home where you belong and good luck with your life." Jill, knowing that for sure that he was an understanding doctor, asked for his personal business card of which she lost later. There was no problem because it was evident he saw Jill only as a troubled woman in her heart. Immediately Jill asked for her belongings from the cage and got dressed. As she started to exit, she realized her cell phone was not there and she had to go back and knock on that glass again. Wow, how non-receiving of another human being can you get! The cell phone was retrieved and out the door into the elevator Jill went. Even though Jill knew there may be no reception, she stated to dial Lori from inside the elevator. It worked and Lori jumped into a cab, for the last time, to get Jill.

This time as they hugged it was all smiles knowing these smiles could remain. Jill made a masterful mistake doing this and realized it was her home she needed to be in to recover with her feelings and emotions. As soon as they got home, Jill and Lori took the car and went to breakfast. This time there was no choking on food stuck in Jill's' throat. The day was spent in the living room discussing what Jill needed to do to start to find her old self. One part of her release was to call the out-patient therapy staff in the hospital on the fourth floor. After several attempts she reached a booking nurse who said there was a four week waiting list. How could this be? Suppose she really needed therapy daily to be on her own? Only to remain out of trouble in case someone checked, Jill placed her name on the waiting list. She never called, and they never called again.

Josh R. Himmelman

Life living lesson: Suicide

Suicide is the process of ending one's own life on purpose. This may be held as acceptable or not depending on culture, ethnic norms, and religion. It may be based on family history, life stresses, and medical and health status as well as age, gender and other risk factors. Christianity sees this negative act to kill oneself and only to be the result of mental illness. But then other societies see a suicide attempt as a crime and others see it as understandable like the suicide bomber pilots of World War II or killing oneself to preserve the honor of their family. A very true example of this would be a young man who jumped off a bridge last year here in the city. His father wanted to see where he jumped and arrived on the scene. Culturally this was forbidden and a shame; hence the father jumped as well to join his son in death.

There are numerous suicides where no-one can say exactly this is what took place. Examples would be; a single-car accident, an overdose, a shooting while out hunting and the man who left his doctor's office with the news of cancer and was the cause of a three-car accident, he to his death. Men are the greater culprits of suicide, and the more successful. Is it bravery, brute strength or the lack of showing weakness to their loved ones, therefore so better to disappear? However, do not confuse self-mutilation to deliberately hurt oneself with suicide; it may be the result of death.

Some true examples of suspicious deaths are as follows: a neighbor on farm land was found pinned between a tree and his tractor while the tractor pushed so hard it had buried its back wheels, an aging man with aids had his son by to visit and as he goes to the kitchen his son jumps to his death followed by his father one year later, and the elderly man in a hospital bed next to myself who suffered pain for years was told there was nothing the medical field could do; his response, do not let me go home—I will jump from my balcony. Are these examples of a chemical imbalance, an innate family history or the emotional quotient never developed to understand life's fears? Something even more prevalent today at least discussed more than in the past is physician-assisted suicide, euthanasia. This is the assisted, deliberate cause of an early death of someone who will eventually die and commonly the terminally ill patient is assisted by their doctor. It is voluntary by a competent patient to ask their physician to provide a prescription for medication, the purpose is to use with the primary intent of ending their life. This way to end a life tends to increase as people age and as well with the number of times a person who desires their own death will repeatedly ask for this assistance. This is a term called "mercy killing."

I believe it is difficult to define a great difference between euthanasia and mercy killing. As always understood by myself, if there are two words used in the same event, then they must have two different meanings. Mercy killing is the killing of one person by another. The victim killed is an individual who will never recover, no matter what age, in a vegetative state or has an injury or illness that cannot be cured and are in their last stage of life. The person is most often in extreme pain in their last days and must request their life to end—an involuntary mercy killing. We speak of euthanasia, but the fact is mercy killing is euthanasia. The difference is that mercy killing is the choice of the individual who is in intolerable pain. Most of the world finds this act to be more acceptable; however it only takes one member of a family to claim a case of injustice. Just because the rest of society has not come to terms with death does not mean people who are dying of chronic illness or even the effects of life itself should have to suffer.

Pain is a very unpleasant sensation with different levels of intensity. In the medical world, pain is measured on a scale of one to ten; ten is the most unbearable! This amount of pain triggers your brain sensors to try and compensate the pain. But normally this is now no longer a physical and emotional pain, it is agony. The physical pain most often is the result of nerve damage which can be in a local area or throughout the whole body. But in suicide it is emotional pain no different than physical pain because both ignite pain impulses in the brain. Without anti-depressants and other drugs, the emotional pain reaches a significant level pushing one's own morals to die before you enter the realm of thoughtfulness, and panic suicide to relieve the pain.

Do not believe I have qualified suicide. There are causes for this act, and most left unattended by the physician or family can lead to final termination of one's life. Neither do we lay blame on anyone, even the individual committing suicide. Perplexed by the overall complexity; that is because suicide is one part of many parts of life that is very difficult to explain, yet understand. Before an individual were to do such, no matter how much information about their pain and hurt they convey to us, we still cannot use that knowledge to understand. No one can be inside another person's mind, inside their emotions or their respect for themselves. We can entertain the idea we can conceive of the idea in a way that a psychiatrist does, but the ultimate ending is in the patient's decision.

The causes of suicide are varied and can be tied very clearly to our society of today. Society has enlightened the strings on many issues; therefore the fear left for the family to understand is not as great as before. The pressures of society more than ever before impact peoples decisions. As an example, young teenage girls who are bullied at school, in the emails they received or their Face book pages; these can very well cause an impressionable young mind to commit suicide, and before the actual deed, no-one would have anticipated such an outcome.

The most common cause of suicide is by firearm and by a male. No pun intended, but the trigger is pulled by a trigger point in their lives, even if real or just imagined. The sad part is that quite often we imagine things and feelings from others that are not true.

Increasing the statistics of suicide issues such as depression, manic depression, schizophrenia, substance abuse, eating disorders, severe anxiety are all treatable mental health disorders. However, a number of suicides are the result of a physical illness. If only a physical illness coupled with a mental illness can be recognized then the probability of that person killing themselves is lowered, and even more so if they have social support.

To understand suicide as seen here we must look at both mental and physical illnesses. Usually the physical illness comes first, causing anxiety and anger with oneself. And with the lack of someone's love as a support those issues intensify and now new issues will enter that doorway that was left open looking for help. Sometimes we just want to keep everything to ourselves and not open up. Maybe the reason is an innate understanding on the part of that person that seeking help will only make things seems worse.

A brief look at the most common factor as a cause for suicide, depression; SAD—seasonal affective disorder is a form of depression due to shorter days and a lack of sunlight. Treatments like vitamins and tanning beds will help make you feel better. Anger can result from depression. Anger will cause the heart to race and blood pressure rise.

Anhedonia, when you feel no sense of pleasure from anything in your present life, also results from depression.

Depression has a wide variance that affects your eating, sleeping, the way you see and think about yourself, body aches and your mood around others and with yourself: how you treat yourself. This is very unfortunate because a huge number of people suffer from depression in today's technological and fast-paced lifestyle. Are we ready for each day as it comes? You are not weak, and depression is a disease that is treatable by doctors and time.

Drugs such as anti-depressants are used to treat mood and thoughts (the way one thinks about things). If treated improperly it could lead to further wrongful thoughts such as self-mutilation. The problem with treating depression is it takes weeks to discover the right pills and then time for them to take effect to calm the mind. In the meantime, you have racing thoughts causing more anxiety, attacks of shortness of breath and you believe you are going to die. Anxiety disorders and serious medical illnesses do instill complete fear; fear that makes the whole thought of self-destruction amplify.

A number of people love drama, and being impulsive is part of who they are. The two together cause impulsive actions rather than thought; the person who blurts out, "I am going to kill myself" most likely one day without thinking will do so.

Very critical for today's fast pace is sleep and the lack of sleep we tend to experience. Even if having the time to sleep and you are diagnosed with insomnia, you may have a serious problem leading to depression. The mind does not want to calm down at night; counting sheep is a ridiculous thought. It weakens your mood, your ability to think, to act in response, hence all qualities that lead to more depression and mood disorders, and finally could direct you into a path of suicide. A lack of understanding of insomnia is not the difficulty of falling asleep and staying asleep but is truly reflected by each individual's own needs for and their satisfaction with sleep. Hence, if you feel refreshed after four hours of sleep you do not have insomnia.

You must have seen on television where a scene is about family having an intervention to make a loved one aware of something they are doing to negatively affect themselves or society. Anyone can try to intervene as well as a doctor with the intent to modify the person's thinking. However, the results could be very weak or strong. Just do not use a measuring stick on the person's success. Thank yourself for caring to help.

Suicide, even if not successful has profound effects on the loved ones, your family and your career. Unfortunately it is seen as weakness and lack of character to many; but these people do not have full knowledge of the process bringing someone to actual suicide. The whole idea is devastating to all, and if the person is successful those left behind are left to suffer chronic grief. Generally, loved ones are not equipped mentally (knowledge) on how to react or feel. They may wonder where God was and did the person think of their soul?

Suicidal people actually ask God, "Please take my life, and give me peace!" Those left behind, if they could only understand for that person how much they just want peace. Peace to them seems so overwhelming to achieve, and lack any direction to go. Like the new born baby bird resting at the end of a tree branch and unable to fly. Where does he go?

Suicide is a progression from suicidal gestures, suicidal thoughts, and the suicidal act itself. Who is responsible to step in and at what stage will you have the most influence? Suicide should not be viewed solely as a medical or mental health problem for some to bear. Most believe there is protection for them, like social support and a connection to the world around them, and this can really help to prevent suicide. It will not be anyone thing or anyone person. But it must start with the person to heal and seek that support.

There is a belief that a trigger of an event can set off a desire in people who are genetically predisposed to developing the disease, or that a trigger causes a certain symptom to occur in a person who has a disease. Look for the warning signs like when you see them making a will, getting their affairs in order in conjunction with suddenly taking a trip to visit all their friends and family. And worse, you see them buy a gun, rope, extra medications, a decline in their mood or finding a suicide note prewritten. Almost all who are suicidal do not release their information to anyone; they do not seek help because they believe they are lost and have tried for a peace that does not exist for them.

Anyone who completes the act usually suffers from anxiety where in itself could be caused from alcohol abuse, insomnia, agitation, loss of interest in themselves and any activity that may bring a semblance of happiness. In their eyes it appears hopeless, and they always predict something bad will happen only to them.

All is not finished if you stop the suicide attempt. You cannot kill two birds with one stone; one attempt to help will not stop this person's second attempt. Hospitalization is required to invoke mental-health professionals to implement a comprehensive outpatient treatment plan. You do realize that after an attempt of suicide without success, you now belong to the state. You have no say and are hospitalized for the amount of time set out by the medical field as a standard and longer especially if the doctors see you as still a risk to yourself or others. Sometimes the person is placed in a psychiatric ward. Once there they realize they are not like these very ill patients. And being forced to remain is enough for them to realize that they need help, but not to the extent that the other people in the psychiatric ward do? But vigorous treatment of the underlying psychiatric disorder is important in decreasing short-term and long-term risk. The first line of defense would be to set a contract with the person to agree to tell a specified person they may again intend to harm themselves. Most important is talk therapy to help them focus on an understanding how their thoughts and behaviors affect others and make others experience guilt.

Yes, now everyone wants to help. The key people are doctors and psychiatrists. In their honest belief, they think medications will help to treat the severe emotional problems that are associated with attempting suicide, and studies show that the numbers of suicides that are a result of being mentally ill seem to decrease with treatment. Mood-stabilizing medications, like Lithium, as well as medications that focus on abnormal thinking and/or anxiety use Clozapine, Risperdone and Abilify (the newest drug) have also been found to decrease the probability of the person killing themselves. Not one of these comes without side effects. Sometimes the side effects don't just alter your mood regarding killing yourself but cause other things, such as dizziness. Look into the eyes of a patient in this condition—it tells the story.

Even though the person wants to escape to what they believe will be peace, they seem to make a lot of preparations before they try suicide. The interesting part is that if they would only try those things before thinking suicide, their life could be better, happier and more at peace with themselves. No suicide thoughts, then. An example would be taking a long overdue trip to visit a friend before suicide. Do it as a part of living and you will not go into the black abyss you believe is your destiny. The notes and letters left saying, "I love you. Please forgive me for what I have done." These notes are a form of reaching out, and it's too bad that we do not find them before the suicide. Have your life as living, and feel the warmth of love; it will be there, even if it comes from your co-workers. You do not feel it because you keep pushing it away.

Looking at the aspects of selfishness and suicide, you are leaving many behind in chronic grief and feeling like it is their fault; "Why didn't I see they were so low?" and "Why didn't they ask me for help, what did I do to them?" This form of grief remains with your loved ones forever. You now have placed your loved ones on to medications to calm their moods of sorrow. Oh how selfish of you to believe things would be better without you. It is better to live, no matter the life, then not to have lived at all. Please realize, "You are blessed!" and just accept the giving of others and from God. How to stop life? This is not the way. Death is eternal.

End of Life living lesson: Suicide

Life living lesson: Cross-cultural love

As you make great decisions around a not-so-great new world, it is all about figuring out who you are first in a multi-cultural diverse environment. How does your culture impact on who you are? And do your cultural beliefs dictate who you are? You do have choices to be yourself or are they redundant? One difference is that we can be defined by the country we live as opposed to the one we grew up in, which may not be the same culturally. We live on the border of two separate countries, on a coastline or inland. Such factors shape a piece of who you will become as an adult. Understand what helps define you as an individual.

There are self-fulfilling people who state, "I am an individual, and I have rights." What rights are embedded in their mind as thoughts/behaviors? If you were born and educated in one place and now live in a totally different society, you must take stock of your whole life experiences. You must love yourself first before someone else can fully love you and you are able to accept their love. Some believe we are forgetting to incorporate the whole past and culture of each to truly understand the person we are in love with. Does all this mean, "Must I tell all?" when you meet someone with whom to be romantically involved. Some issues should be left alone, the most common mistake that can begin the destruction of your present relationship is to tell of all your past loves and mistakes. It will lead you to more questions as a result of previous failures in your past loves. We do need to explain ourselves. However, be up front about how our families fit into our lives, the amount of education we pursued, our types of friends and the activities we like to do together. This helps our new partner to understand the present you because all our living of previous makes the person you see here today.

No matter how much of your previous life affects you, cultural difference makes top grade. The obvious cultural differences that exist between people are language, dress, traditions, their concept of morality, and interaction with their environment. We have come as far as to not allow a parent to physically spank a child. If this were done and noticed, the parent is subject to interference by the police and a form of family services.

Human values with beliefs generate behavior, personal identity, and a sense of worth. Two different backgrounds, two values that say what is good, beneficial, important, useful, beautiful, and desirable and appropriate are very difficult to compromise.

Thanks to the human needs to procreate, we today have more cultural diversity in relationships than ever in the past. Cross-cultural love and values are a part of every culture. But how will diversity be preserved as we move on into the future where numbers increasingly against diverse peoples co-existing or even exist? More than ever today we cannot ignore the Hitler regime and his legacy even today in countries like America, where some people argue there is no need for a number of languages spoken in their country or even in the world as a whole. We have a lack of cultural diversity and it needs to be kept for the sake of human dignity.

Love and being in love with a person from a different cultural background, a different ethnicity and morals makes the relationship more difficult to sustain. It is easy for many different people to attend the Saturday market of one culture and enjoy their tastes of foods and differences. But is it so easy to live with a person from a different culture?

As a couple, how do we keep our own human rights when we clash cultures? Cultural background is one of the primary sources of identity. For partnerships, peoples of different ethnicity inter-marry, their cultures interact and intermix, and a cultural difference represents a change and a new type of culture. This process can be enriching, but disorienting. Today you may not notice it through the media or on your street, but there is an insecurity of cultural identity that is reflecting changes in how we define and express who we are today. What happens with two different sets of values? Families need traditions and they are evolved from values. This helps them to find importance in their day-to-day lives. To think of the past as an example, if two different religions were to marry, one religion may not recognize the marriage and second, what church will the children attend? In some families even the children are split: sons went with the dad to his church and daughters went with moms to her church.

Within a couple, depending on how strongly each holds on to their own values, some may be destructive in their bonding through love. To co-join in a relationship you must understand the values of each, beliefs, and assumptions that motivate each other's behavior.

A personal value is a relative ethic value, which is a set of consistent values. Each individual harbors a principal value, the one where a foundation upon other values and integrity are based. Not much different from cultural values, personal values include: ethical and moral values; religious and political values; social values and ethnic values. Individuals most often take part only in pieces of their own culture as their personal values, because they do not agree with the norms, values of their whole culture.

As in a relationship, one or both partners will do the above to better have the cohesive family so much desired. One might say on each behalf, they show a certain amount of selflessness. If not, you have a couple where one is quite selfish and is concerned only with placing his own needs or desires above the needs or desires of others, his partner and their family. That is an extreme strain on family rearing and the home environment.

Even as a couple, today each wants their own personal life. This is not a European personal life but a Western culture evolution. The different facets of European culture is evident in their countries' style of dressing, the food they eat, their music and folk dance, their literature, simply all aspects of their national life. The church has played a major role and is the strongest influence of each country's culture. As opposed to Western society, it is more of work-life balance. Hard work never killed anyone, especially since it gives you the choice of anything you want as in hobbies, foods, education, the two family automobiles, lack of attending church and the individual freedom of choice.

Canadian culture as an example is similar to old European culture maybe because of it connection to Imperialism, the French and the British crown. It in itself it has many artistic, musical, political and social elements that are representative of Canada and accepted by people all over the world, unlike some cultures that are individualistic. Canada has a multi-cultural society that sits within a hard-core established system for all of Canadian society. Canada keeps true to its country's place in the world and remains complacent or active within the necessity of the needs of other countries.

In the eyes of the world, the issue of Canadian identity remains under scrutiny, simply because of our multi-cultural society and its elusiveness. In an opinion other countries should be so wealthy with different human societies and cross cultural acceptance.

Maybe the more passionate couples are those who have cross-cultural perspectives and hence different sexual desires. The major cultural groups within Canada are more similar in their views of love, sex and intimacy than those of a single country with non-acceptance of differences. As Canadians, we are left to be individuals with our own personality that shapes our attitude and behavior with equality and a pursuit of pleasure and avoidance of pain as desirable goals. Canada is seen as creating trends toward marriage for love, sexual desire and greater sexual permissiveness.

Cultural and gender differences may often be less powerful than individual personality differences in shaping attitudes and behavior. Canada has equality for men and women. But facial expressions show language barriers as well. Even though we are more accepting of different cultures we must learn what information an expression says. Can there be emotion without facial expression? Can there be a facial expression of emotion without emotion? And how do individuals differ in their facial expressions of emotion? These are all parts of communication in a relationship and once again, if the couple is of different cultures it is one more avenue of learning for each.

Here in Canada we focus on the eyes. This means we have difficulty distinguishing facial expressions that look similar around the eye. Again in Canada with the diversity of couples, human communication of emotion is very complex. It is not reliable to provide emotion in cross-cultural situations. Compared to European emotions, mostly the mouth is used to convey an emotional state. Cross-cultural research on facial expression and the developments of methods to measure facial expression are shown through smiles (in case a not-so-friendly smile is one where the smile makes fun of the other person and ridicules them). As well there is a case that can be cited for the wrinkled brow that expresses sadness, anger, fear, or disgust. The wrinkled brow can mean deep thought but here doubt, frustration and disbelief may be the cause as well. A sad expression is conveyed as not happy. That means it expresses discomfort, pain and helplessness. Angry expressions are topping the list as daily stress and frustrations are on the rise. Anger is in this case includes interpersonal aggression conveying hostility, opposition and personal attachment. A fearful expression conveys apprehension of danger, threats, fight or flight, or the possibility of bodily harm. Anxiety between couples is related to fear and both create unhealthy physical effects. Finally and necessary to understand this couple is disgust. They are part of the bodily responses to another seen as revolting and obnoxious. This is shown as comments on anything the other partner would do to make them a couple.

What predicts people's life satisfaction? Personality factors such as self-esteem, optimism and a positive emotional experience. Often it is these factors for each other's personal internal attributes learned through their upbringing and environments that predicts one's life. Relationship harmony answers the question.

End of Life living lesson: Cross-cultural love.

It was time for Jill to face the house and all of John's things clinging to the heavy air of emotions. It was the same as a death of someone in the home. You need to pack all of their belongings as soon as you can because otherwise it is only prolonging sad memories. Jill decided to be a perfectionist, as she always had been towards John, and treat all of his belongings with respect. Since it was nearing Christmas, the local hardware store was selling oversized Christmas totes for storage. Jill started by buying four, then four more and then finally ten more totes to fit in all of John's things. It was now into the second week of December and it was spent folding and labeling everything on sheets of paper for John. No throwing of things making them seem impersonal but even pressing of some clothes that were wrinkled and tossed about by John himself. He had one whole bedroom in the house claimed as his walk-in closet with floor to ceiling clothes racks, and they were full. It had to be the way he grew up with this need to have ten of one thing because he had none of anything as a child. To watch him shop it was like a paranoid curse of neediness of material items. Everything with John was a want and not a need.

During this time Jill went back into depression very quickly. After all, this confirmed her loneness to be permanent. There were many tears that went inside each tote as it was shut and taped up and sealed so that it should not open. Jill was unable to pull herself from depression, and Lori could not stay home from work any longer.

Lori knew Jill and John had spent some Christmases in Mexico and thought it would be a great idea for Jill to get away this Christmas from the house she had tried so much to make a loving home. Maybe not such a great idea, but Jill agreed and went to the same town and condo where they used to stay. Christmas was to be spent on the beach, the perfect getaway for a holiday where by you seem not to notice you are alone. Everyone is laughing and sun tanning on the beach with a great gym nearby to work off your frustrations.

Jill really did use every ounce of her strength to travel south. Because she booked last minute, she had the milk run; three different planes to her final destination. It was so difficult for her as soon as she landed, taking the taxi through the city she once was so happy with John by her side; it all brought deep memories so that Jill could hardly maintain her tears in public. All she could think of was getting inside the condo. Arriving at the condo front desk, everyone greeted Jill, remembering her many stays with them. Even some of the permanent residents were standing there as well. Excited handshakes were exchanged and then the dreaded question, "Where is John in laughter? Did you run away and leave him at home?" Jill knew this would happen but still was ill-prepared and had no set answer to give. With a nervous smile, she only responded with the information that she was on her own now. Looks of shock were in the room and there were no further questions. In public around John and Jill, John always made it appear as if they were the happiest couple.

Jill knew from past years that here there would be little evidence of Christmas. Decorations and music would not be evident, only the odd poinsettia. The locals were Catholic and celebrated Christmas on the twenty-fourth in the evening. It was more about family gathering than lights and huge presents. Jill went shopping on that day and everywhere there were families together buying clothes they needed as gifts and, unlike Canada, the more elaborate the better the Christmas you had. It made Jill feel like it was not even the Christmas season, something of which she always cherished for herself and others. In years past, of course, without the help of John she made the home look like a gingerbread house. A nine foot tree trimmed with antique ornaments stood in front of the lead glass windows of a one hundred-year-old home, the fire place draped with strung cranberries overlapping the Christmas socks and enough presents for the whole street to open. Now this was no more, and as Jill thought, even back then it was a dream of family happiness. On the outside it all appeared to others as wow, what a home! But inside Jill knew but failed to admit it was just an empty house, no affection. Then to be in a little town in Mexico with so few lights and a nativity scene by the church was exactly what she needed, the true meaning of a family time together.

After checking in and all the hellos were said, inside the elevator Jill turned back to her old self: worn and depressed. When she opened the condo door there was a beautiful hot breeze blowing the curtains high in the air. The sounds were climbing from the beach over the balcony into her room as if she were right there sunning on the sand. She was right at the water's edge and could see the hang gliders and the sea dogs passing by—all laughter and screams of fun and joy. Then joining the sounds was a band from the restaurant below.

Jill dropped on the bed with weeping tears. She could not take all of this at once. She closed the sliding glass door, whipped the drapes shut, turned on the ceiling fan and crawled into a ball shape on top of the bedspread. This time it is quite the opposite of any previous trip. By now the suitcases would be unpacked, shorts on and out the door to greet more people and have a cool drink. Instead two hours later she awakes only to be sweltering in the dead air of the suite and wanting not to unpack but to come home.

Knowing her charter would not leave on a return for a week, she started to unpack her belongings. Unpacking was unlike ever before: no neat hanging of clothes, no folding of blouses, just place whatever there was in an empty spot. She knew as soon as she appeared on the street she would be within the surroundings like a second home, of which Mexico came to be. So many people with cheery faces kept greeting Jill that finally after a quick bite she had to return to her suite. She brought with her two greatly needed international tools, a cell phone and a laptop. It did not take long before she was on the phone with Lori. She might be a grown woman but as soon as she heard her voice she bellowed in tears. This was her first call to Lori, and she had a rough time trying to control his emotions. She felt she needed to come home and wanted Lori to find her a flight. But Lori knew the medicine she needed was to get out and face life. Be a part of what you lost over the years. Talk for you, and when others came up to her, it would be for her. No matter what the expense, she wanted to fly back home. Lori convinced her that would be the worst thing she could do to herself. Jill needed to be away from her home. Not sharing the thought with Jill, it became apparent to Lori that it was a mistake for her to be in Mexico. But then she realized that Jill always called it her second home and she should stay. Jill told her about his great suite, but she could not open the curtains and windows and see and hear the sounds of people's happiness. Lori demanded her open the glass doors of the balcony, pull back the curtains and sit outside to enjoy what she had deserved so much. Jill refused, and as if to punish herself again kept crying and hung up the phone. Her weak energy and now her emotions caused her to lie down on the bed. It was only seven in the evening, but Jill did not leave his solace not even to remove her clothes.

The next moment was a morning stream of sunlight flickering perfectly over her forehead through the crack of the closed curtains.

She had spent twelve hours in that bed and awakened to realize nothing had changed. It does not matter how educated you are, how mature you are or how old you are: when you are depressed, you are depressed. She picked up the phone for the second time and phoned Lori. It was the same story all over again but this time a little less fraught, probably because she had at least rested her mind with sleeping. Lori asked her, "What do you normally do in Mexico when you wake up for the day?" Jill quickly understood that she needed no plans, no grand ideas but just to be. Is what used to make her happy when in the sun getting away with kind and accepting people? Jill said, "My days used to be filled, never stopping to have a late afternoon nap, and early dinner, then a short nap and dress for the clubs. Lori said, "Jill, the next day will be a repeat of the last day until the time comes for you to come back home. Lori with a calm voice said, "Jill, start your day as you should. Soon your days there will be gone, and then you will be back at home with renewed energy to do what you need to do."

Jill's days in the south would be envied by anyone. "Good bye Lori, I need to have a shower and get going on with my day." Showered, popped contacts in, shades were placed on like a movie star and a backpack was filled with all the necessities for a complete day on the run. First stop was the same little café for breakfast, seated outside by the railing against the cobblestone street with the smell of old gas fumes from beaten cars bouncing by. Sounds dirty but it were her heaven. Jill was a familiar patron, and even the cook came out to say welcome. You know a good waiter when it has been six months and they ask you, "Do you wish to have the same, mum?" In moments Jill's breakfast arrived just as she remembered, and with two cups of coffee later disappearing she takes the lead down the sidewalk.

As she walked along this first day, she looked like a very stern woman, shades, no smile, and confident. But all of this was done to hide the inside of her shell. Inside was still that unhappy woman. Jill knew she had to work hard at this and learn that there were people like her, not just like John and her. Because John would do all the talking, Jill felt she was seen as no value. She learned soon on this trip she was wrong.

With an already soaked shirt, she went walking to the local bus station which was no shelter but only a small street where all the buses stopped. No matter, every year was the same for Jill she could never remember which bus took her to the local gym. Finally using poor

Spanish, Jill got on the right bus, and off on a bumpy ride over the cobblestones to sign up for a week at the gym, her favorite part of the day.

All ready for an immediate workout in the gym, Jill spent the rest of the morning rebuilding her old gym routine that she had lost in the past two years. Many locals at the gym smiled and nodded to welcome her because they remembered Jill could not speak Spanish. She tried so hard to smile, choking back emotions of remembering her and John at the same gym. To finish off a good workout is to belong to a gym with a nice wet sauna or Jacuzzi. Fortunately this gym had both. Sitting with her head dropping into her chest in the Jacuzzi, a middle aged obviously happy couple walked in. Jill could tell they were discussing her. She looked up and they said "Hello," and "Are you okay?" Jill just wanted to offload to anyone, dump her sins of emotions, her negativity, but then why hold a strange couple hostage to such dribble from a stranger? Before Jill knew it, she was asked to have lunch and the words "cheer up" were attached. Because they had been a couple for fifteen years they did begin to talk. They too had had many problems similar to Jill's but pulled through, out of love. That even reaffirmed to Jill that John did not love her. John was truly a selfish man as seen by everyone else but herself. In actuality Jill left lunch feeling like she was okay, not a failure in relationships.

Leaving lunch and before the evening Jill kept her routine and continued her day with her backpack hanging over her left shoulder and jumping the cobblestones on the streets and window shopping and taking too long to stare in the bakery window. Jill made a promise to herself, a reward if she allowed herself to enjoy the rest of her stay; she would hit the bakery and gorge in their fabulous sweets.

Back to the condo, and now it was three in the afternoon. Jill never cared too much about lying out in the sun, so later on the beach was better for her. A quick shower from her walk, the air conditioner flicked on to cut the humidity and then the six different bathing suit changes to find the right matching bathing suit and t-shirt combo. Jill did this routine every day, and today she looked and found the last Palapa hut way in the back away from people. She liked to sit there drinking only water and a coke, no beer in the sun: too much of a headache. Usually a people-watcher for fun, this time Jill buried her head in a self-help book. Even though it was hard to read in the sun, Jill struggled to look busy. Then a shadow appeared like a jump rabbit in front of her chair. As she looked up, it was a beautiful woman, with the biggest smile and an overly friendly hello. As Jill and other gym rats would say, she was ripped. What a woman! Definitely a gym bunny or a dancer! Turns out she was both. At first the conversation was, "What are you doing all by yourself here in a corner of the beach?" You are much too beautiful to be hiding." Jill was hiding in fear that she wasn't attractive, and it was pleasant that she had come over to speak with her. That was her life with John. Jill was never allowed to speak a word on the beach or almost anywhere if there were other people present. John was the song bird and Jill was the seed that attracted other mates.

Jill and Kim had a great chat for hours discussing gym routines, selections of books to read and then the dreaded question to come and join her up front. Jill was never really comfortable as she also remembered there were a lot of problems in being married as well. Jealously seemed to be a common problem, no matter what the relationship was. It was a nice awakening for Jill; she realized no relationship is without problems. She always remembered her mother's advice. When Jill would complain that during life as a couple, they never had any money, never owned anything, house or car, her response was, "Who you think you are. No one owns anything anymore?" Jill got the same advice about partnership arguing. Everyone argues. Jill thought how true and how intelligent for an eighty-three-year-old lady who went through so many changes in all the years of her living. No one owns anyone, it would be nice, though, if you both just want to be there always as the vows of the marriage ceremony portray.

Jill refused the invite knowing that Kim would get some sort of message. Being confused, she gave a little left-hand wave and a big smile and started to walk back to her Palapa hut. Jill felt so inept for throwing away an opportunity to laugh and meet her friends that would have been her new acquaintances in Mexico. This was enough for her today, and she started to walk back to the condo pushing soft white sand through her toes.

Her routine was on schedule, and now it was time for a nap. Setting her alarm, she lay down for two hours because at darkness in early evening everyone comes out like the ants going as troops on a feeding frenzy, and Jill wanted to be a part of this tonight. She went alone to dinner only to hear the waiter say, "You are alone Madame?" It just did not end; the impact of being alone meshed into her whole self, not only by herself attacking her insides emotionally but from strangers as well. Because she was alone, her table was in the back of the room. Nice and hot by the kitchen doors. Jill wondered why he was in this place in his life.

In the evening for entertainment in town there were a number of small local bars and one huge dance bar. The couple invited Jill to meet around ten p.m. and Jill was pleased to have one place to go and not be alone, and second, to have someone to speak with instead of looking like a loner, no partner, and no friends and on a recovery holiday. In places like these, there are a lot of nosey people watching for entertainment. Cocktail hour approached and a decision had to be made. Does she go and revisit the New York couple or do like always, run away from the possibility of making a friendship because she felt unworthy? There was no coin flip, but for Jill a turn on the street to the right. Jill sat at the bar looking like she was supposed to meet someone, the look every time the door opens for that familiar face. After an hour no-one came through those doors that she knew. Jill knew she was being watched by a table of six guys all making bets on why she was alone. Soon one of them got up and invited her to join their group. Jill felt it was more out of curiosity then to have an intellectual conversation. But they truly wanted to chat and change her emotionless face to a smile. Hence, Jill did meet more new people and they seemed to enjoy her company. The most talkative was a seventy-five year old man, so gentle. Jill knew this man was settled with all of life. All of life's incidents, good or bad, had passed and he had found calm and peace. Jill at first wanted to be jealous but could not be because this man had earned the right to be so at peace. Jill loved their conversation and felt once again this was destiny for her to meet.

Everyone was getting ready, downing their drinks to stroll over the bridge to the dance bar. Jill never was in favor of such a bar and declined. Two of the chaps, a couple, invited John back for the next evening to have a rerun of great conversation and as one said, "A cheering up session for Jill." At this point she agreed because Jill was tired of hiding all her negative self behind a long scowl on her face.

Sleep that evening she did not. Too many memories were haunting her. No matter, she was determined to keep her routine the next day and for the remainder of the week. Jill arrived at the beach late again and was totally unaware of being watched by a young handsome dentist. He approached with big smiles and invited himself to sit down. The conversation was pleasant until Jill said it was her turn to explain why she was spending Christmas alone in Mexico when she had a huge family back home. With hesitation, he began to tell Jill of his brother who has been in and out of drug rehabs since he was fourteen. He almost lost his dentist's practice trying to help him. His mother had disowned him and now he was deemed to be the care-giver for his brother by the judge. He told Jill, "I just need a break before I break!" He said every time his cell would ring, it would be a new problem with his brother. So, he decided to take a week for himself and the rest at home would have to cope with it. Again, Jill was thinking, "Is this destiny again to meet someone so close to her own personal problems?" God was teaching Jill she was not alone. So many had the same problems, and Jill needed to see that. It was now close to Christmas Eve and Jill thought why not invite him to join them for dinner? Why should both be alone?

The next day, the next continuation of her routine was the same. This time she ran into the New York couple again at the gym and asked them to join her for Christmas Eve dinner. Jill went back to the restaurant once again and asked to change her reservation to a table of four. Happily this gave them a private table now on the beach, surrounded by torches sitting on the sand approximately four feet away from the surf rolling softly over the sand and a canopy of stars shinning above.

Jill made the last day a change from the routine. She was not sure if the stores would be open on the twenty-fifth, the following day, and she wanted to purchase only two things on this trip. In appreciation to Lori, she wanted the best she could find in silver earrings. What she found were beautiful and just meant for Lori. The second item she wanted was a solid silver rosary. Jill needed to pray more and felt this would capture her prayers and hold onto them and keep passing them during the day to God. She searched from jeweler to jeweler for hours. Because it was Christmas Eve, the selection was not very appealing. Finally she found the perfect rosary. Maybe it is a sin to haggle over the price of a religious item, but the price was enormous and out of her budget. Finally, the owner said, "We sold nothing today and to sell your first item in our custom brings good luck to the store and the purchaser. So, I will meet your price and we each have luck and a God's peaceful day." Jill's day was ending with no time left for the beach, but little did she care.

After her evening nap, a much shorter nap, she kept thinking what to wear that would seem like Jill and not what John would tell her to wear. It was an hour of decision-making because it had been years of not choosing for herself. Very much like the husband who constantly tells his wife what to wear to go out to dinner or over to a friend's house. This was all too wrong.

The restaurant was below the condo, not far to go, and was considered one of the best in town. Jill was there on time at eight and found a very giddy dentist, boyish like, all excited. Then in walked two other couples one behind the other. It was his New York friends, who asked if it was okay to bring another couple. Of course, and the couple Jill had had drinks with for two evenings jumped forward, big hugs and said, "It's us." Jill looked up at the stars and wondered could everything be so kind after all he and John did to each other. Six people shaking hands, criss-crossing of arms and finally everyone meets. The hostess immediately sends the waiter to place two more settings at our table. The guests all looked at Jill with big smiles in anticipation of sitting at such a large table right on the sand. What a perfect night for Christmas Eve! There were so many conversations, no difficulty in ordering appetizers to share, and the main courses were superb. The best of all, everyone was being to kind, wanting to talk with Jill during the whole evening. Jill forgot, forgot her recent past and the past eleven years, and she did remember what it was like to talk for herself. Three time glasses were raised to the air to cheer Jill and Merry Christmas to all, with low voices echoing across the beach. The only small amount of sorrow in Jill's heart was she had to leave the next day. It had to be that way because of the season. These were the only tickets available, and the only space available in the condo. After that day everyone would be arriving for New Years Eve. Huge hugs were exchanged as they went their separate ways, everyone leaving a feeling of comfort and calm inside Jill, her perfect Christmas gift.

Jill went upstairs to her condo and spent a long time on her balcony. The Jill she first feared looked up at the stars, God's home, and the universe full of love. She took her rosary in hand that she wore to dinner that evening and prayed a thankful prayer this time. She felt like she was worthy for someone else to share a new life with.

Morning arrived too soon and Jill overslept. Frantically she packed her belongings and had a renewed feeling of hope different from when she arrived. Off to the lobby to hail a taxi. Everyone said their goodbyes in sadness, and with tearful eyes Jill now realized she was on her way home. But to what?

The airport was chaos. The evening before something had threatened homeland security in an airport and all flights to everywhere were delayed. This small town airport was not equipped to search people in private. Standing in a long line up for four hours, they all watched as each person was checked over and over. It was very orderly but tedious. Because the plane left five hours later, everyone missed their connecting flights in Denver, and it was now mid-night. Line-ups quickly grew at the customer service desk and tempers grew as well. Finally, Jill received a hotel voucher and was checked in at two a.m. She had to be ready for a pick up at seven a.m. to make it for a new flight. Jill was exhausted and to make things worse, these flights were delayed and the searches were the same as the day before. What normally took Jill six hours to get home, took two full days. All that she achieved on holidays, all the restfulness and peace were gone. These two days sitting alone in airports brought Jill back to reality. When she arrived home, Lori picked her up at the airport, and she knew this would change the good that Jill had found back into her old self: depressed and lonely. Jill embraced Lori tightly with a long tearful hug, as she knew what was facing her at home.

Arriving home as she opened the front door and there were the eighteen Christmas totes, with other belongings filling the whole downstairs, waiting for John to retrieve them. That was supposed to be done while Jill was away. Lori begged Jill not to let this bring her down to the place she was when she left. But to Jill they were John's belongings—a reminder he was gone for good, and no matter how he treated Jill, Jill saw the loneliness. She walked through the house touching each box and dropping tears along her way. The only space to escape would be to go to her bedroom until these things were removed. But John did not keep his promise, and he would not answer his phone.

Jill was held captive in her home for the sake of not seeing any representation of Christmas. If she went out during the daytime there would be music playing in the grocery store. People knew Jill everywhere and when they saw her, one cashier even asked her if he had cancer because he looked so bad. Jill thought what a strange thing to say to someone! But maybe she thought so much of her presence when she was around that she was truly shocked and felt sad for her. Usually Jill would go to the entire sell-off sales after the holiday was over, but not this year. She had received some cards, and even they were placed in a drawer in the foyer. She kept asking herself; Why? And her only answer was for pure loneliness, her biggest fear. Jill has seen people mistreat their pets, kicking them aside or smacking them on the back. Always a pet quickly forgives and comes back, more loving with a gentle voice and rubbing their head against the owner's leg. Now that was pure love and forgiveness. You may say an animal, a pet is dumb but they are not. We all could learn from them, firstly love and forgiveness. John did not call or come by; there was no love or forgiveness in him. A true representation of no love for Jill as always shown by John for a long time remains the same. Lori finally got a nasty call from John who said he would pick up his things on New Years' Day. Jill could not understand why John would choose such a day but then she realized his cunning ways. John knew Jill always believed in what happens on the first day of a new year would represent the rest of that year. John was going to leave his last cruel mark on Jill.

SECTION THREE

CHAPTER *EIGHT*—The *BEGINNING* of Jill and John

Saturday, January 10, 1997—March 2003

I need the message to be loud and clear. Please understand again, these are life living lessons for our society today, and my desire is that you will always be a learner starting here with this reading. It is not meant to cause dissent in a relationship but open communication to freedom of trust, respect, and honesty. Please make your home a lasting, loving place for both to grow and seek the future with desire.

And so it will be written. It is now time to uncover the truth of the past. This is the grim source of unfortunate displeasure that was never meant to be their ideal of a relationship, but which very quickly took root.

John and Jill had met on a very cold, unwelcoming January 10th, 1997. Is there karma in the type of day, the actual day of the month, the actual month of the year that one should meet a possible true love? Alone and lonely looking at the fireplace at home, Jill could not have another Saturday evening by herself. Peering out the living room window through the venetian blinds, like her kitty Sweetie did never-endingly, she decided to leave and go downtown. After all, she only had to call a taxi van. Nothing could stop her from passing through each street with ease. She was full of excitement with the memories of a little girl on the farm and jumping in the truck to go to town. Still the little girl now, with an excited jitter she passes over each snowdrift to find her way to what would become the next eleven years of her life.

Bad karma or good karma, you decide. Yes we are life learners but do we need to learn so many lessons in one precious life?

Jill was not sure anymore of the blowing, drifting snow in the streets and the lack of any living creature flurrying about. It all seemed to her she had entered into darkness as she drove towards downtown. If your own touch is cold and causes within a shiver of discomfort, then maybe it is not the moment to take on the newness of a stranger. And you are actively taking this on because you are in a place of meeting for that purpose, the local bar.

Jill finally reached the nearest bar, and the lights were still on. Parking was in abundance for a change; the taxi parked the van in a snow drift. Inside she went to find all of three people at the bar. It was here she had a choice of who to speak with. All three people looked sane, lonely like her and just wanted to be somewhere where there were people. The choice for no reason other than he was the closest to her, was John. Well, that evening Jill embraced life slowly with John, giving nothing but a nod. Jill was unaware of John watching her wherever she went. He followed her until the moment and place was right to say Hello! Jill recalls the moment so clearly. Jill responded with, "I am still so cold from being out in the storm." John smiled a boyish smile and said he could warm her up. He started to touch her hands, and Jill was done. Jill truly loves a man's man, and he was all of that. They left the bar together and only exchanged emails at the door. Neither wanted to give out a phone number; they had learned to be cautious from previous pursuers who would not take "no" for an answer.

Within 24 hours they emailed each other and spoke somewhat of their personal lives and decided to meet at his hotel the next time John was in the city for work. Two weeks later, Jill arrived off an elevator in the airport hotel to see this guy with a concierge moving his luggage. Jill walked right by him and then turned around at the same time John did. It was John, and Jill did not recognize him; it was strange and Jill should have recognized it as fate to be adhered to.

There is a message in this for Jill and for you. It is the saying, "Clothing does not make the man!" Well, she disagrees and most people do as well. You can change your whole perceived personality and character by the type of clothes you wear. You see a sixteen-year-old with the crotch of his pants down to his knees and you think "No respect." Well, as a teacher this is mostly false because despite the way they dress they are great young people. John's clothes that day were a whole different representation of whom Jill had met in the bar.

Well, John and she laughed, went into his room, jumped right into a heavy conversation again as they went on their way to the hotel lounge. What a delight to feel so comfortable! It was obvious John felt the same and that was why they exchanged phone numbers this time. Obviously there can be a comfort zone in closeness with another, even if you do not know them so well. That comfort zone was what helped make that moment so great.

John lived out of town and came into the city about three nights a week. Those nights soon became their nights to be together. Within one month, Jill started to have John sleep over in her house. John at one point gave Jill a laptop computer and began to show her how to use the laptop. There was a red flag for Jill right then, when she noticed John was so insecure and nervous. Maybe it was because John was showing her sites and chat lines, something Jill knew nothing about. It was crazy to think parts of what drove them apart he had taught Jill to do. As for red flags, you should know what that means: stop doing whatever it is that you are doing. Why is it that we never pay attention to the obvious? Jill should have called John on his insecurity and figured it out. This is another part of the reason why they are not together today, and it all started at the very beginning. Do you understand? If something does not seem right and it is so obvious, you must treat it or it will become infected, fester and turn into a disaster. Relationships with enough small infections and eventual turmoil will have nothing left to salvage.

Within months, a friend of Jill's made a plea to move in her place. Jill agreed because John was only there two or three nights a week, and also Jill was starting to drive to John's home for the week-ends. Sam, the roommate was hated by John, and soon became Jill's ally. Sam stayed in his room. Within a few years, and being in his room upstairs, it did not prevent him from observing the troubles of John and Jill. Eventually Sam asked to move into the basement apartment that was empty. He could no longer take the arguments that John would start. As well he told Jill, "I cannot watch you be hurt time after time."

March blew in like a lion and remained in a roaring commotion the whole month. Even before Jill met John, the previous September she had met a girl from Texas who just wanted her to visit and see Texas. The bad part was this girl had already bought Jill a plane ticket.

So, during the March break she was supposed to leave for Texas. John wondered what was taking place. At the time, they each did not give the impression they were not in love, nor did they discuss love or even a relationship. It was simple for Jill, she left for Texas. She arrived there on a sweltering day, called her friend and waited for her standing alone on the sidewalk. Jill's heart sunk deep. She knew she had made a mistake. She wanted to go home but there was no way she could. They arrived at her friend's house and Jill was very cool. She had to tell her she now realized she has fallen in love with this man named John. And he was a jealous type and may think I am here in Texas for different reasons. The whole next day they sat in her back-yard, her doing paperwork on a picnic table and Jill as far away as possible on her phone trying to get a flight home. Eventually, she was able to leave the next evening, and then Jill calmed down. Of course, she called John several times to say, "I want to come home!"

    Jill arrived back to the city, took a cab to her house and John met her after his work. Immediately John started a story of talking with his best friend in Edmonton who gave him good advice. Naturally, Jill had to ask what this good advice was. Jill had told John about this girl she had met last fall who has become her best friend. While she was in Texas, John made it his purpose to find her friend and make it his own experience with her! He felt he needed to tell her because Jill had called from Texas and had said "Nothing happened here, I need to see you John!" John now was quite guilt-ridden. His friend told him to come clean and Jill would understand. His friend was right, but why was this the only time in the remaining years he came clean? John became a compulsive liar, knowing from that day Jill if she knew would never accept a lie. The truth and its possible hurt are always better than a lie. Because he told her, Jill grabbed John, kissed and hugged him passionately as to never to let go, like he had imagined he would do on the plane coming home. Out came the words. Jill said, "I love you, John, and I only realized when I left!" From that moment on until today, Jill believes she stills loves John, and even today after all you read she still feels love for him. Jill said she really knew, understood and felt love. Never with anyone, not even her family, had she experienced such love. Her fantasy was to be able to place love on a silver platter so it could be displayed, observed and touched. Seriously, how many of you can say you feel or felt real, pure love in your whole self, the all of you?

A love affair it came to be. After the first year they took their first trip to see his best friend in Edmonton. He too had a new partner for three years now and was quite happy to share his new life with John and meet Jill. The four of them together as a group put her on top and for the first time Jill felt like she was living life. She had never had much in relationships before, another whole story. John's friend even threw a party in his home and invited all his friends for them to meet—a very exciting night for John and Jill. There were about fifty good-hearted people all in one room, and seemingly normal. John and she were given the guest bedroom since the house was crowded. The next morning Jill sort of fell out of bed and as she looked straight ahead she noticed a silver watch under the bed. Picking it up, John grabbed it and said it must be his friend's watch. Breakfast was called and they happily took the watch along, like little beavers dragging something to the den. It wasn't funny when his friend said, "This is not my watch." Oops, the jig was up! Apparently, while John's friend was working, the not-so-employed girlfriend entertained little friends in the guest room. Not soon after John and Jill returned home they got an email saying they were no longer together.

The next year started nicely with a trip to the Dominican Republic. Jill could not swim so he would lie on the beach. Unfortunately one day, John saw these lovely towels in a hut. He grabbed them and said they were a part of the hotel, so it was okay. Off they go towels in hand to another part of the beach. A shadow was cast over them as Jill laid tanning; she opened her eyes to see six security guards and a very angry Spanish couple. In very loud, poor English they were accused of stealing their towels. Jill should have known from there on, travelling with John would be a very different experience from her own travels.

Soon after they ventured off to a Caribbean Island where there were mostly nude beaches. That was a whole new experience, a staid, passive woman as herself walking naked on a beach. Add to that a safety vest so she could go into the water. Yes, a different and lovely sight to behold. Too many little old ladies, nude of course would walk by and smile. Not sure if it was the Bay Watch life jacket that got the smiles or the woman in it, Jill. Another trip was traveled and, yes, a troublesome experience like always. If there was an off-limits area to be found, John would sniff it out. Sure enough, he found what locally was called a no-swim zone beach, some huge rocks and scary crashing waves to a non-swimmer like Jill. Yes, there were locals there as well. Jill had a choice to leave or stay but was not aggressive enough. Gathering shells and colorful rocks which was her passion, they managed to stay there for the afternoon. She soon heard a voice from the shoreline, which was a high hill, "What are you guys doing down there?" Yes, the local boys in blue showed up, chased us and history again.

All remained the same at Jill's home, Sam as a roommate in the basement apartment, John staying three nights a week, and Jill alone with no friends, only Lori. Eventually, John started coming home from work very late. Dinner of course meant nothing and from John's cell phone Jill could hear the noise of his co-workers in the background from the bar. This was not several evenings but multiples of multiples. Jill even gave up the gym a lot of nights so she would be home to heat up his dinner or throw it out because he had eaten already. Eventually, John realized and started to invite Jill to dinner instead of his buddies. Jill ignored the previous months only to be happy to be alone with John. But when that behavior with buddies took over the special times you planned and there was no remorse, you had better check on his respect for you; something was wrong. Take off your blinders, instead of only looking straight ahead, start checking the corners.

In their fourth year, 2001, a change in their relationship was beginning to take place. Jill's observation of a deteriorating relationship brought a sadness that still exists with her today. Sadness can eventually be healed. Look for the blessings of God that surround you daily, the ability to smile and laugh are with you. You have to choose not to be sad. The longer you are sad, the more your body becomes tired and irritated. Sadness is not depression. Depression is much deeper and can only be treated with medications and therapy. You cannot ask within yourself to have your depression not exist. But you can with your sadness, a simple walk, a comedy at the theatre, repeat the things that used to make you happy. Eventually the cup of sadness becomes half-empty. Let your life of family and friends help you to dry and polish that cup of both feelings. Sadness is the most obvious; you can see it hanging on your face, like a mime with a painted face. Your sad face is without the paint but has the same effect, sagging chin; drooping eyes and grayness are all visible. But depression appears more on the inside and affects your thoughts and behavior. You become weaker at heart more deeply than if you are sad. Jill was more than sad, and depression, like a mold started to grow inside her.

They were in their fifth year now and the relationship with John was in a different place, due to John's reaction to everything. He even began to look different and act differently. Jill, who naturally worried in life, even over the small things, was now more deeply worried about John and what maybe she had done to change John's attitude towards her.

Jill's worry started to consume her peace of mind, and she became agitated and distressed. This was the beginning of what Jill still is today: left with insomnia. Jill just could not please John. Everything she said or did seemed to be wrong. Jill started to have pains in her chest and was diagnosed with chronic anxiety. She tried to discuss her issues with John, but his comment was, "Get over it. Act like a real woman."

Jill tried to see John's point of view and to believe he was right. No matter that Jill's every thought was about John and her guilt-ridden contribution to the deterioration of their partnership. Jill soon became helpless and extremely sad. One day she even went to the local emergency thinking she was having a heart attack. They took her seriously, performed all the tests only to discover Jill was experiencing pure anxiety, a heavy dose.

Maybe Jill had some good reasons to be worried. Things started to happen in public and that was John's sacred domain to keep everything about him as a wonderful guy.

To make Jill feel even more compassion for John, John arrived home from one of his week-ends at his house. John was in tears as he walked in the door. His older daughter had just told him off saying, "You could show you have love for me but you do not. All you think about is what is good for you." She actually jumped out of the car with her cell phone in hand ready to call 911 against her own dad. She felt he was abusive to her verbally and physically. The physical part came because John jumped out of the car as well, grabbed her arm and tried to force her back into the car. His other daughter was in the car crying hysterically. This was not John's behavior, something was wrong. She ended with her last words to her father and to this day has never spoken to him again, "You are an asshole!" To this day John has made no effort to repair that damage. But at the time of the event, and then when he saw Jill he finally opened up and cried heavily from his heart. Jill, who was so much in love with John, felt all his pain but had no words to make it better.

Weeks went by and now John's behavior everywhere became erratic and not understandable by any of his friends and especially by Jill. It got worse and brought the quiet, formerly gentle Jill to begin to defend herself. On one outing for dinner in the market square, John kept accusing Jill of looking at everyone in the restaurant but him. It became a whisper fight, but a heavy fight. When they left, as always, they took a walk down the street to see what was going on that evening. Much to Jill's amazement, John started yelling, "You are looking around again. If you want to walk with me, hold your head down and look at the sidewalk." It was such a mean and unforgiving remark. But to keep the public peace, Jill complied. Jill was not a scene-maker, plus a lot of people were acquainted with Jill as a teacher, and she felt horrible not being allowed to smile or acknowledge their hellos. For the first time, Jill spoke out and said, "Let's get back to the car." John was now stomping along, definitely not the man Jill knew. They got into the car that was parked right outside the restaurant windows. Jill as calmly as she could asked John, "What is wrong with you? John lost it and with cold black eyes he yelled, "You are nothing but a flirt!" Jill replied that this was so far from the truth, "I love you so much John. Why can you not see it?" Without looking, John abruptly pushed his car door open to jump out in a rage and a passing by cyclist slammed by his door. She went flying across the street, cuts and bruises and a flat tire. John's mood changed in the snap of a finger. He was so kind and forgiving. He offered everything to help her but Jill did not know why she refused; she just picked up her bike and walked away. John was very lucky. Not that he deserved it at that time. Jill was in shock of what had just happened and so were all the patrons inside the restaurant, half of whom knew us as a great couple. A part of Jill's mind was wondering how John could be so apologetic to a stranger but not to her.

It was enough, and the engine got started with John driving too fast towards home. Both were very quiet, but Jill could not take the speed, so she asked John to slow down. There was no response and a heavier foot hit the gas pedal. Then it happened. For the first time and as an excuse because of his behavior and what his daughter recognized, Jill called him an "asshole". Name-calling in a relationship is low and dirty, going too far without discussion. There should never be name calling between two partners. Teenagers are not given enough credit for their observation of life and how they can see the truth, especially with their own parents. John's response was hitting the brakes and pushed Jill out the car door onto the roadside and sped off like an idiot. Jill was in total bewilderment and shock of what has just happened. She had to cross a second roadway of the highway to reach the side of the causeway. There she sat in the grass trying to think that this was too much. The relationship has reached a level of crazy, but then as always in Jill's mind in crept an explanation to forgive John. She felt his reactions were because his daughter had just written him off as she said, forever. She has kept her word even until today.

Hailing down a cab, Jill got home and thought, "I need not be afraid, this is my house. I should have no fear of entering." John's car was in the driveway but was nowhere to be seen. Jill went upstairs to find one of the bedroom doors locked and with no words exchanged. Jill went off to bed alone.

This was the first explosion by John that had been building for months showing unexplainable emotions and behaviors. He seemed to withdraw even more, pounding his way through the house and causing little arguments about anything to upset Jill. As regards for Jill there was no understanding, no awareness of what was really taking place. Jill's friend Lori could offer no help, no solution, nothing to help her try and solve what was taking place in her home life. Lori could only see a crushed woman who kept blaming herself for the failure of their relationship.

Then John started to disappear several nights every week. Soon it was on a Friday or a Saturday all night only to see him during the day. Jill kept quiet because she was not an argumentative person and actually lived in fear now of John's forked tongue, and his wrath. Jill could never answer quickly enough in first response to John's arguments. Later she would think of the response she should have given John.

This was when Jill was introduced to John's real cheating. He would get up early some days, sit at his desk and rushed putting his work papers together for the day. Jill's intuition kept bothering her, and one day she decided to follow John. Jill had now moved into a new form of living, the stalker, a very suspicious woman and really started to believe in her intuition. Nothing seemed right this morning because John ran out the door, no kiss, no goodbyes. Jill knew what the point was, but she drove right to the place she expected John to be. She found John's car and her heart was racing and empty all at the same time. Never would Jill forget the image of John walking along to his car, knowing he just met some girl in the apartment building and whether ignorant or not when he saw Jill, he yelled Jill and smiled, "It is nice to see you." He was not nervous, no guilt-ridden explanations just a "Hi Jill." Jill lost her composure, started to cry and asked, "Why, I am at home, your loving partner and you abandon me for this action?" Jill hit the right note and John began to cry—the first and last time when ever Jill found him cheating. It became a hobby and he became less caring of what Jill thought.

This all became too much, too many unanswered questions. When the first fight took root in the bedroom—that is the last place any couple should fight—then Jill knew it was becoming unsolvable. And one day when John was in the bedroom fighting he ripped Jill's blouse from her back. Jill still felt it was her fault and was still sympathetic towards John.

Jill wanted this new beginning, but was she was uncertain of John's intentions with this new breakup, Saturday, March 5, 2003. Even though he promised to go through couples' therapy again, and promised to stop cocaine, Jill's intuitive sense told her John would never agree in his heart. As for therapy, it was not in his culture to do therapy. In realization of the facts, Jill knew she would have to help the one that was meant to be helped, and Jill did not know how.

Jill thought about her previous parental guidance which she felt had been of little consequence. It should have constituted all the building blocks for a strong emotional and thinking individual. Jill felt cheated, and every time as an adult she brought up these issues her parents would say, "Where did we go wrong?" or even worse, the most common response, "I never should have had children!"

Jill did not need that so-called advice; she did not need to hear that from the people whom for all those years she had tried to please and emulate. But as she observed in later years, she did not want to be the chip-off-the-old-block and for that, she is who she is today. Emotions, thinking, decisions and taking action were all askew.

When Jill needed to think as a child she went to the one place familiar to her as a child. When she felt troubled she would go to this great beach nearby and sit on the sand dunes pondering about her days and mostly about her future. Fortunately, this city had a great beach as well, and it became Jill's destination for deep thinking seated on a rock ledge.

Jill had a different request now with John. She asked for help because she was in immense emotional trouble; disabled by her own thinking. She could not understand why her own parents in the past had no answers for her life. When Jill recalled this day, she realized that thought was wrong because we are responsible for our own answers. It is our thoughts and the emotions attached to them that give us the answers. But Jill, still hurting, felt her own parents were ill-equipped to help in any way. The best possible answer from them was, "Go to church and pray for guidance. Believe in God and he will see you through troubled waters."

Does all of this with John say Jill has no self-worth? Worth is not dollars and cents as in the pay check. We all have to have to sustain some form of living. Jill felt her worth was in deep jeopardy. Even though she wanted John returned home, it was not totally for the right reasons. Jill knew that loneliness and co-dependency were her killers. They had caused all her pain in life, even more that what all the Johns could do to her. Jill realized now she had less sense of her values, morals, intrinsic and extrinsic behavior and just a sense of self, and nothing to give to John.

Intuitively Jill knew a huge part of her life was missing. That was to have her own child to rear and let him develop into a fine young man. But then that was one of the reasons why she wanted John. He had two daughters that Jill could be mother to with lots of love as well.

Josh R. Himmelman

Life living lesson: Can you feel alone and be in an intimate relationship?

Being alone can be in the form of physicality or of emotion, or both. It is a complex place, somewhere all on its own. If one of your senses picks up on a past event, you cannot stop your mind from jumping there. If you feel alone, try to jump ahead, not behind, and train your mind to follow the right decision.

Intimacy is the feeling of having a close personal connection and belonging together deeply through knowledge and the experiences of one and another. In human relations, intimacy requires verbal interaction, your thoughts with each are transparent and you are vulnerable with each other. You want everyone to see you as a known intimate couple. In human relationships, the meaning and level of intimacy will differ within your partnership. To develop an intimate relationship it takes a dedicatedly long period of time. It takes on all forms of communicating: verbal as well as non-verbal, and importantly body language.

Your goal is to maintain a degree of intimacy through the years, and this takes both to show their emotional and interpersonal awareness. It requires for both to be together in participating in an intimate relationship; intense loyalty. Intimacy between two people is developed over time and if either person has the inability to do so, because they struggle to find their boundaries, to constantly keep their connection, they do not even have the skills to keep a best friend or even move too fast, which is a poor management skill as regards being intimate for a lifelong relationship.

There are two important different forms of intimacy: emotional intimacy and physical intimacy. Emotional intimacy develops in sexual relations only after physical bonds are established. It means falling in love, but could be tainted by body stimulation from sexual attraction and by talking after sexual interaction, also physical intimacy. Emotionally intimate relationships are much stronger and will live through even ongoing disagreements and arguments. In new relationships today, sexual intimacy develops in a very predictable way. Couples have seen their parents whose divorce rates today are very high. Couples realize that they should not rush, that they keep their own apartment space and seem to start a right beginning. But those who rush quickly are noted to be the most likely to break up.

With emotional love you can have either passionate love or companion love. You expect passionate love to be intense; there will be unknown facts about each other and you are waiting for the next moment to happen because you do not know each that well. Companion love is almost friendship love; your best friend tells you all their secrets and desires. It is a more peaceful and calmer form of loving between two people.

Ask yourself the following questions: Does your spouse see you as an equal? Do you feel you are treated with respect or exploited? Do you feel your spouse will always be there? Can you count on them? Can you share your inner thoughts with them, especially sensitive issues? And when you disagree do you both take action to solve the issue or is it just discarded as an issue, left unresolved? Your relationship needs closeness. You should count on always repeated interactions and your needs being fulfilled. This would be a relationship where two people like and love each other romantically and sexually. You should not have to ask the other partner for emotional and personal support. It automatically fulfills your need of belonging to someone and the need to be cared for.

Love is the factor, not just like in a physical and emotional intimate relation. People who are in an intimate relationship should be called a couple and proud to be called this in public. To be alone and think you are in an intimate relationship can be quite devastating. You can lose a sense of self, who you thought you were emotionally and physically. You are alone if you expect your happiness to come from your partner. You need to give as well as take. To feel not alone, respect the fact that not every issue between you is solvable. Create a trust and a safety net that you can both cocoon in keeping your communication as common grounds to understand each other's different viewpoints. You cannot have it always your way. Keep yourself open to discovery and not in the backseat hiding. You can learn from each other and contribute equally. When you contribute be truthful to yourself first and then share that truth with your partner if you want true love. Do not create a disconnection. When something turns into a mistake, say you are sorry. Do not be the person who can never take the blame, but equally, do not keep a tally of past arguments and who gave in.

To be really free of the fear of standing alone, appreciate your partner. Be sensitive and say that you do not want to argue and let's look at ourselves, who we are and what we started with as our expectations. Remember, you both need love, intimacy, affection and affirmation that you will be in a permanent togetherness as a couple. You do not need to be or to feel alone in your relationship.

End of Life living lesson: Can you feel alone and be in an intimate relationship?

Life living lesson: Do not argue in closed, restricted spaces, or with your back against the wall.

Many years ago I developed a close relationship with a female co-worker whom now has become my confidant and personal advisor. She was like a personal 911 rescue unit, always ready to stop and have a coffee with you. And, she knows it was not time to savor the coffee bean, but I am once again in a personal rut and need help. Yes, we are having a deep conversation in a public place with reason, even though we each have our own homes.

A piece of advice learned that was very personal for her to share. Her and her husband found a way to work through a disagreement, an optimal mode of arguing would be in public place. As newlyweds, she was given the kind of advice that I must share with you. No, you do not schedule intimate sexual moments and you should set a time and place to argue. First rule is never to argue in your home, your car or on any place that means something to you both or either of you personally. Remember your classified memory banks, and do you really want to associate your dining room table as the common battle ground? Never let your needs be remembered as a place where an argument took residence. Instead, choose a restaurant, a table in the open and have your conversation. You have one thing in common, respect, and here you must respect everything attached to an argument because you will not make a public scene. You cannot raise your voice to send chills through their body; name calling will only make you look like the underdog instead of fulfilling the intention to hurt your partner's self-esteem. Keep it calm, keep it together in your resolutions, it smothers the flames into a simmer and hopefully a fizzle. A peck on the cheek in public after a discussion helps to really solidify honesty and respect in your decisions and a movement forward in the relationship. Compare any part of this with an argument in the bedroom, slamming doors with sleepless nights. Which one do you want to try on for a continued, understanding of your relationship? The restaurant represents non-confinement. You are not limited or restricted regarding physically leaving, a sense of freedom that helps you to focus more on the argument instead of the space holding you physically and mentally.

The term "open discussion" if truly adhered to by both partners is a valuable tool to understand and know what each of you are thinking, your belief system and personal values. It is a time to ask questions by each to make it clear where you both stand on an issue. Such knowledge can then help you reach a mutual agreement on how to work together as a couple.

Do not believe there will never be an argument or a fight in your relationship. And until time together has passed will you even know how intense the fights may be or even why they may be in your partnership?

Would you ever think the person you love so much because of their passion for life can also be the fighter? All too often, that passion is used to go to the limit, then reaching unnecessary words, phrases and name calling that cannot be erased. Yes, it is normal to argue; after all you did not grow up together in the same household, hence the different opinions and upbringing. And let's throw in culture, religion, finances, educational background and your own understanding of anger.

How do you decide what will become a regret of yours? It is very easy, because in the heat of it all we become very confused. We forget even who started an argument and the blame is redirected by you. It is always easy to blame the partner for everything while it is you causing the fights. Causes are no different for any couples: non-trusting, jealous and as in some, a feeling of being taken for granted.

The advice to improve is, "Become the learner in your relationship if you want to stop fighting or to fix your problems." You need to show and make it known that you are intending to make everything better. Even recognize every fight for what is was worth but do not bring up old wounds. That was a learning process. However do not dismiss what you learned because each argument provides benefits to learn more and how to grow together. After all the fight had a reason; then work on that reason.

Look at verbal abuse within fighting as definitely a form of mistreatment, like being placed in physical entrapment. You want to believe either would never physically want to touch each in an undesirable manner. It is okay to feel sorry for yourself for enduring a physical conflict and degradation. It has reached this way of problem solving by treating you like a stranger. You will keep saying, "I love you, let's fix us, we can be better," but a new variable has entered the relationship—worry. If you ever hear the words from a partner, say the next day, "I really enjoyed that fight," your relationship is lost.

End Life living lesson: Do not argue in closed, restricted space or with your back against the wall.

Life living lesson: Time out! Giving space and freedom in arguments—is it a must?

In sports a "time-out" refers to a stoppage in the match for a short amount of time. As a couple, can we call a time-out for each to step back and look at the problem? A time to think or even only to be alone and not have your thoughts influenced by their physical presence. Do you need to go as far as move out for a week? Go see the grandmother and read a book calmly. Moving out is a separate whole new ball game in trying to resolve a partnership problem. Out of sight, out of mind; is a little phrase that should mean nothing if you truly love each other.

If you physically separate your living together you are putting a physical distance between you both. It can cause an opposite effect by creating an early distant past. It can start you thinking beyond those memories and moments of togetherness.

We keep referring to time. The use of time, the nature of time and of various issues related to time. There are believers that whatever will happen in the future is already unavoidable; no one person is able to prevent it from happening. Is this a reason not to take a time out with couples, could it be fatal? In true love, thoughts of tomorrow's events should predict that whatever will happen, it will be for the good of each in the relationship.

Every argument is relevant and when that time comes you both decide either it has no true value fight now, or else it needs to be further discussed in a deeper detail to keep it from happening again. It is all on the value you place on the importance of this argument now. It makes sense that if this argument reassumes later it may have a different truth value. The same argument in different times will have a different value placed on its importance as part of your relationship. It is essential this argument be resolved the first time.

Does each argument actually have a pin pointed beginning? Many times we try to determine when the initial issues began but then why look for more fuel. In fact, whether there was a beginning to the argument building, it is the present that holds the importance and needs a resolution. If you do not solve completely the issue, it will tend to branch off into other areas, now used as fuel to ignite a new argument. You could now have a forest fire with hot spots burning or you both bring yourselves equally to extinguish the big fire. Do not let the hot spots smolder because they will be, at any time, ready to burst into possible bigger flames than the first original fire.

What if one day things in your relationship came to a sudden halt? All conversation is frozen, tight lipped. During this time do you think nothing has changed, that it is possible for there to be a period of time without change? Obviously it would follow that your relationship will still exist without any interaction, physical or verbal. But this empty partnership, lacking of any events will be only empty. The partnership will only continue if you start to place some events to fill the voids. There are only so many days a couple can co-exist physically and not be there emotionally. The relationship, the container that holds your loving memories will begin to crack like a damn. Eventually that crack will break and depending where that crack is in your relationship, there could be a huge flood of arguments, misinterpretations and indecisions and together it may take too much to try and resolve all of them pinned up issues.

Time in a relationship is thought as being equal. But truly I believe noting is exactly equal. Time means different things to different people. The only identity of time that is the same for a couple is the duration of their relationship. In today's society we have taken a turn and see time is a finite entity, one day the relationship will stop and never be again. We seem not to start out by thinking we both will see the finish line together. We have become within ourselves too personal and subjective. You look for your time together to fly through existence; joy and contentment but if not together it appears tortured. You will do little to make it last forever. You need to see each other as close to whom they are and not isolated by events and time spent. Try to keep it as both you, let your relationship be the first and the last for each forever.

Did you decide it is time without restrictions to give freedom to your partner to evaluate your lives? When you love someone, you imagine tying your heart to theirs and never want to let go. With true love, you will always be thinking of them and you will want to make them always feel your love. The time out should only be time out of your lives for each knowing you will always want to be there with them and make them happy.

End of Life living lesson: Time out! Giving space and freedom in arguments is it a must?

The month of March 2003 was more difficult to endure. This time Jill not only has cocaine to face but cheating was becoming just as big an issue but not more prominent in the relationship. Cocaine was his favorite again, and apparently five years before Jill even met John after his separation with Cheryl, John learned the pleasures but unsavory costs of cocaine. The heaviness of tension and slight of eye contact, and doors smashing all became so bad, yet Jill was so ignorant of what was going on in her own home. Sam could not take what John was doing to Jill. Sam could see pathetically that Jill thought she was hurting John somehow. Jill knew she needed many answers and even asked some of his friends. One response was dead on. Sounds to me like Cocaine.

Does getting an answer that you been searching for make it right to discuss your partner's behavior with a friend behind their back, behind their own knowledge of this taking place. What made it worse for Jill was that she believed John would never suspect she would do such a thing because of embarrassment; especially all the negatives in their relationship. Because of this guilt, Jill at the end of every argument would say, "It is okay!" or "It is just me!" Or the one she was fearful of saying: "It takes two." Jill too many times asked herself whether it was a habit to keep apologizing even though you were not wrong. Who created this apology? It could have been either her or John. It is an erroneous habit like a smoker in a hospital dragging his IV drip pole alongside of him as he exits the building for a smoke. They found the energy to do this but not the energy to ask God for help in healing. Like in a couple relationships as John and Jill, who loves whom? The smoker outside quite often is joined by family members, drawing back the blue smoke of heaven. It is their habitual choice to choose death. Continuous arguments are habitual choices for the death of a relationship.

Jill's friends all know about her living situation and her neediness to be with someone, now anyone. They have joined in the habit of asking drilling questions the same as Jill does. They ask Jill leading questions about her life to get her started on a rant about private scenarios at home. Sometimes Jill expressed the wish that she could stop talking negatively about John. Maybe that was what was making it harder to forgive John. Jill might have been pleading for a different type of response, not just listeners but for someone else to control the conversation. Jill knew what she said drew the energy from her friends and the worst was now they knew the dirty truth and saw her in a different way. That was not the way Jill wanted her relationship to appear. She wanted it to be envied by all as the happiest couple. Many times Jill spoke to John telling him that others admired both of them and not just her. But the jealously always got in the way and John would not let them be happy inside the door of their home. A great showman in public, but at home a few blouses were ripped off Jill's' back in arguments. Their life was not a bed of roses and that phrase was wrong anyway. As Jill said, roses die and you are left with a dead bed. When a relationship dies, there is nothing in the bedroom. And if you notice, a rose petal dies from the end inward. A relationship dies the same way, starting on the edge of small imperfections and spreading inward into the hearts of both. In their relationship, the tip of happiness had already gone.

John's brain was becoming like a hot plastic sealed container. One more little prick and it would burst. John did know that he was stronger than he thought. We are all stronger then we think. When John thought of all the negatives in their partnership there seemed never to be anything positive in the forefront of his memory.

Sunday morning of March 05, 2003, there was another argument but this time it took on a calm presence. Jill left the house looking back at John and said, "Decide what you want; this has all become too crazy." "She did not say, "Leave" or "Pack your belongings." Jill just went out the door.

A phone call was made to Lori by Jill and she asked her to spend the day. They went to her local pub, had lunch and obviously discussed John more often than anything. Hours later Jill's cell phone rings and it was John. With hesitation he said all of his belongings were packed and he would be leaving soon, "So you can come home." There was a lull in John's statement and Jill did not ask why but she did ask, "Are you leaving?" and said, "Maybe you should not." Jill was so distraught that she was not thinking. There was a second call made by John to say his car was packed and that now Jill could come home.

Within minutes the bill was paid and Jill very quietly drove home, there were no thoughts in her mind other than the craziness would stop. As Jill walked in the door she almost heard an echo. Yes all of John's belongings were gone. Jill was hit like a swinging wrecking ball from a crane. Jill sobbed and rolled on the sofa. She kept saying, "Why didn't I stop him when he called me? It was obvious that was what he wanted."

Two days before Jill had just bought a new car. John that day was very happy for Jill. That evening, after John had left Jill immediately jumped into her car and over the speed limit she went to reach John's home. Jill ran to the front door and knocked loudly with John answering. At first John had a smile and was glad to see Jill but coldness came over him and said "I do not want to see you anymore." John allowed Jill in and kept saying, "You are not a kind woman." John was being as cruel as he could. He kept saying, "You kicked me out," and "You do not love me anymore." Jill looked around the room and all she saw were green garbage bags stuffed with her beloved's belongings. This even made it worse for Jill and she kept apologizing to John and saying, "Please come back home."

John started to be what Jill saw was a different self. He started yelling and crying uncontrollably. He told Jill he had made a big mistake and then curled himself into a ball on his sofa chair. Jill tried to comfort him, kissing him but was turned away. Jill could not understand who this new John was. It was very intense, too abnormal and finally John literally kicked Jill out of the house.

Jill had to teach school the next day and it was already three a.m. After school she called her doctor for help, to please give her something to calm down. But as Jill knew any pill would take weeks before you could see its effects. Jill was stuck in what she thought was limbo and turmoil that she did not understand herself. Today Jill understands that it was a solid case of co-dependency. Back then Jill started to call every fifteen minutes into John's cell, but he would not answer. It drove Jill into a panic because she could get no answers this time. Soon Jill found out that John was staying in a downtown hotel because he had a number of clients to visit here in Jill's town and needed to be close and not travel such a distance each day to work. Now that Jill knew the hotel, she started calling and leaving messages on his room phone, but still no response.

Jill found a therapist and knew she had to speak with someone who understands this lifestyle. As Jill arrived for her first appointment, her cell phone rings causing Jill to quickly check the phone number. The ring was from one of his friends who said John was soon going to call as well. He proceeded to say John was at a bar downtown as they spoke. To Jill this was her assurance the suspicions were correct. Entering the therapist at this time, Jill was so emotional her words were all garbled.

The cell phone rang again and it was the same mutual friend. He said, "I have a message for you from John. He wants to teach you a lesson."

From that moment on for weeks, Jill went different times of the day to find John's car by that club. Jill even went to a psychiatrist out of desperation to see what she could do. Jill got lucky once at least she thought and found John's car. Jill went inside and found him in a room dealing drugs with another guy, counting out money and discussing the evening. This same guy came to Jill about six months later all hyped up asking for John's families phone number. This was on the street and Jill wanted to know why. He said, "I had another guy like John who bought Tina from me and lost everything. John was going down the same path and he was too far into the drugs." Jill could not give out those numbers even though it seemed the right thing to do. But when dealing with drug users, what do you believe? John in the club that night was unrecognizable totally wasted. He saw Jill standing in the hallway. Before Jill knew it he leaped on top of Jill and shoved her, asking where she was standing in the bar. Jill had to tell him, and as they walked there John was very possessive and shouted, "You stay here and I do not want to see you speaking with anyone." At first Jill thought he actually cared, but then she realized it was more about the drugs influencing John then anything. Jill left defeated, not being able to convince John of his soon-to-be demise.

Jill later went back to many voice messages. Except this time John would answer her back. There were two daily messages from John. In the evening it was the drugs speaking, cursing Jill and so on. But in the early morning waking up from his night he would send another message, crying and saying he was so sorry for what he did say. This went on for a week; and Jill would not stop. She was relentless in trying to help John. Jill's voice was always calming and loving; she never spoke harshly or remarked about his messages. The morning was the true John; the John that Jill wanted to come back home so she could take care of him.

Finally John left a message for Jill and said, "Come down to my house on the weekend and we will talk." Jill was elated and planned for a week what she would say, what she would offer for reconciliation because Jill still believed it was her fault that John had turned to drugs.

The meeting finally took place, and surprisingly John's home was all in order as opposed to the last time Jill had been there. Jill wondered how could that be since knowing what went on in the past three weeks for John. Jill did not realize that cocaine gave endless energy and a drive to complete what you are doing. John stood there in front of Jill so tired, sleepless and beaten emotionally. John decided it would be best if he came back with Jill and that meant a second chance, Jill's wish. Jill helped him pack what he would need for now and they drove back in one car since his was already at the hotel in town. John, after all he did, asked Jill if she had cheated while he was on a binge during the last three weeks. It was all too weird for Jill but she now had John in her car. So what! This might help in the reconciliation.

During those three weeks Jill needed someone to speak with about John's behavior so she could understand. She met a truly nice guy at the gym who was only interested in helping Jill's obviously acute guilt. He spent every day coaching Jill about what to do and promised it would work itself out. He was right, and John did agree to come home. When they arrived home in Jill's house, John started to laugh. He admitted to Jill that for one year he had sat at the dining room table, supposedly working. While there he would watch the back of Jill's head and snort cocaine. "You were so naïve Jill." Jill was so hurt but realized she had brought John back and wanted to fix a broken partnership; a new beginning and forgets the past. You can forgive but never forget. They sat down to talk and John as a part of coming home made a solemn promise not to do anymore cocaine. Jill believed in her John and the idea meant everything to her. But then John asked Jill if he had made any friends. Jill said she had met one guy who had helped her to understand what was taking place. Jill admitted that he knew nothing about drugs and needed this man's help. John turned red and demanded Jill to give him the man's phone number. John then picked up the phone and dialed the number; Jill could hear his new friend's voice answer. John said abruptly that Jill would no longer be his friend, "I am home now and never call here again." Jill was in shock and asked him why he would do such a thing to another good person. His response was that this was a clean slate; you do not need him anymore. Jill asked John about all *his* new drug friends since he was to be clean from now on. "Well, they are my best friends and I have no intentions of letting them go." Jill started to wonder what she had done. This last action by John made Jill go to her room and sulk in her emotions over John's even worse behavior. Jill still did not understand what the use of cocaine can do to a person. John came upstairs and they both went to bed tired and only ready to sleep. John lay still on his back and said to Jill, "Kiss me to prove that you love me." Jill was okay with this, hoping it would lead them into a renewed sexual connection. When Jill went to kiss him, John tightly kept his lips perched shut, no movement on purpose and Jill was kissing an emotionless hurtful man. This was so hurtful to Jill; it was like he was still punishing her for all his mistakes. You could not feel such sadness that Jill felt. The next day fortunately was a Monday, a work day for both and time spent apart to think before seeing each other that evening. That night was different. It felt like almost three years ago and they did start a new but cloudy relationship with but a tainted past hanging over each.

Jill had to mention Spain, the soon immediate trip that summer which has started to be only one of many. You are wondering what really was wrong with Jill. Are these tales of truth? Well they are true and some can be proven by real people. Others can be proven by emails Jill grabbed off the computer. Others can be proven by recorded voice messages from John bashing Jill quite badly. Lori heard those and cannot believe just how disgusting and belligerent he was to Jill and upset that Jill still had not done something about her life. In Spain, with a stranger in the condo next door who heard all their arguments finally came to Jill's rescue. John wildly held Jill down on the bed, tossing her around the bedroom with two syringes in his one hand yelling he was going to either blind Jill or stab her in the heart. This went on for a good thirty minutes. Then John stormed out the door and Jill ran next door to get help. Then John returns yelling that the whole building could hear. Why Jill didn't call the police, or someone living there, she does not know. He thrashed around their condo for about ten minutes, and then started banging on the neighbor's door where Jill took refuge demanding to open the door to let him see Jill. John yells, "I know you are in there Jill and I want you out." John leaves again and the neighbor with Jill ran into Jill's condo to find all of her belongings everywhere, trashed and difficult to put together in her suitcase. They just got out and he returns again, yelling up a storm banging on the doors for Jill. He leaves yet again. Jill called a cab; drove to the airport and never got out of the cab. The cab driver thought Jill was nuts, in Spanish, of course. Jill went back into town and rented a hotel room next door. You cannot put into words what her heart and mind were doing that night. This was the third day in of a fourteen-day holiday. Jill already paid half of the condo fee and she deserved that space. A bigger problem: Jill could not fly out because they were on a tour flight which only returned after two weeks. She would have to wait for a space to open up on a charter just like the way they got there. The next day Jill went to the condo and asked for her room key. It was already gone and the concierge said John just left, he believed for the gym. Jill fast paced followed through the streets only to miss the bus John would have been travelling on. In such a chronic state, Jill got the next bus and found him at the gym around noon. They talked slightly and Jill said she needed to stay at that condo and she was coming back to no more arguments. They leave the gym to return to the condo where John went upstairs and said, "If you want to move back, go and get your things on your own." Therefore with no help Jill went to the other hotel and dragged all her belongings back to the condo. When John got inside, within those hours that Jill had been gone John had taken this two bedroom condo and laid all his personal belongings out in the two bathrooms and two bedrooms. Jill asked why? It was really weird. No real answer. Jill asked him why he did what he did. Were you on cocaine? "Oh no but after wards I went out and bought cocaine, after you left." Well John was injecting steroids from a vet as soon as they had arrived, so Jill forgave it all because she felt it was not her real John who did this but a man strung out on drugs, so it was not his fault. But this experience cannot leave Jill for a very simple reason. Later that day, John looked at her and said, "I really loved pushing you around and pinning you down. It felt real good!" Needless to say Jill had two more weeks left of learning how to forgive a partner who can make such comments. "I love lying to you, it is so much fun."

    Wow, Jill was sitting there and he could not bring the recent verbal abusive lines to the forefront of her brain. She was so disgusted that she could not allow herself to think. John used to say he was sorry. Sorry for the panic, the flutter he caused in Jill's chest. The best part was after John would say it was going to be okay and offer some conciliation with it he would say, it takes two. Jill said Sorry as well, but did John really get the big picture? That picture was the hurt in Jill's face, the need he had for this not to continue to happen. Peace within this partnership sometimes cost too much and usually one paid a bigger price. How quickly John would settle into old conversation and old ways after these words were spoken. And not often enough were these words spoken. One has to wonder why it was so easy for Jill to forgive and forget. You say, "It takes two." Was it a control freaky thing John wanted over her? Was it the fact John knows guess who was in the wrong and John was getting away with it as well?

How many times did Jill want to hear the word Sorry from the same person? The more you accept, does it mean you love them a great deal and your feelings do not count? Oh yes, since Jill really does love him, she believes she should forget, but Jill was forgetting as well her own ideas, values, beliefs, needs, wants, attitudes and a whole lot more to come. Was this who she really wanted to be? But, Jill does love him and realizes if they argue or he fights back, all may be lost. If this was true, what did he really have anyway? The result was who was at fault here? And Jill lives her biggest fear, being alone.

This relationship now was a façade, an outer shell of a physical structure. As well the outer layer of your emotions and behavior because nothing felt deep. Take a close look at your partner. Do you really see what you are getting? Open your eyes and dig deep because most often there was something hidden. At one point Jill and John took a tour of Venice by boat and saw all its beauty, its facades. But behind that beauty were massive decay, mold and rot due to an interference of the outside forces, like drugs decaying one's mind. No-one is one hundred per cent and that means your partner as well. You must learn to see beyond the facades of even your most beloved. I am not telling you to distrust or disrespect them. Then you will destroy your relationship, but just be aware. It was very difficult to look at an image behind the mirror but it does exist in reverse. You have to look at the composition of the image and then you can see what lies beneath. Look at the all of your other half and see if you find something lying, an image below their façade hopefully to be kept hidden.

Life living lesson: Cocaine

A drug, usually called "coke or "blow," cocaine is a white powder from a plant grown mainly in South America. It is a stimulant of the central nervous system and an appetite suppressant and it is highly addictive.

Cocaine is most often used any age, demographics, economic, social, political, and religious or just about any livelihood. There is an enormous demand for cocaine in the United States market particularly among people who have incomes with more income than necessary to sustain their life. That includes professionals, single adults and as a status of being luxurious.

Cocaine in its purest form is a white, pearly product. Cocaine appearing in a powder form is a salt. On the street cocaine is altered or as they say "cut" with various powdery fillers to increase its weight; it is sold by weight. Fillers to enhance quantity of cocaine (and diminish its purity) would be substances such as: baking soda, sugars, and local anesthetics: such as Lidocaine or Benzocaine which add to cocaine's numbing effect on one's mucous membranes. Altered cocaine is often a white, off-white or pinkish powder. Cocaine is usually sold in small baggies by the gram.

Cocaine is used by snorting with any device like a straw a narrow line of the powder from a flat surface. The effects come on gradually and it's most affective after about fifteen to thirty minutes. The effects are a sudden increase in heart rate, blood pressure and breathing. It definitely leads to feelings of confidence, alertness and euphoria.

Another common method to administer cocaine into the body is to rub the powder along the gum line, or onto a cigarette filter which is then smoked. Obviously it numbs the gums and teeth, giving this type of use names like "numbies," "gummies" or "coco puffs". After all, when you inhale through a straw, there will be a residue left on that surface. This is when the small amounts of remaining cocaine are taken care of, none is wasted. Another oral method is to wrap up some cocaine in rolling paper and swallow it, called a "snow bomb."

To explain better, be aware of a user, the adept hide this habit for a long period of time. It is better you understand closely what you need to observe to maintain your own self-preservation.

Orally taken cocaine takes about thirty minutes to enter the bloodstream. A bit of a waste of the family hard earned cash and only one-third of an oral dose is absorbed. Because it is so slow to be absorbed it takes about an hour for ingested to give a maximum physiological effect. Therefore, if you do only one line and stop, it effects are slow but the effects are maintained for about sixty minutes after it peaks in your system. Hence, the reason for doing several lines of cocaine repeatedly in an evening is to remain high the whole evening. As your tolerance level builds rapidly in the short-term (one evening), many lines are often snorted to keep a greater effect. Either way being oral, ingestion or sniffing results in about the same amount of the drug being absorbed. Compared to ingestion, the faster way to absorption is sniffing cocaine with results quicker with the maximum drug effects. Their effects are maintained up to sixty minutes after the peak of the drug is attained in your body.

"Snorting," "sniffing," or "blowing" is the most common ingestion of powered cocaine. The reason, it coats over the mucous membranes inside your nose and is absorbed through this entry point. Not necessarily is everything absorbed through the nasal membranes and is therefore collected in mucus and has to be swallowed. There can be damage inside the nose because cocaine highly constricts the blood vessels; therefore blood will collect in that area. The various ways to inhale cocaine, which is very fine in consistency, are called "tooter" by users. Some of these tooters require a straw and can spread blood disease such as Hepatitis C.

Drug injection provides the highest concentration in the blood. The immediate effect after administrating is a ringing in the ears lasting up to five minutes, referred to as "bell ringer." It is a much faster way to reach euphoria; it is already in the blood stream and is very toxic and can cause blood clotting from the substances used to cut the cocaine. "Speedball" is a mixture of cocaine and heroin that complement each other and are responsible for numerous deaths.

Last here is the form of inhalation. Smoking is another way cocaine can be taken. Cocaine is smoked by inhaling the vapor from solid cocaine that is heated. Smoking cocaine or crack cocaine is done using a pipe made from a small glass tube, sometimes called "stem", "horns," "blaster," or "straight shooters." The cocaine and crack cocaine, which is the solid form, are smoked by placing it at the end of the pipe and when a flame is held close it produces a vapor which is then inhaled by the smoker. The effects are almost immediate but last only several minutes.

Cocaine and crack are both very short acting leading to using too much too often. Eventually you are addicted and a compulsive user has many side effects: depression, agitation, anxiety and paranoia. High doses or more frequent doses have caused seizures, strokes or heart attacks. Obviously, repeated snorting can cause damage to the membranes of the nose.

Not everyone who uses cocaine becomes addicted but if they do, it can be one of the hardest drug habits to break. Addictions cause people to lose control over the drug, an intense need to have more even though intellectually they know it is harming their body. Eventually cocaine can become the most important thing in their lives. Any method of taking cocaine can lead to addiction. Without the drug they can crash, their mood swings rapidly from feeling high to distress. Additional symptoms of cocaine withdrawal can include instability and suicidal thoughts because of the craving for more of the drug. The memory of the euphoria derived from cocaine use is powerful and causes the person to experience a strong risk of relapse to continuously using the drug.

You by now have to ask yourself, why? People take drugs because they want to change something about their lives; they want to escape; they are bored; they want to rebel or simply experiment. Because drugs are so common, they think drugs are a solution. But it becomes their new reality, a whole new different problem.

The consequences of drug use are always worse than the problem one is trying to solve. Their biggest detriment to the body is how they directly affect the mind. They distort their perception of what is happening around them. It can only result in odd, irrational, inappropriate and even destructive behavior. The drug blurs memory, causing blank spots. They make them feel slow or stupid and cause failure in life, like losing a partner or their career or end up on the street hustling. The harder life will get and the want of more drugs to help deal with the problem. Eventually, drugs will completely destroy all creativity and happiness.

End of Life living lesson: Cocaine

CHAPTER NINE

Sunday, March 27, 2005—Thursday, November 19, 2007

Jill is afraid of Tina, one of John's favorite drugs. He once told her, "I love my drugs." So she has caught him in the office with the window open puffing out Tina. It was so pathetic to see him jump as Jill approached and to hide the pipe between his legs. Jill asks, "What is going on?" and John was so black and dark in his face that, yes, Jill was afraid of him and walked away.

The two addictive drugs, cocaine and crystal meth, happen to be the easiest ones to hide. The user can hide this even at work and that was what John did. Christmas as Jill said used to be her favorite time of the year. John never did take an interest in the holiday and Jill worked continuously to make it a special day for John.

The Christmas of 2005 was the one that affected Jill for the rest of her life. Every evening the fireplace would roar until bedtime but this year there was no bedtime for John. Though he had never taken any pleasure from the Christmas traditions, this year because of his drug use, he stayed downstairs with the fire and a nine foot tree with blue and white lights. Every evening John lay on a blanket on the floor looking both at the tree and the fireplace and never once came to bed. Jill was happy to see that finally John was taking an interest in Christmas. For a few evenings Jill would come down and kiss John good night on the cheek and asked if everything was okay and went back to bed feeling all was just cozy. However, one of those evenings, as she leaned over to kiss

Live in the Present and Learn Valuable Life Lessons to Improve Any Relationship

John her hand fell onto of a weird looking brass pipe. Jill was confused. Why that was there and asked, "What is this, John?" He replied it was only an old piece from his repair kit from work. Jill did wonder why that would be there on the floor under the blanket at two a.m., but in her ignorance and trust, she let it go.

A month later, a previous co-worker of John's called and asked them both to brunch. Jill was worn out from doing all the work for Christmas and declined. John being his usual self who always wanted to shine was embarrassed that Jill was not going. John and his friend left and Jill decided to clean house. She found an empty beer bottle standing on the floor behind the desk. On the bottom, inside, were loose ashes, white in color; there was no cigarette butt, and the ashes were powdery. John does not smoke and always proclaimed that he could not, which Jill knew to be true. But apparently you can smoke Tina (crystal meth) and it is not the same as inhaling a cigarette. Jill knew it was her fear that John had defaulted on his promise not to use cocaine but Jill should have made the agreement not to use any heavy drugs. Jill was certain it was crystal meth (glass) and like a mad person, went searching through the back room where all John's belongings were kept. It took all of five minutes to find a pipe and the glassy crystal powder in the side pocket of his work briefcase and of course stored beside his drugs was a stash of condoms. Jill immediately called Lori for advice. Lori could not believe what she was hearing and tried to comfort a once again distraught Jill. Lori invited her over for the day, but before Jill left she finally found something inside her to fight back. Knowing for sure his co-worker would come into the house after their brunch; Jill put a small table (the one she used to hold her suicide drugs) in the center of the living room displaying all of his drugs and pipes.

A few hours later Jill gets a whispering phone call on his cell. "What are you trying to do? Being first through the door I saw what you did and quickly threw my coat over the table. Ha, Ha, Jill, my fried did not see anything." "Too bad," Jill responded because you need help, "more this time than with the cocaine. You are using a killer drug and leaving your family with a dead father." John raised his voice and said he would not be there when she returned.

Hours later Jill returned to find once again most of John's things were gone. She also noticed another beautiful card from John was lying on the table in the living room torn to shreds. That was the blow that put Jill into acute grief. She had done so much for John. All these years she had given him. Jill still could not see this was out of her control. But there were no tears this time, only questions beating through her head of what to do. She knew she still wanted him back because that is who Jill is as a person, a caregiver. Jill wondered if she should call his family this time or his friends for help or just let it settle for a few days and definitely not react like the past times.

About four days later Jill was driving through the market and she spotted John's car. She went on a search and found him again at the local bar. Jill pleaded with John to leave with her and go to the car where it was private and where they could talk civilly. They sat there for hours talking and more promises were made. John promised to return home and once again Jill went to John's house to repack his belongings and drive them back to her home.

Unfortunately in Jill's mind the trust was gone. John was not honest, nor did he respect Jill's idea of two understanding partners in a relationship, sharing and relying on each other for help.

In the next two years John kept one promise. He used Jill's house as a safe haven. He was very quiet and unforgiving of Jill in his demeanor. He never slept with Jill but instead always bedded down on the sofa. This was now a sexless, loveless partnership, leaving Jill to fall further into a depressive state of mind and behavior. Jill became very sad and could go nowhere because of the obvious fact that she was depressed. She had lost her great smile, which had given her an aura that people loved to be near. This time Jill's heart was shattered. They became two co-habitants. It felt like two strangers had found the same ad in the newspaper and decided to become roommates. Jill had lived with roommates before but it had never been this distant, never this cold or non-responsive to any offers of sharing even a simple dinner. In the house John became a loner, missing most of the time and only coming upstairs to use the computer and the bathroom. This was an extremely unhappy place to be, more like a place to die.

As a couple, it does not matter what form the relationship takes, the bedroom should be as natural as picking a daisy from the garden, smelling its beautiful odor and handing it over as a representation of your love. Search for your answers, your desires that you both openly agreed to as the direction of closeness and they may be as simple as holding hands any time. No matter how long you are together, how many flowers or how many times you hear the word "Honey," you need to feel your love is everlasting with feelings and emotions of a warm touch. Sometimes it takes one of you to take the initiative. That is fine. Just do not count your number of times or say, "It is your turn." All of those things at the end of the day mean nothing. Just be and stay in love. We all show our feelings differently and to survive as a couple you need to recognize your differences and needs. Once you even think that some of the above has gone astray, most often it has not. People have so many stresses in life that the one we take it out on is the one we love the most. The reason is because we know they will forgive us and be understanding. Do not turn a wonderful person away; it may become irreparable.

Sometimes we say things do not add up but the more questions you ask will only intensify the problem areas unless clear communication is established. If you don't communicate clearly, you may have put your partner in a defensive place, not the most desirable place to be. You have that power to not even start but once started you have given a power to you partner to question you why you are raising an issue. It can be a no-win situation if you don't respectfully communicate with each other. You can have whatever you want: win-win, win-lose, lose-win or lose-lose. Obviously, everyone wants a win-win in their relationships but we cannot help ourselves from agitating the waters. All that said, you have the right as an individual and as a person sharing your life with another to ask whatever question you need an answer to for your feelings to be secure and at peace.

Josh R. Himmelman

Life living lesson: Crystal Meth and Methamphetamine

Crystal meth is not what you will hear when a user is looking for a dealer. Currently the street names include: speed, meth, crystal, crank, tweak, go-fast, ice, glass, tina, and quartz. It is taken inhaled, smoked or injected. For the novice, he can acquire a low dose in a pill form. It resembles small fragments of glass or shiny blue-white rocks. Its effects are highly powerful and addictive. Its source is man-made as a stimulant that causes aggression and violent or psychotic behavior. From the drug dealer's point of view, it is the "best" one to sell because users of drugs, once they try meth, they become "hooked", that is addicted from the first time they use it and also it is the hardest drug to treat.

As with any substance, it has immediate effects and long-lasting ones too. When it is first used it affects sleep patterns and causes nausea, delusions of power, aggressiveness and irritability. Usually, users are not happy with only a few puffs. They need to keep taking it once they start. In higher doses it has a greater rush, causing increased agitation, and the user could be violent. Most common manifestation of this was insomnia, confusion, hallucinations, anxiety and paranoia; if taken in sufficient quantities, it eventually leads to convulsions, causing death.

If you survive the initial stages of using meth, there is no true road ahead to euphoria. Eventually there will be damage to the blood vessels in the brain leading to strokes or an irregular heartbeat, and eventually a collapse that may lead to death. A continued user will suffer brain damage and memory loss. If and when they get treatment to drop the addiction to meth, most often they are subject to memory gaps and extreme mood swings.

Dealers are all too aware of its effects, but more concerned with their profits. They will say anything to get you to buy their drugs. They will tell you that "cocaine will make your life a party" and that "heroin is a warm blanket." They do not care if the drugs ruin your life as long as they get the money. Dealers have been quoted to grinningly say, "Their buyers are pawns in a chess game."

End of Life living lesson: Crystal Meth and Methamphetamine

Life living lesson: Does cheating really improve your sexual relations at home?

Okay, some people are neurotic and never comfortable with the real truth. They keep pushing and pushing for some answer they want to hear. They are so certain something is wrong that they themselves cause the relationship to break apart. It is very easy for the partner to recognize what is happening, but they are left defenseless.

It is not meant to hurt, feel pain especially if acting in ignorance. Be smarter, not suspicious. At times it is all self-induced and prolonged agony thinking that when your partner does something out of the ordinary, they must be hiding something. It can be looked upon as a life equation; left life equals right life: two people that need to be equal in emotional strength, intelligence, education, career-orientation, keeping healthy and fit and religious and spiritual. Do you need all of the left side variables in the equation to meet each individual's variables on the right side of the life equation? Two political parties in a democracy serve the public: left wing *versus* right wing. But when it comes to major issues, it is opened to discussion and debate, and a final decree is passed. Could it be so simple in a relationship to communicate so well that there are no worries of infidelity; no worries of any sort; just a peaceful life? Like identical twins connecting and seeing the same reality. They are a good representation of a partnership reality: you need to compromise as a couple with thorough information providing you with the necessary knowledge and your resolution will be easier. Most couples see their personal lives as theirs even though they have a signed contract to honor and obey. Most contracts have today removed the "obey" phrase. This leans more towards keeping individualism, even though they are sharing a balancing act to be in conformity.

"If I am not perfect, I will not find someone to love me, therefore it will be only me." There is only one definition of perfection that will satisfy you: that is your own definition and no-one else's. It is very difficult to change one's perception of self, simply because we have to live with ourselves. Back to the same issue: in a relationship you have to live with each other. We live with our thoughts not necessarily exposed in conversation, making our equation equal; however thought creates your behavior consequences. If you find you are unable to love another, you are not in balance. The simple truth: "you need to love yourself before anyone can love you."

You feel you should be the emblem of perfectionism, like a Sunday school child in Bible class who did his homework. Do we need to try to find that someone who can say, "I am a perfect, me, I am unique and I only need to answer to myself only for you. The consequences of life are sometimes threatening to your being you, for example accusing a spouse of cheating might arise from an encroaching insecurity. A life is your creation from all the developments in a black and white negative film strip. Are you as a couple on the same strip each to be referred as a negative yet to be developed? A picture says a thousand words, but does it say so in black and white?

Your Emotional Quotient, E.I., is your ability to control and evaluate your emotions. Your Intelligence quotient, I.Q., is your ability to learn or understand or to deal with new or trying situations. As an example, some people misuse the word "smart" to mean knowledgeable. Though one can lead to the other, it does not mean that they are the same thing. It is suggested that emotional intelligence can be learned and strengthened, while parts of your emotions are an inborn characteristic. Your fulfillment of success, peace, and happiness in your relationship will depend upon the correspondence of the E.I. and the I.Q. of the two partners.

A break-up due to a breakdown in communicating and trust is a break through. It is not meant to cause hurt for either but to finally fill the ignorance you each maintain about your living together.

Do we look for the signs of a cheating spouse or do they just pop out at you. And how do you feel? Ignorant, confused and betrayed? Yet you still should be uncertain of your beliefs. There are warning signs of a cheating spouse, mostly in their behaviors around and with you directly. Say that our spouse returns home from supposedly work smelling of a fresh shower. Not your bathroom soap or hair shampoo but a foreign smelling substance. At what point do you address your observation? Sorry, it all depends upon when you are ready emotionally. To do this you need to think what type of affair I am suspecting? Is it just physical with no emotional involvement, therefore he still loves me? Or is it a fully fledged romantic affair that may leave you struggling to keep your partner. But how far do you struggle without pushing them away for good?

Think about what is present in your relationship today. Are we still equal? Did one of my variables fade away, such as an interest level in sex? Who is at fault now? If you realize it could be better then gradually show more interest, but do not show up in the bedroom all at once in shocking attire to attract him. They will know you suspect something and that evening of saving your partnership may turn into turmoil. And it was not an accident you broke the egg open. Does it fry or splatter or become cohesive like a hardboiled egg?

Couples are together to create a future together. Think of everything you accomplished and your plans to reach elderly status in a union. With this information in mind you may be able to think, "Does this cheating have the potential to end the relationship, or would they just never leave, even if the reason would be to save the appearance to family and friends?"

So what are your warning signs? The worst would be your partner wants out but feels trapped. Then you are only going through the motions of a relationship. The opposite is they confront you with leaving. Do you make it hostile, or thinking he is in love with someone else, believe if it happens now you be concerned that it may just happen again? Has your life become a game of checkers, having to move strategically so to be crowned the prize queen and a little more power over the relationship? Nothing wrong with a little unnoticeable power, slight of thought then talks.

"The truth is rarely pure and simple." (Oscar Wilde)
Wilde, Oscar: Bing. Retrieved February 2012 from http://www.bing.com/search?q=%E2%80%9CThe+truth+is+rarely+pure+and+simple.%E2%80%9D+%28Oscar+Wilde%29&src=IE-SearchBox&Form=IE8SRC

Now your life is full of uncertainty by discovering infidelity and deception. Think about your own acceptance of lying, infidelity and cheating. Can you in your rearing as a child accept any or all of these characteristics of another, whether a spouse or a friend? Most of us cannot. When do we accept to rebuild trust, we must remember how long it will take. For most of us it will truly be an indefinite period of time. But you decide if it is worth saving.

To answer whether your relationship is worthwhile you need to answer why your spouse cheated, if it really was cheating. You may interpret your spouse's behavior on the internet as cheating where they honestly believed that they had done nothing wrong. Second, you need to ask yourself, why they would lie to you. Was it to save your feelings, not to hurt you, or do they believe it will help the relationship because cheating and returning shows they still love you? If there is one lie, all chances are that there are more, and then it becomes compulsive lying.

Look back at your beginning and how you fell in love. What qualities were there that are still there today? Then you can make a more informed decision. Is that person still that same person who has simply made a mistake? It is quite possible that life beyond the home is not as bad as what you think, what you suspect. Jealously is very hard to overcome, and even with pure honesty and proof from your partner that all is great, nothing has changed, you still feel some jealously. You either want part of their life or you gave up part of your own. If you gave up your own life's ambitions, it most likely was your decision. After all you should have learned the necessary skills for decision-making. If not, you may be maladjusted and this created a different set of partnership issues. This does not create a healthy relationship. Anything that is seen as unhealthy, whether a plant, a person or an animal, needs a helping hand, some nourishment and tender loving care.

Once you have opened the door to your suspicions, it can be the beginning of rebuilding that much-needed trust. Trust will either tear you apart or bond you closer. You should not even use the word trust in communicating but demonstrate that you do trust. Physical action here takes precedence over verbal discussion, but both will help. Have you learned how to talk, discuss your problems and even your individual successes? Remember the jealously factor. Even partners are jealous of each other's success. Some people use the term, "closed mouth," meaning they just cannot talk issues through to a resolution. It is like having the 'flu and if you could vomit the symptoms would be less. You are not on your way to recovery without talk; you cannot repair any problem unless discussed. Remember back to when you met, you must have recognized this and therefore developed different approaches to communicate. It is very difficult to be with someone who does not talk.

You approach the situation as the spouse suspecting cheating and your concerns are "Once a cheater, always a cheater." If you believe this whole heartedly, then you might as well walk away from the relationship.

The desire to cheat is complicated, and it is not solved by feeling sorry or making a promise to change to your partner. To change your behavior, you need to realize how that behavior came about. What causes a spouse to cheat could be a combination of issues or simply one incident in their relationship. It could be like the opportunity on a business trip away from home. They think, what happens in Vegas stays in Vegas. Another reason to cheat would be the obvious problems in the relationship at home, and one spouse says "enough." To retaliate, the first choice usually is to cheat. Cheating hurts most to your partner, and you want them to hurt. Not sure which is the most common feeling from cheating but it could very well be the excitement of someone and something new. In their mind they may think it will help at home because a hidden need of theirs was fulfilled.

Not unlike the story you are reading, many factors that influence cheating may have a genetic background, determined by a sexual addiction. Cheating is like the idea of taking a risk playing the roulette wheel at the casino. Usually the person cheating does so with someone they are attracted to. When the partner hears or sees the cheater's other choice, it cuts deep into the unanswered question, why? Maybe there is a reason why you should not have married this person. To better understand your future, look back at dating. Was your partner a cheater then? For example, when you were dating was he multi-dating, several at one time? That could indicate they will always be a cheater, even in a committed relationship.

Sexual relations at home will change because you bring different sexual habits to the bedroom. Who will notice, but your spouse? When two people are close, nothing goes unnoticed. Does this mean you should be afraid to try something new because you were thinking it as a thought to spice up the homeland? This is a hard question to answer, because it will depend upon the couple's communication ability. Forgive and forget, or go cheat yourself. It all depends on your own belief system in life, and most people are good people and will not. They hold onto their respect for themselves and onto their morals. Forgiveness is the start, but to forget is the hardest and longest challenge. Both keep your trust, honesty and respect.

End of Life living lesson: Does cheating really improve your sexual relations at home?

Life living lesson: (Needs vs. wants) and their effect on honesty, respect, and trust).

We are all living, experiencing and co-existing between each other. We are social creatures and we desire the love and affection of others. So not to be a social outcast, we will act like the others. Different culture means a different amount of love and acceptance.

We all have wants and needs in our relationships. These are very confusing and not necessarily interchangeable. So what do you want from a partner in a relationship as opposed to what you truly need in order to make it work realistically and effectively?

Wants are anything that you personally do not need; but as a couple your combined wants may have to change because your partner must have those wants as well. You can live without your wants but you may be bored. We desire the love and affection of others which is a want. We receive that love and affection when we are like others. To gain social acceptance we may have to change what we want because in our society it makes you different and not part of the normal circle. This could be an argument as a reason for wants being needs. To give up on a lot of your wants, you also give up on the norms of society. We have a strong desire to fit in, to be loved and to be accepted.

In your relationship, are your wants truly needed in order to make it work effectively? The needs of your relationship are the recognition and valuable qualities, but remember they may not be romantic. Does everything you do as a couple have to be romantic? Are you not in for the long haul, good or bad. Not being romantic sometimes is not bad.

Which are more attractive in a relationship, wants or needs? If you both live on the same premise, e.g. each just wanting their needs fulfilled, is that a better partnership? Some needs that are accepted: trust, pure honesty, loyalty, and humor, all there to understand and to accept when each are both difficult. If we go only to having all wants in the relationship, we experience: only desires, no over the top for romance, argue but calmly, travel together without passion, and working casually and lazy or messy when we give each other attention. Obviously a want is the desirable trait because it has no limits. Can this couple have everything they want or are they better only to desire with their needs?

As the relationship grows with thoughts over a period of weeks, eventually you either love or you lose interest in your partner and then you will find certain deeds are required. The reason is because your needs are necessary for survival and those wants are only what you would like to have.

As you both experience together parts of wants and needs, the whole idea is freedom to separate for downtime when required. If you decide that your wants are needs, your wants are likely to keep you from what is really needed, that is to follow the things you enjoy in life.

Needs and wants are different. We simply want things because they are entertaining, things that maybe put us more in the social link or even make the relationship easier. We all have wants and needs when it comes to our relationship and it is very easy to confuse the two.

As each partner considers their wants and needs, they must decide how much they trust the amount of honesty between each other and respect for each other's decisions. Trust is a shared belief that you can depend on each other to achieve common sense. Honesty is the easiest way to see one's character, willing to accept the responsibility of what comes with it. It is your heart that overrides the lies and the mistakes bound up with pretence. Respect means to be treated with consideration and esteem and in turn to do the same for each other. You listen, hear and give full attention to the other person when they speak. You have empathy for other people's feelings. Respect each other for their needs, especially emotional needs and their sense of needing to belong.

You want to build a strong, solid foundation in your relationship. Then respect each other for what they are. Respect is belief that others can contradict us, but we honor them because it is a right thing to being a human that is to be respectful. As a couple you need to have the same goals, first to believe in the relationship. To do this you each have to know that we are only human. You cannot be ignorant because you may attack the other's identity, a major part of who you are. Respect builds trust in your partnership and a continued want to keep building. When you argue with respect for each other it better leads to a positive outcome instead of destruction. Positive outcomes are new beginnings to start new opportunities together peacefully.

Your respect allows the much-needed compromise between two people working together with an accepted outcome, and definitely the decision will last longer. Children learn to put personal success and craving of power above anything else if their parents are the same. The child looks at people as a way to advance and sees no other value, no respect. This type of individual growing up chooses to have friends and a marriage of his convenience to get further ahead. Knowing the right people may mean you should honor and respect them as well, but this is difficult when you never were that way to begin with. Their success is being a part of the social heights and having the largest house on the street all built off other people's trust in them. A typical phrase used to describe this type of person is, "He would sell his own grandmother to get ahead."

Respect is created—it is not innate—but can be learned from the home environment, education and basic learning. It is created when people treat others as they want to be treated, "Do unto others as you would have others do unto you." Do not insult others for reasons of being different, such as a cultural difference. Spend the time to learn something of their culture. Listen and be fair in your trust and if you are in an argument, step back and recognize the issue in the problem, not each of you. Speak through the issue, be understood, and listen to make sure you are understood.

If you have respect for others you can help solve problems by using what you have learned. Remember, mutual trust and respect will make any partnership last much further into the future.

Respect leads into trust, or is trust built from respect? Mutual trust is a shared belief and you will always be there for each other, working for the same goal. You can rely on each other's words; you have integrity and really important is consistency in your relationship. You may have noticed one key word for each; it is "mutual."

Trust must be learned from information given through conversation. Your partner will know when you respond with a reply directly in relation to their message. They can trust you were listening. Cultural differences are difficult; the use of certain words or gestures during communication can be misleading but if you listen, repeat, and reconfirm you will understand what the meaning of the message is.

The bonding of trust exists in empathy. It gives us an insight into what others are feeling; hence we understand them better as to why they react to a situation. You must take care of yourself first, respect yourself and your partner will see you are in this for both. Whatever you do, you are partners and do not exclude them from your side of life. Exclusions cause them to lose dignity in the relationship. It is called mutual respect, the key to almost nothing going wrong. Out of respect will come love for each other? During discussions, if you feel hurt, say so. Do not blame. Just ask for them to make things clearer. Apologize if you make your partner feel hurt, but do not do it out of guilt from them. Give each the respect and support by giving time to think first before any conversation or action. Be brutally honest, whether it is good or bad. Trust is as important as respect. The best way to receive respect is to give it first. To do this allow your partner to give solutions to problems as well, do not exclude anyone. The nicest thing you can do is take a moment and when apart give a little call and show your love outwardly. It also shows at any time you are willing to communicate and give them no suspicious thoughts or a reason to think they should distrust you.

> *"Problems in relationships occur because each person is concentrating on what is missing in the other person."* (Wayne Dyer).
> **Dyer, Wayne: Bing. Retrieved February 2012 from http://www.bing.com/search?q=%E2%80%9CProblems+in+relationships+o**

Trust that your happiness is yours to have and you helped to acquire it by participating in the conversation. You would love to argue to be right, but this is a step backward. A healthy trusting relationship is sharing each other's experience, and then you love and share and learn from those experiences. Remember, if there is no mutual agreement, it does not mean you or he is wrong. You or both should step away and approach it as a more valuable learning experience. What has happened is you both equally contributed and this is how the relationship will grow and you can work even harder to move on. The important factors here are: always tell the truth (to yourself and your partner); step back and look at what you each expected; (see your behavior); be responsible (always respond and do not shut down); and laugh (laughter brings humor, relaxation and a bigger connection).

End of Life living lesson: (Needs vs. wants) and their effect on honesty, respect, and trust.

Life living lesson: When it is time to give up on a relationship?

Giving up means you have moved on and if you turn back you give your spouse a new control. You may not want to acknowledge that lying and deception have become an element of your relationship because they do not equate with romance. Remember that these can fester in relationships for several reasons. You will need to make some decisions.

Should you ignore it when you discover something makes the issue of lying impossible? This will violate your trust, and the bedroom, the dining table, and the ride in the car all become changed with a feeling of frustration and your conversation you need to have is resting on the tip of your tongue.

Hidden secrets are alive but non-accessible. If you feel your relationship is about to end, to whom do you turn? Does your best-kept secret stay secret until a For Sale sign goes on the house? You need to address the issues before it goes this far, to have good old fashioned advice. Signs of trouble do not prove that there is trouble in your partnership. Think very clearly because once you are upset, your perception of everything is biased. Any behavior or change in behavior can be interpreted in many different ways. The big one is your trust in them that causes you to overlook the problems until they become almost non-resolvable. Does that mean you should ignore trust? Definitely you should not.

Is your relationship worth saving? People see what they want to see. Maybe you are the one looking for a way to cause dissent and possible separation. Fabrication of a false truth is a trait we all unfortunately have within us to some degree. Problems are there for both and they seem to add one on to another, giving a different perspective of your lives. Look at what is positive in the relationship and what might be concerns you need to address.

It is simple to see how your relationship should last or dissolve. Look at its quality. Like taking a questionnaire quiz inside a magazine about some topic, like does he love me or not? You can always go and pick a daisy and play the game, pull each petal off one by one, he loves me, and he loves me not. As we get to the end, some cheat to get the coveted answer, he loves me. It is not like that in real life. You cannot pull out more issues to throw away thinking solving only the last one will make your relationship perfect with love.

Here is my questionnaire for you to see: Are we as a couple on the right Y in the road or did we start taking separate paths? When you disagree with each other, do you work and try to resolve your differences? Or is there disregard for the disagreement? Are you anxious in the bedroom that you cannot say I really do not feel well and they will truly understand? Inner thoughts are your most private ones; most share their thoughts comfortably on their own but if you are being prodded to tell your spouse all your supposed secrets, you will always feel trapped, even when you are not.

The logic of math works when $X=Y$ because both have an equal value. Is there equal value and fairness in your relationship? Are you pushing your affection on them, hitting a wall as it simply bounces back unanswered? When you have a discussion at home on how to curb appeal the house or out in public trying to buy a larger home, do you mostly agree, or do you become today's free movie for the onlookers? When you go to bed, no matter at night or an afternoon nap is there a smile in your heart thinking of them? And your last thought, do you have the same values, goals and interests? Do you enjoy doing the same things together and maybe find part of an event you both experience brings laughter to each of you? Your answers are there; do not ignore them for the sake of "saving face" (a phrase that should never have been coined), just save your heart, emotions, and your thoughts.

We all stand before someone and pledge our love. The experience of being in love is not the same for each of us. People have different ideas of what it means to be in love. After all, is this not a common affair we should all realize? To understand your idea of love you must understand there is more than one kind of love.

Love can come with a lot of intimacy and intensity. This union has a strong sexual and emotional component. You feel as if you each have the same emotional and physical closeness, hence passion. Romance is the beginning of a relationship but often that is where it remains: at the start. You have to work hard to keep the romance as it is the bonding glue later in life. As you will read here, love is treated by some as a game. They win, you lose. What you lose are your emotions. What they gain is control, and you cannot expect anything but cheating, lying and deception. You very seldom gain back any control because your weak spots have been exposed.

Another form of love is the co-dependent love, the care giving, a selfless type of love. What is left for you, you do not care because it is all about them and as a co-dependent, you are happy with that.

A truly star-bursting love is the one you started with your best friend. It evolves and constantly blossoms and then it becomes genuine. It will take longer but the end will always be the same as the beginning: at peace with each of you and you are truly in love.

The next best of my thoughts of love is the practical love. Keep it simple, running like a finely-tuned sports car. Once in shape, it only needs a little time once and awhile to keep it moving forward.

Another love that makes for good partners is seeing each other through your observation of them over a period of time; like both being a member of a co-ed volleyball league. You spend the summer learning through their verbal and non-verbal languages, about their type of friends and overall personality. Your love appears practical but then why not? A car with too many options always spends more time in the shop for repairs. You have eliminated the options.

The last approach to love in my mind and my least favorite one is the crazy, intense, out-of-control love. You are falling out of love before you knew you were in love. It is sort of like burning a candle at both ends. It burns bright, one side quicker than the other, but when you meet and burn out quickly, it was the delusion of each lover, at each end of the candle.

When do you begin to walk, sprint and run in a separate direction from your partner? What do you base such a life-changing decision on? For each of us, it is obvious that the answer is different. It is one or some of all the forms of love we have looked at here, or is there a hidden needle in the haystack. How can I deal with jealously? Does jealously evolve out of the issues of mistrust, betrayal and conflict seeding anxiety and despair with yourself? Do we mislabel what we see as jealously when in fact it is suspicion? One thing in our heart is labeled correctly, with these feelings; you are threatened and imagine you are going to lose your partner to someone else. All too often, and it is easier to say and do today, when one sends a phone message, a text, a Twitter or a Face book blurb and does not receive what they perceive as a timely response, you jump to an immediate conclusion: they are ignoring me because I am no longer number one.

These negative thoughts, doubts and being really insecure often lead to more of the same. Try this and find very quickly you can go crazy and you do the same to your partner. What your partner did was nothing wrong but you turned everything that was okay into a wrong because of your suspicions. Not many people can or even want to try initially to live with such a person. And it is very easy for the partner to turn and run because all he sees is a controlling, invasive and needy relationship blooming, like dandelions on a field. If this happens at the beginning there will not be a relationship. If this begins to happen after a period of time, it will be like small grenades turning into bombs. Eventually they hit the target and the target disappears.

Today's world is full of crowded streets, tied up traffic on the highway and one reality television show followed by another. It has to happen: your mind goes into overload, and then it is empty. With emptiness comes fear and negativity. You have now created unnecessary turmoil of negative thoughts and cannot begin to develop positive solutions to your problems in life. Not easy, but all of your success comes from within you: part and parcel of the mind. Every mind is capable of great things, and the best you can always do is to fill it with positive thoughts and eventually the darkness will lighten like a dawn—sun through the fog. See yourself walking out of the fog; visualize answers to questions that really were not ever a question. They were empty, negative thoughts.

Everything in life eventually results in a feeling. Even emotions are true in feeling. Emotions are unconscious thoughts about things, and thoughts are conscious thoughts about everything. To follow a math theorem of logic, if a thought results in feelings, then our emotions will also result in feelings. Weird as it may be to understand, your emotions are your feelings. Who wins at the end are your feelings.

Emotions, thoughts and feelings together are a focus on one certain thing. Life is feelings, you are never without them. At times feelings are from thoughts you do not understand. Thought comes from facts and information that caused your feelings. Thought is then about feelings. Feelings are what provide the motivation to arrive at an answer in your thought.

We hurt ourselves when we hurt others. None of us, no matter how much we have not been accepted in life can be intentionally cruel to someone else. Hatred is only fear. That hatred causes us to do and say things our heart does not agree with. We watch each other, every loved one; every stranger and we know we are connected because of our emotions, either full or lacking in intensity. Emotions are shared; it is the one thing that is common, sadness passes through a crowd and the saying, "Misery loves company" is true. And as tough as you may seem, when we hurt someone, we share that hurt.

Why do we hurt ourselves when a relationship ends? Hurt comes in many forms, such as not sleeping or not eating; lying awake at night and longing for their touch, taking the phone to bed with you so you will not miss their call. You just want that one call, one apology to have something to work with to rebuild. Your problem is you are in despair; and with your vision in the mirror, you see there is no beauty. No gold star placed on your emotions in wanting a person who does not want you. There will be no collection of anything peaceful waiting for someone to do what you want them to do. You are lying under the cool damp sheets of disappointment. It is your shroud, and it belongs only to you, not them. Your fear is it will never be lifted from you because you do not know how to. Imagine a flat screen image in the air just above you. See your great qualities and worthiness not to allow you to succumb to an apparent meaningless broken heart. If it had a meaning, you would have a place to rebuild from. Your partner has not offered a meaning, the worst exit, the cruelest way to end and find your own recovery. Where do you truly begin? Begin by not waiting; move on, they will not do what you want them to do. You are wallowing in your own disappointment and fear of the next minute. Always remember, you are not the first sufferer of love's harsh blow, and you definitely will not be the last throughout eternity. Yes, you will love again, but the advice is taking your time.

End of Life living lesson: When is it time to give up on a relationship?

SECTION FOUR
RECOVERY PERIOD

CHAPTER TEN

January 01, 2008—Depression

This is the beginning of rescuing her life from the "Woes of Jill." She realizes that most of her life belongs to "Guess what!" and "Woe is me!" You may wonder if these are dilemmas that cross our patterns in life. Maybe they are your pattern of life, your cross to bear, and the albatross that hangs around your neck. Does this sound heavy? Try to carry their burden on a continual basis. If you believe you are either one or both of these, then you experience a level of stress and discontent. Stress because your mind does not relax from the outside factors around you. People, things, and situations seem to spark one of these reactions, "Guess what!" and "Woe is me!" That leads to a panic.

She knows that too much of her life is placed in her belief. She does not really want to do this anymore. She does see some improvement in her way of handling her life, but it is not enough. She wants all of her life so that she can live in truth within herself. She finds that she is able to take back her life when she is alone. She feels more relaxed, more at peace all around, and she can create time for herself. She does try to enjoy her life at these few times. If she would allow herself to do more of this then she could feel calmer and would be able to allow more truth within herself to emerge. This would help her see what it is that she really wants and to act upon her true self. If only she were able to take back a little more of her life from the "Woes of Jill."

Life living lesson: Depression.

Depression is a disease that requires treatment from medical professionals. You are unable to treat yourself. It is an illness and treatable with medications and therapy. If it were not treatable, half the world's population would have an illness from being confused individuals with a low, miserable mood. We say confused because the individual themselves cannot identify the difference between feeling gloomy and being depressed. It is evident that the state of depression is not so clear. What is clear however, this illness is all too common.

To be depressed is not a weakness. But society does judge and likes picking on the weak, singling them out of the heard and leaving them behind. There is a common phrase, "Oh, she is depressed again," meaning "Do not bother with her issues." This would imply that if you are depressed, you can offer no value to others, especially to yourself. What is forgotten is that a depressed person does not choose this way of life: it mostly comes from family genes or an earlier life experience, mostly stressful like a physical illness, a certain drug treatment and more importantly the recreational drugs you choose. Jill's' depression was the result of her partner's recreation.

Depression and stress both let you feel down and in a low, intense mood. The difference is a depressive illness lasts for a much longer period, possibly months. There are many symptoms for depression, but here we will look at: losing interest in normal life and having no energy. Most common are getting out of bed and looking reality in the face for the day; a loss of self-confidence; finding it very hard to make any decisions; the feeling of uselessness and just a waste of others' time; and the most common are loneliness and the thoughts of suicide. These are signs of clinical depression; they are serious and a cause for concern. As seen, most are often life-threatening.

To determine if you are depressed, there are no blood tests, no CT scans, only the symptoms: a persistent low mood that causes the person not to be happily present in everyday life. Every individual's experience of depression is different, from the signs of depression back to its cause. Hence to recover, it is different for every person and the depression treatment will be unique.

Anger is also more and more common. Maybe that is why depression is widespread because depression can be anger turned within you. You are left with no optimism, full of fear and a sense of loss of a future. Depressed people turn away any offers or signs of possible happiness because they feel guilty, they do not deserve any pleasures. A common feeling is everything is dark, like heavy black out curtains blocking any light of hope. The person with a depressive disorder is often seen as having acute grief. Acute grief is characterized by body aches; crying spells; low energy and libido; and being unable to sleep. In real terms, the nervous system changes the brain that causes many physical symptoms that result in a lack of participation in life.

Depression can increase the risks for developing HIV, asthma and unfortunately more mortality rates than any other medical condition. Depression most often co-exists with other mental health illnesses, causing it to be even more difficult to treat the other illness.

Recently as in the past decade it has finally been realized that a type of depression occurs when the days become shorter, therefore less sunlight. SAD, seasonal affective disorder starts in the fall and continues throughout winter. Treatments are simple such as taking more vitamins and making a weekly visit to a tanning salon.

As we know, society can be cruel when someone appears weaker. There are myths about depression and its treatment that society needs to be aware of: it is an illness, not a weakness; it will not go away by wishing it away. You hear people say they feel suicidal, those are not just words for attention, they actually do mean it. As well it is important to recognize the many types of depression; mood disorders; major depression; dysthymia (less severe but longer lasting); bipolar disorder (manic depression) cycles of moods. The mood most recognizable here is the bipolar disorder that is often chronic and recurring. The person's mood switches dramatically and rapidly. This type of disorder causes the person to experience any of the symptoms of a depressive disorder. When in a manic cycle, often the person has trouble thinking, poor judgment, and acts out socially, causing embarrassment. As an example one would practice unsafe sex or make unwise business decisions.

Throughout the mood disorder there are crying spells. These result as a loss of one's self; you are irritable with your own life, restless about your future and its aspects, suicide attempts, unable to concentrate or remember things. Crying spells are simply the underlying cause of these outcomes, simply because crying depletes all energies, causes a weakness of self and with a lack of energy to care for oneself, any of the above may prevail.

Treatments for depression generally involve psychotherapy. This means just talking your problems through with someone, not even a doctor is necessary. But it is recognized that counseling in the form of cognitive behavioral therapy (CBT) or interpersonal psychotherapy (IPT) usual results in a better outcome; but depends upon the illness. They are as effective as medication, and unlike medication there are no side effects to deal with. Remember, even some medications for a different illness can cause depression as a side effect. CBT can be provided through most GP practices. During your therapy it will help best if you allow your partner some space. As the partner who is not ill, try to be there for your loved one. Act as if they are recovering from a serious illness; do something nice for yourself, because being around a depressed person is draining. Remember that this period in your life will soon be better, and the depression will be gone. But the ill partner must recognize that they need medications and other forms of help.

Medications such as anti-depressants will help to correct the low mood, do not change your personality, and better yet, are not addictive. Hence you can try at different times several types and be okay. The worst part is that it may take weeks of using one medication to determine if it will work. If not, you have to start over again with a different one. Even worse, you must gradually remove yourself from the one you are trying by reducing the dosage gradually. This means more time invested and, all in all, may take up to months just to see no result from a particular medication and having to start again with another type.

Patience is very difficult during this process, but if want to get better, it is a must. There are many guidelines for the above procedures, all of which should only be decided by a doctor. Your doctor must control the process, keep in mind these pills appear to act on chemicals in the brain to correct the abnormalities which causes the form of depression you are experiencing.

Whether using a psychotherapist or cognitive behavioral therapy, most likely you will be using some form of medication. Importantly, you need to take it on time and regularly. It will take weeks to take effect and you will need to continue after you feel you are better for another six months. In all seriousness, looking at treatments and symptoms is a long road.

Depression will affect your sex life and your relationships whether with a partner or with family and friends. Depression affects every aspect of your life, and when one partner is depressed, the relationship will suffer, sometimes badly. When you are depressed, you will heal better through a loved one's understanding, but if they do not care, a huge resource for helping to getting better is gone.

In a relationship if your partner is depressed they will be withdrawn from about everything that means something, even the partner. The other partner feels unloved, in the way and could see the depressed partner as wanting to leave the relationship. The perception by him is your partner is acting strangely and is unhappy. Like some people who cannot stand to be around a very ill person, they leave permanently.

In all relationships as we know there are trials of some type to test each other's love, trust and respect. Depressions are one of these and recognize you are the same people who are in love. Truly, patience is a virtue. And at this time patience is greatly needed.

End of Life living lesson: Depression.

Josh R. Himmelman

Life living lesson: Does running away from you help?

Is this what you should believe to be God's plan, run away or face your problems? After all, is it not our physical body here to help its soul learn and carry on through eternity the lessons learned through its bodily host? God's plan, though, is your own direction you take; you choose the path. It is like your parents telling you what to do and what to choose as your career. This is only done in the best interest, but still each person must choose their direction based on life living and a desire for a particular outcome. In a religious family, some children will say, "You are not God!" This is a frustration for you who is struggling with their life already and know they must live the life before them and that the ultimate control lies within you.

The beginnings of adulthood are usually coupled strongly with love for another. You have one of your first big decisions to make, keep the relationship but let's test them because you are uncertain this one is for you and during this time hold onto to a fading flame unlike a burning candle. You need to expect of yourself your direction because direction will lead you to a resulting outcome sometimes never to be changed.

After all, it truly is your life, not unlike a relationship between a parent and a child. This is a connection that could be at odds. Ultimate decisions are each other's and if your plan does not connect well, the light to illuminate your path will fade as you walk further in your chosen direction.

Personal growth is seeing yourself as you want to be. It is about you and what you absorb from time. You can believe the idea you can do it all, but really no one can, hence depression and anxiety. How to achieve a balanced quality of life, make time for you and recognize the selfishness from others. Your state of mind has a major influence on how you handle your decisions. Interact with others and most importantly see how you view yourself. That will determine your quality of life. Does running away from yourself, your life's problems, really help you?

You deserve to live your life exactly the way you want and need to. Do not let others determine the quality of your life, you do this for yourself. But what happens with us all is the voice within ourselves which has mostly negative thoughts, for example, if I do this no-one will be happy, and you forgot your own happiness. This is why you need to take care of yourself and make yourself a top priority in your life. If you do not and you keep running, the neglect of you will cause you to fall. And where you fall may be your worst fears for yourself. You can run but if it is the wrong direction and you took the wrong road and therefore you were left with the wrong choices to choose from. Remember, no matter how busy you are or how busy your mind is, there is always time available to do something healthy for yourself.

Yes, there are times when you need to escape. Your stress levels, your whole life is pushing for something you have that is running low. Make a schedule for yourself to do something that you forgot from your previous living for example, chilling and listening to music or eating your favorite foods. You recognize you not only need time but space as well. Running from your problems does not fix them. You are only pushing them aside. In a relationship a breakaway is a very good and healthy thing; you see you do not really know why you have it until it's gone. So even if it is for a few days, they will soon realize they miss you. And stop pushing them; take it one day at a time and maybe even you will see that you do not need them in your life. For some, everyday can be a nightmare, the thirty texts and emails. You believe you understand why they need the space, but most likely you do not. You are afraid that if you run for time to think it may not work out for the best. The space drove you even further apart. Now you have guilt to understand as well as not understanding what just happened.

Do not feel guilty. Do not put such importance on the decisions others make; make your own decisions for your life. Especially if your relationship is separated by miles apart, do not hedge your existence on the fantasies of some other person, it would be insane. Then judging from their responses to you, you may have to change the way you do things to keep them. Maybe you should run away and find better happiness. You have allowed another human being to become your entire world. That puts a huge responsibility on to the person you are obsessing over, and this is no longer just affection. No one wants that burden. If they know you are at home obsessing and panicking then that too is a big put off. The best is for them to see you become a strong, confident person with an interesting and full life of your own. For the partner, they may seem to be secure, but no one is one hundred per cent secured. But to be insecure to the point of panic is pathetic.

Also, remember that if your partner runs to need space that means you cannot move forward in a relationship, and you will not ever forget that experience. So run yourself and do not give any more attention. In most experiences, if a person wants space this means that there is something about the relationship that they cannot take anymore.

Moving on you could mean that you are depressed from the problems and also that you are experiencing a feeling of abandonment. You could even go as far as to say "devastated." You may not want to run away, leave your home and move away from the memories, but again, what are the choices? Your biggest gain would be something else to occupy your mind and get your life on a new road forward. It can be hard to do, but instead of dwelling here on what does not work in your life, step back before you do anything and be grateful for what you have.

Either running or staying, you must find things that you enjoy doing, and do them. There is no true happiness if you depend upon others to make you happy. True happiness comes from within and is a constant choice. Crying can help too.

Running away from what? It could be you. You cannot run far or fast enough to do so. Are you trying to fit yourself into another mold that really would be strange for yourself? Are you choosing the unachievable? Will it give you an understanding within yourself of a truer place to be in the world?

No-one can escape from them, and eventually it is like a thief, the police will catch you. There will be only unhappiness and trials of your life's events. But one thing positive is that you learn along the way, and after running you can take these experiences and learn to be at peace with yourself.

End of Life living lesson: Does running away from you help?

January 01, 2008. Unfortunately for Jill, the only period of time that had consistent events was last September, October, and November. It was a time of uncertainty, realization of the inevitable loss of a partner, and hence of stress and depression. Each month seemed to have its own period of impetuous drama within Jill's dreams. When Jill would be on the mend towards the end of a month, a new month would appear with a whole set of fix-it-up,-Jill and find-yourself-in-this-new-living, new program of life.

January began with New Years Eve. Jill has hated anything to do with this celebration. No celebrating a new resolution or a promised future as it seemed always to turn out to be a disappointment. Jill just wanted no more grief but peace. If that meant for her a world that appeared to others as emptiness, fine she would be very happy.

Lori, on the same downward spiral on New Year's Eve, for many years had actually disliked them more than Jill. These two should have slept that night for what is an evening of celebration around the world. So a pact was made that they would spend it at Jill's home, eat lots of junk food and watch rented movies on the television. Jill was very pleased with the plan because she did not want anyone around her now, not even wanting a phone call from her mother. Daily, her mother would call Jill but recently she had been avoiding her calls. Sometimes when Lori was there, she had her answer the phone so her mother would not worry about her daughter. Lori would tell a few white lies that Jill was busy outside, or shopping or anything to prevent her from suspecting that Jill was having a difficult time. In reality, Jill's voice had a deep depressed sound to it and was difficult to understand on the phone, another reason to avoid her mother's calls.

The pact was for Lori to arrive at around seven p.m. and stay the night. Jill went grocery shopping and movie renting for their evening together. For once maybe New Years Eve would not be a failure. As in the past, failures on this night seemed to trail along from year to year. Jill fell into another trap again this year, an even bigger disappointment. Around 10 p.m. Lori finally called as Jill was edgy and not wanting to push her, said I hope you do not mind, but maybe I will arrive around 11:30, if that is okay. What could Jill say to her only friend but, "Sure"! Lori felt that since that evening was meant to disappear, it did not matter when she arrived. She forgot that Jill was unable to take any new emotional disappointment. But for Jill, she hung up the phone and fell into her new leather recliner she bought to treat herself, but certainly did not make her feel better. Tears automatically began to form on the outside corner of each eye as she thought yet another failure to begin another year. Why she asked herself out loud do I always get let down?

She had treats laid out on TV dinner tables around the room as if she were having a party for thirteen. She gathered herself together, took all the plates of chocolates, cakes and Christmas cookies and threw them into the garbage. After all she did not have a Christmas either, this was meant to be both together. This was a huge disappointment for Jill, but she was determined not to break down when Lori arrived. For her it was more wasted goodwill on people, kindness that she gives and goes unrecognized. She felt again and again, "Just why am I here on this earth, what is my purpose struggling so often. Is it some joke of a group of sinful souls hanging out there in the universe making bets on how long Jill will last?" What will Jill do next? We bet three to one.

The month of January was filled with grief and more grief every day. Who is left but herself? A self that was still waiting for a phone-call or a knock at the door from John. The huge red Christmas totes stood around the downstairs staring at Jill from every corner of the house. She could not escape the presence of John. John promised to pick them up between Christmas and New Year's Day. He never showed or called. It was torture for Jill to be surrounded with these each day, and that is exactly why John left them as long as he could. All present in the house, one simple fool. As a child you saw grief of different intensities; the loss of your neighbor who always made you fudge, the family pet dying, all the grandparents dying, and you learned to grieve. Jill did not learn how to grieve the loss of a life love. It was suggested to her to start writing in a journal to let her feel like she was talking to John. That lasted all of two days, and the fireplace became its home.

Jill finally told her mother, so she would understand her cracking voice, that John had moved out and she felt lonely. She kept saying both to Lori and her mother, "I should not be alone. Why me? I am such a good person with a huge heart to give!" Lori's advice repeatedly was, "He was no good for you," and "He did you a favor." And Jill's mom was wondering why she was so upset. This was acute grief with underlying depression about to blossom like a pest of a dandelion. If John's intentions were to sabotage Jill's mental state by leaving his belongings there so long, he was succeeding.

Yes, suicide was beginning to surface to her thoughts a little too often. But again, the thought of her new home at the psychiatric ward if she failed was certainly enough to deter those thoughts. Also she considered the reality of such a selfish act and fear of living your life as not your own is not warranted by anyone, especially not by yourself.

Jill did not return to work this month, she was nowhere ready to face a room full of students. Plus she always said that there is no lonelier job than being a teacher. You are in a classroom all day and never to see your co-workers for more than five minutes. When you walk the halls, even the students who were just in your class walk by almost brushing your clothes and ignore you. They do not believe that as a teacher you have human feelings.

She searched for the answers, but they were not there. One answer, yes, was there that tore her apart every time she thought about it: it was abandonment. Life had abandoned her. Life had dropped her off on the side of a bridge and drove away spitting dust and rocks that flew her way. Jill was chewing on the grim of life, her life. Someone needed to tell her these were all her choices and she could change everything. But first you need the desire to do so, and where was Jill's desire? It was back on the side of a road, forty meters above a raging river.

The worst part of the month was when John came to pick up his totes that Jill had so neatly packed for him. They were the red oversized Christmas totes meant for tinsel and joy, not clothes and belongings to take on their last trip from Jill's home. She knew she could not be there when John came, but she needed someone to open the house and give him a hand. Jill called on two of her friends. One was her handyman, who gladly said yes to help out Jill and a female teacher friend who had always helped Jill over all her bad relationships. Jill drove away and found a little diner where she sat in the corner booth, head hanging low into her overheated coffee. Lori was at her own home; she certainly did not want to confront John and knew he would be brutal with her.

A cell phone call came from Jill's friends, "Where is he? It is two hours later and he has not shown." Jill felt like a heel dragging her good friends through her garbage, but asked if they could please stay and, of course, friends help friends. About three hours later her cell phone rang again while the waitress was staring her down. "Okay, he has come and is gone." Jill bolted home and walked through the door. The once overcrowded downstairs was now empty. It was all over. With anxious breath she wanted the details of the move. It was not nice. He was wild with anger. John called first to the house and asked for Jill but was almost disappointed to hear she had gone. Then he asked if he needed to bring the police since he was told to stay a distance from Jill. Her friends had told him no, just come, everything is alright. Jill's teacher friend said she had never seen things move so quickly out a doorway. Jill had left for him a USB of all his pictures and contacts from the computer. When her friend gave it to him, he smiled and said, "This is for me?" and almost started to well up in his eyes. But that was stopped by one of John's friends who Jill knew well, and who knew what John was doing to Jill. He had said, "Come on and get out of here and never come back here again. Do not even look around or back. Get in the truck!" Jill heard he was not hurt anymore but angry. John's friend who knew better should have intervened long ago to stop John's drugs and help us. After all, he said he was a friend of both of us. The saying "blood is thicker" is very true. Both John and he were from the same country, blood of their culture sticks together no matter what the circumstances.

Everyone left and Jill stood in the middle of the living room. There was so much space and so much emptiness to see and feel. To escape she appeared to enter into another time zone, a time of seeing nothing, never looking back, never seeing the past, a place non-judgmental of the past living and of seeing the present, the now. She was finding her understanding of this day, knowing this would become her past and that they would grow apart, no intertwining of soft embraces and the arguments had finished. No more communication together, no taking a walk, no trying to work it out together.

Jill was now like the great façade of Venice, sinking under water with little anyone could do. She was sinking and disappearing, breath by breath.

February, 2008—Co-Dependency

Jill had waited enough time, enough of what she saw as suffering. A co-dependent does suffer with frustration. Then they are unable to accomplish their nurturing and experience total lack of doing for themselves. There was no devotion to anything, only that of reaching John. Every moment and even at work she would multi-task, trying to teach but focusing her mind every second of how to reach John. Jill felt every second of every day. Her chest was anxious with waiting for a response from John. If she checked her email once a day it would have been thirty times a day. Such actions are delusional, and her actions in life full of incoherency. Jill, you could say, lost a month in her life. She accomplished nothing, unless you call waiting by a computer screen productive. To let out her frustrations, Jill started to email John not once but too many times. With each email she unknowingly turned John further away. A known fact, people need space to think and calm down before they are ready to broach the very lack of communication that caused the present failures in commitment.

Josh R. Himmelman

Life living lesson: Co-dependency, Parts One to Eleven.

Co-dependency can be a true destruction of oneself. "Co-dependency" has become a very common expression to mean when two people form a relationship with each other because neither feels that they can stand alone. Neither person feels capable or self-reliant. It is as if two half souls were lacking wholeness and that only now together do they make one soul. From this feeling one believes they are psychically complete. In Jill's case she spent most of the last seven years attending and using all her time to assisting John to recover from his drug addiction.

Co-dependency: Part One

Health—Depression—(Stress-Anxiety)—Suicidal. How do you stop yourself from falling in love with the wrong person? Maybe personal sites have the answer. People submit their answers to the same questions, and boom! You have at least one first date and several similarities to discuss over a glass of wine with duck. This opened a door to a second date and as every date goes further, the more the door opens, this allows them to enter side-by-side as a couple

Co-dependency: Part Two

Definitely by doing this she avoided her own needs truly because she did not want John to leave and then experience exhausting pain. It is supposed to be that John, the partner, needs Jill to deal with his addiction, grateful, yet angry because of interference. As a deep co-dependent, the partner feels then let down and taken advantage of, for example losing her own desires in life as living. As for the partner with the addiction, he complains and argues about the relationship to avoid dealing with his own addiction and neediness not to be alone.

Co-dependency: Part Three

True as in "truth be told" is consistent with facts or reality as it is never false. To be true as a person you are genuine, accurate in what you do and because of this you are seen as a reliable person. You always conform to what a group in society wishes you to be, whether it is a type of person or a standard, like a Philips screw driver required to function properly.

Co-dependency: Part Four

You will act your thoughts and the information that makes up your thoughts. You are that individual who might be able to change your self-concept but not totally who you are. You are supposed to be normal and have a healthy state of mind. Working to help a person with an addiction you are taking on something more than who you were meant to be. You are no longer yourself. As a co-dependent coming back to one's self as in "normal" according to society will almost never happen on your own but only with therapy such as cognitive therapy. Looking at the semantics, to come to oneself means to come to one's senses. The word "self" has the connotation of being without a companion, hence alone. Hence, everything you do is by your own effort; you stand on your own two feet. To be one you are considered normal or usually, just "self."

Co-dependency: Part Five

Co-dependency is exhibited by a partner who lives with an abuser where the partner has difficulty leaving and takes on attributes unlike his true self to be there for the partner. This becomes a dysfunctional pattern of living where the co-dependent is the one who suffers the most. The partner who is co-dependent is maladaptive and suffers from the pain and stress of something in their past. As for John, divorced by his wife and losing his girls meant trauma, and that is when he began to use cocaine and continued without Jill knowing when they met. After a number of years, this new relationship for both and the experience of living it becomes very toxic, unreliable, and the cocaine user is emotionally unavailable. Therefore, the other partner loses control as well, but of her own needs.

On a very sad note, a co-dependent person will still be such; and will choose people in life that will use them, and the unhealthy behavior continues.

To recognize the co-dependent behavior you need a friend, an outsider to point out to you your own caretaking behavior, intimacy problems, distrust, episodic stress, and avoidance of your own feelings choosing to see the partner as too needy.

Co-dependency: Part Six

Each and every one of us has at least one co-dependent characteristic. Are we so blinded by a pseudo-needy partner, friend or maybe even a co-worker? Society makes it hard not to be co-dependent, beginning maybe with our mother's behaviors to our own growing into an adult. Then the question is, "How do I become more fulfilled and feel better about myself and simply the life I am living?"

The diagnosis is a self-defeating personality disorder beginning in adulthood drawn into relationships in which he or she will suffer and prevent others from helping them. As an example, the person responds with depression or pain in a sense of negativity, rejecting pleasures surrounding them or helping others to, but not doing it for themselves. The worst outcome is the loss of friends because they see a lack of self-confidence and that brings down another's self-worth who does not have those attributes. Results are illnesses, unable to have energy and a feeling of being unwanted.

Co-dependency: Part Seven

To start pulling yourself out of being a co-dependent, if someone you care for has a problem, for example with drugs, examine how you are reacting. Are you enabling, and are you yourself becoming sick because of this other person? What you are looking at in yourself is confusion, low self-esteem, fear, anger and shame because of your partner. The core issues could be over dependence in a relationship with fear of abandonment, difficulty trusting them and others who may be there to help you, or just taking on excessive responsibility for others.

After these forms of behavior are recognized one would hope you recognize a need for counseling. It can teach you assertiveness and listening skills in communicating. It can help you develop new and healthier coping skills. Again, as in choosing the right doctor for yourself, you need to interview your counselor to see if they fit your needs. There are also self-help groups, like AA called CODA groups. But as seen in different situations, for me this time the other members did not help much.

Co-dependency: Part Eight

I am afraid you will leave me if I help the abuser get better, therefore I must keep you needy, as I am. Where does dependency come from? It usually starts in a progression of living as an adult. We become interdependent adults because we were born both dependent and needy. An example would be bonding with your mother. Then growing as a child we do not seek dependency; I am no baby! In a co-dependent relationship, such real progress is a threat to one's stability in a relationship. A co-dependent believes that if the partner does not need them, then they have nothing to offer. Things are just black and white. The sad component is the person who lives in co-dependency does things for others because they want approval and love. And when others do not return the compassionate treatment, they feel betrayed.

Co-dependency: Part Nine

The development of interdependence and independence is the end of being co-dependent. It is a scary position for the formerly co-dependent individual, who wonders "What now will happen in my relationship?" They need to look for better ways to keep the relationship alive and thriving. The first step is to recognize the problem and reach out for help. Help is there, and receive it with open arms and remain there until your mindset changes. Look for support from your family and friends as well from yourself. Most co-dependent relationships do not end in tragedy; but they do keep people from living full, rewarding lives they could be enjoying. Enjoy your life. Build up your esteem and say, "I am good, people will want me, and therefore I need to change this behavior."

Co-Dependency: Part Ten

Learn to change your life and see how you will benefit from focusing positively on the here-and-now, so that the decisions you are making today will help you create a positive, successful, and productive future. Find the determination and believe in yourself. Keep positive, and your thoughts will become a new energy for you to work with yourself. If you do not lead yourself down this path, you are most likely to cause destructive behavior upon yourself and only yourself. Examples would be: self-punishment, clinical depression, misplaced priorities, self-inflicted wounds, a lack of self-confidence or even used as an attempt to drive other people away.

Co-dependency: Part Eleven

In some sense, all relationships are co-dependent. Many people have low self-confidence and it is always there. But there are people who have enough self-esteem that they can adapt to it and work around it as well. But others can be more aggressive. They get more depressed, develop addictions and the relationship suffers to possible destruction. They end up anxious, depressed and suicidal.

End of Life living lessons: Co-Dependency—Parts One to Eleven.

Sunday, February 28, 2008

Jill had a difficult time forgiving herself for the month of February. She was really tormented. Did she seek this forgiveness so as not to blame herself for antagonizing John? After all, Jill did get what she wanted: his phone call. It seemed so right to her at that time. But as Jill read through the last message in her email, Jill did say she would be out for the afternoon and John should call that evening. But John called in the afternoon. Now and only now Jill realized he had no intention of speaking with Jill. John's call to Jill was at 2 p.m., and she is sure that John only expected to leave a very succinct message and the contract that Jill pushed for by email had been fulfilled.

Without regret, Jill was there and answered the call, the last time John's number would show up on the call display. To this day, Jill has not removed his name from the callers. John's voice was calm, almost sweet. Maybe he thought he was speaking with an emotional nut case. Jill in her emails sure acted as such, with regrets. John knew Jill very well and not to respond to her emails was a way to frustrate her and drive her into an anxious frenzy. John's tone of voice was meant to be understood. Jill held her composure and did not let go of her emotions. There was no crying, no pleading and no threats. Jill tried to explain to John that this whole conversation seemed one-sided. John's side was very negative of recalling the dirt of eleven years.

John said this call would only be a few minutes but it lasted an hour. Jill listened to every word, shaking her head slowly to the left and then to the right in disbelief at John's words. Everything was about little fights and arguments that in her opinion every couple has. He kept shooting them off, one by one, not allowing any explanation from Jill. John was only dwelling on the arguments and never once showed any emotions about the numerous good times they had had together. At the very end John was trying to control Jill's thoughts to believe their life together had been a mistake, no relationship, but just passing through time. Jill had to agree to keep him on the phone, but was so against what John said. Jill was furious inside with John for berating what Jill had done for him for eleven years. That was always to give forgiveness and bring him home. Jill felt at that moment that John had either a lack of intelligence of love or maybe it was his culturally engraved way of thinking and living. Maybe John was high, which gave him the power and euphoria to say that he didn't need her or anyone. Yes the conversation now became long and abusive.

In one sense at least for a while it caused Jill to feel angry. Anger is definitely a trait Jill never took ownership of. It would have helped her tremendously if she could have only got angry. At least she would have released some anxiety, stress and depression. On three separate occasions Jill asked John, "Do you still love me?" John was silent for about thirty seconds and changed the subject. Jill will never know what that meant, and probably that is the way John wanted it. Jill believed that if she admitted to herself that he still loved Jill, he would have met Jill in person. Once they met in person it would be like the last two times. Forgiveness and back to a well-seeded young tree that grows into knots and will not bear fruit.

As Jill hung up the phone, the teacher in her needed to make notes of the conversation in case something was to come out of the conversation like a lawsuit. As Lori warned Jill, it would be all one-sided, just like over all the years, John was "a motor mouth." His conversation was meant to be the only conversation. Jill could not even talk about her own work, and John answered that question for her. There were two final statements made by John: one positive, which truly shocked Jill and, yes, one negative. He told Jill nicely to keep writing, you are very good at that. And please do not call me a "druggie."

Jill was not only suffering from chronic grief, the loss of a loved one and the future she had planned but also chronic depression. These both held Jill in a state of sadness for which there is no pill to treat. That little anger was not held on to long enough, and within the next few days, Jill once again because of John, withdrew into a depression bubble, purposely not allowing herself to take any advice. All Jill kept saying was how could John be so unforgiving? Not to recognize his life was like living in a hotel. Everything had been done for him. Jill asked John about all their dreams of owing a boat, travelling back to Europe to see his family and his only response was, "Maybe in fifteen years when we retire, maybe all could be forgotten."

As Jill's friends, we tried immensely hard to show her the unending mistakes and hurts laid onto her by John. When you are such a frozen state of mind, you need the sharp prick of reason to break apart this unhealthy whole. Jill's whole sense of herself was still John, it was so obvious. Jill could never see herself as anyone but John's wife and partner. So much therapy by friends was sought on Jill's behalf and waiting lists of six to nine months were pending. Not very encouraging for someone like Jill who sees life sometimes with no value and could do the worst thing ever, suicide. The costs associated with any therapy were astronomical because Jill was a teacher, so she would have to pay full price. Little did anyone know her true financial picture; maintaining full house expenses, a mortgage and supporting John all this time.

We were all afraid that Jill may slip as far back as she did previously, and then we would lose a great, giving and loved person. Jill could not see the love portraying in cards and emails to her at home. So many young people appreciated her, missed her and said she was the one who helped shape their lives. To this day, Jill still receives emails from past students thanking her for her guidance. Was it selfish of Jill to think of herself today? As her best friend, Lori, she would have to say "no." Jill invested another huge chunk of her life and received less than nothing in return. Lori and Jill's mother finally convinced her to begin reading more self-help books if for no other reason but to keep her mind busy. Jill could not stand music or television because it brought too many memories of the two of them doing something generally nice together. Lori knew Jill would always come back after an outing with John and say you never would guess what he did today? Maybe because Jill was so reserved and passive that she saw John as her real alter-ego, what she wished she could be and do. That is the only explanation Lori had for Jill's preoccupation with John. With a lot of prodding, Jill then stated to eat literature, one book after another because her friends were right. It did change her mind compulsion she had had with John to a different level of consciousness and feelings. For once Jill felt good in herself because she was doing something that was finally just for her.

<u>March, 2008</u>—and still learning

Jill's mother has read the Bible cover to cover three times. She has urged her to read the Bible before going to bed in the evening because that is what religious people do, and they are happier and less stressed about life. Jill questions, "Does this connection with God be so positive, so fulfilling that it will give one the willingness to be more accepting of their own health issues that most likely cannot be changed?" Will this make one more optimistic and have a reason for being placed here on earth? Does the Bible inadvertently enhance your ability to handle stress, anxiety and depression? How early in life should one start reading the Bible or look at the stars and feel you are a part of something huge? Jill was still struggling for peace, the peace she asked God every night to give her. She also asked for calm so she would have the opportunity to move forward with no mistakes.

Life living lesson: When you need time for yourself, take it.

Take time away from your suffering. Be dependent on yourself and devoted to your beliefs. Liberate yourself from emptiness and loneliness.

Time as it goes by, is very real. We live in time, but time can only be used to measure a part of something happening. There is no shortness of time, we make it short. The only definition of time is our personal belief of existence. Time does not move or travel or take up space. We all do things because we schedule ourselves. Our emotions and our need to understand our decisions in life can be directed to time as in how long it takes to help ourselves. But time will always be there: with no beginning, no middle, and no end. There is no fence to jump in time. We try to imitate time with articles like an hour glass; which only has significance if you say so. We say, "Take as much time as you need." This truly means you are limited in time only by the issue you have with what you ate doing.

Time as an illusion in Buddhist thought. In other words time is truly unreal. As discussed, time is space, like the universe; this again has no center, no beginning, and no end. However Einstein showed that if time and space (the universe) is measured using a test of light bouncing between two mirrors, then the constancy of the speed of light may be measured as time in space. Do not misunderstand: time is needed to change your self-concept; your ability to relieve yourself of co-dependency or simply even of a misunderstanding in conservation. Time is important and essential to being, to life and to living as a learner.

Temporary measurement of time is used as a motivator to navigate and follow astronomy. We do see periodic events and motion as standards for units of time. To understand, watch the sun rise and fall followed by the moon or the swing of a pendulum, or the beat of a heart. There are standards of time such as a second. At a personal level we are aware of the limits of time such as that encompassed in a human life span.

When do you need time for yourself? Is it devotion time, hibernation time, loneliness time, suffering emotions time or happiness time. Can you split your time evenly? Of course not! Does the amount of time you have depend not only on you but on outside forces around you? We put too much emphasis on time that really has no measurement. How you feel should be the indicator where your focus has to be. Try to choose wisely and build upon the one that needs the most attention. Simple devotion can lead to happiness which can then lead to answers for what you see as problems in your life. But to hibernate is to put off for tomorrow what you must fundamentally uncover and start fixing today. Hibernation can be peaceful because you are away from the compulsive behavior that upsets you. Going to bed and trying to sleep it all away is not hibernation. Insomnia, not being able to sleep is non-productive time. Even a second can make a difference. The little peck on the check as he walks out the door is only a second but really not measurable because of its impact.

End of Life living lesson: When you need time for yourself, take it.

Life living lesson: Religion and spirituality

Religion and spirituality enhances your ability to deal with stress, anxiety and depression. Religion is a faith or a belief system, a belief concerning the supernatural, which is divine. It uses sacred teachings of moral code within institutions as a place of refuge for those who need to belong. Is it mankind's relationship with the universe? Religion developed in many cultures and hence in many forms. But it still is worship of God or a commitment and devotion to a religious faith. With religion there is a belief system, and the powers, the principles, the sacred morals that exist. Religion is society's way of conforming to a system of religious attitudes, beliefs and practices. To keep your religious faith you must keep your principles, beliefs, and practices.

The universe is your true self through your soul. We seek the highest level of truth in our mixed-up affairs, our system that seems not to work today as it did in the past. It is a belief of reaching a higher level of our mind giving us memories of life experiences. If you believe you feel as an awakening to these feelings and want to seek higher answers, then you are more spirituality and more in tune with the universe.

God wants us to experience in relationships the kind of love that is focused on the other person. It is better to give than to receive. This could be viewed as co-dependency, but not if you experience God's love for you. You must learn your own experiences, the true you before someone can share love with you. God is love and when we turn to God and accept his forgiveness, and then we begin to experience his love. God will forgive us and cleanse the sins for which we asked forgiveness. We base our love on an instructional list of love because we want to fulfill a check list for God. God's view of love is totally different than what society believes love to be. His forgiveness and love is ours for the asking. It is a gift to civilization. But unfortunately many does not pray, many not ask for forgiveness believing there is no such God. We are the ones who cut ourselves off from finding truest fulfillment, true intimacy and true purpose in life. Put his love into your heart.

What God wants for us is to have life, not just today, but eternal life. By choosing to reject God, we choose sin, which is death and eternal separation from him.

Our lives will balance with the trust in God. Faith and prayer in God lets him forgive us. We will have peace by letting it be a dependence on him. Forgiveness will cleanse us from sin, self-centeredness, our deepest problems or struggles we have in life. In a relationship, as you grow together, not only spirituality, but socially, mentally and emotionally, you are able to be honest, caring and have an intimate relationship which will be fulfilling and exciting. The sexual union can only enhance this foundation. Prayer expresses the desire of your heart. Placing your faith in Christ will result in his coming into your life as promised. This will be a relationship with God. Your life will take a whole new dimension as a spiritual one, bringing more harmony and fulfillment to all of who you are.

Spiritually our value system states that all human meaning is derived out of a fundamental fear of death; where values are selected when it is allowed for us to escape the mental reminder of death. It is a power within the universe and a connection with all living creatures; an awareness of the purpose and meaning of life: one absolute value. It is your own personal way, not a divine way as in religion, to find meaning, comfort and inner peace in your life.

Spirituality is a living that refers to an individual's awareness and choice of lifestyle that reflect the way of life with their attitudes and values as a group. It is an intentional living choice based upon one's fundamental beliefs. It represents an individual's effort to live with integrity in relation to his environment.

Spirituality places little importance on a belief system but is concerned with growing and experiencing. Spirituality to God is seen as only a way of love, no judgments and only acceptance. Spirituality feels these sins are ignorance based on a false belief of who we truly are. God is seen as high in a heaven. Spirituality has the presence of God felt as a living presence in our own heart. There are many religions all with their separate beliefs, but spirituality feels that all religions have validity, all leading to the same goal. Spirituality is acceptance of all the world's religions. Religion has earthly houses to represent God; some believe the bigger institutes are better for humanity. Spirituality defines what is important in what you seek in your inner attitude. This can be called an inner shrine within your heart.

Spirituality and religion can be interchangeable. Their boundaries are fluid and are the only true difference between a human religion and a divine religion. Hence, spirituality is a form of religion but a private and personal form of religion. Religion is spiritual and spirituality is religious. Spirituality is your private self, but religion uses public rituals and organized doctrine. There is no clear distinction between the two because they all use a belief system known to all as "religion." There is no better or worse for either religion or spirituality.

End of Life living lesson: Religion and Spirituality

Life living lesson: Visualization will help

Why do some people have it all: the willpower, strength (physical, mental) and emotional stability? They see the world as a challenge and each new day with open eyes, and comfort in their own self. A feeling of oneself is who you really are, and stable to withstand the little and big traumas that life brings you. You can go searching for trauma or you can let it in, thinking this is what fate and karma has to do in your life. You can accept it as payback and you must endure this to move forward. Or you can be the opposite, in control of what is good for you and those in your circle of life, and feel fulfilled.

As a small child you first crawled to choose, your choice of where you would go. With success achieving your goal most times, what you whole—heartedly wanted would be taken away from you. Then you got better, you began to walk ; stumble your way at a faster pace to beat out the takers. You realize there are the givers, rewards for doing so well and the takers, the micro-management group that scoops up your success. If we could talk to this child, we would ask how you felt. But this child is learning, taking in the data around him, processing it as information and knowledge so the next time he will have a much better chance of succeeding. Hence he develops happiness, the idea of fulfillment, loving relations, vibrant health and being very creative in his endeavors. Can we visualize back and see the wonder in our life then and how we really had what we wanted? We can look back at never giving up, you never settled but kept pushing forward. Today, have you given up on creating the ideal life you once dreamed of, visualizing your happiness?

Refocus where you are at and you can create the life you want. If you desire to expand your potential as a person and if you want not to need or have a stronger impact on your world as it is, the information is there, just like the living room gadgets that were available in all directions for the taking. You and no one else have to manifest your visual future self. Transform your desires into reality.

There are many forms of meditation, I shall let you research all of them, and if you see the value here, then start learning the art of meditation. You are seeking should be seeking meditation with self-hypnosis, creative visualization with affirmation for setting goals.

Learn how to identify your mission in life, as confusing as it may seem, you must believe you have the creative mind to transform your life, especially if it is an everyday poor relationship. But do not think that you can achieve anything you desire only through the use of your mind. Spiritually you must begin to accept that to achieve what you think you should do, you must look at what you were sent here to do. So many people do not receive the things they want in life because they are not naturally entitled to or even deserve. You may have deserved the candy on the other side of the room as a toddler because of your efforts; but in true living unless you believe you deserve it, that spirituality it is your destiny, you will never walk/crawl to have that candy.

Believe in the universe and accept religion and spiritual living. You are born for a reason, and if you stop yourself from learning that reason in life, you will have the wrong, unsatisfying career, poor health and a troubled relationship. But when you find your life mission, no matter how your life is today, it will change, it will because fulfilled with self-esteem and happiness.

Begin by accepting your intuition that we all possess to understand what your purpose in life is. You now know how to learn to use your mind to create coincidences that you need to accept and not be afraid or else you will never move on. The factor that holds all of us is we just do not know how to make the right decision. We are lacking the decision skills necessary for the life we deserve. Once you control this process, your relationship will be what you were promised.

The now is how to achieve what is right for you. Even thinking it is the right relationship for me. That is why we hold on to someone because of the worry that the decision will be wrong. Too many people see their lives full of roadblocks, boulders they cannot move because they lack to see their own power outside their present life. To encourage the healing you need healing in every direction, not just in your health or to build different coincidences you must absolutely be sure of what you want and that want fits your purpose of moving forward. You must read and find specific self-management techniques to help you overcome any roadblocks to your happiness and to help you achieve your life's successes. Your readings have to be about affirmations, goal setting, positive visualization and meditation. It will deliver results and will change your life. But be ready for life's changes in the form of acceptance. Ultimately it will be your decision; no advice will do that for you. You and only you are the master of your life and through acceptance of spirituality your destiny will be laid out for you.

How do you believe famous actors, gold medal winning Olympic athletes and successful people are where they want to be? They visualize, set a goal, have affirmations and meditate to see themselves in that place.

Meditation is a deep inner self-connecting all senses of who you are. It's supposed to help depression, control pain, slow down diseases, invigorate the immune system and reduce health issues like blood pressure. It has been studied to be a solution to a range of illnesses. When you learn the art, it will only take one day to relax your mind and body. Get rid of that stress and anger that clouds your decision process and move forward. Imagine having intuition that can always help you make the best decisions and send you towards your destiny. Use the stronger intuition you now have to know what lies ahead and which can give you the ability to have success, happiness and fulfillment. Imagine complete peace in your life from visualizing, intuition and meditation. You must believe in your spiritual self. Feel the awareness that can overpower you when you allow it in. You are able to strengthen troubled relationships.

Once on the right path nothing can stop you; you can create coincidences to push you as if a hand were on your back, towards solutions and moving barriers like you are the world's strongest man. Believe, and you should have any goal, better health, better relations, increased wealth and a greater creativity in your thoughts of what and where to be. It will not be temporary but with you for life. Once you learn it you can always have it at your disposal, it will be your ability to achieve calm, peacefulness, happiness, health and safety in your life.

While in sleep mode, if we fall asleep with good thoughts for tomorrow, goals for the future, your consciousness will bring you answers and guidance in life. Some people wake up and feel the warmth of sunshine caressing their face, yet there is no sunshine peering in the window. This is your sole purpose and you have to be ready to achieve it, there are no silver platters at the front door like winning the publishers clearing house sweepstakes. You can recognize your self-improvement but definitely you cannot have everything you desire. The world would be full of no mistakes, a utopia.

Do not shut out the universe, the part of your soul's path for you. Your intuition can give you a direction, but your soul will provide your Life Purpose. If you think you now have a goal and it is barred from happening, then of course you chose unwisely, you can however live a life with your true purpose and make the right decision in all aspects of your life. In your intuition, you must clearly see not only just for you but for the better of all that is needed to fill your soul's reason for being here. Believe in yourself that you have the tools you need to have guidance and a higher intelligence to prepare yourself to succeed the way you should in life. Nothing will happen until you believe. Look at your life lessons and learn from them, believe in them and look for the answers. See your weaknesses to overcome, start by seeing it happen, a spiritual awakening, the control of your destiny of happiness. The problem is you and I may achieve this but too many people see it as normal to go through life without ever using their sense of intuition and their mind's ability to create goodness and circumstances to meet their goals.

Intuition is a part of you, recognized by you but uncertain what it is or if you should trust in it to make decisions. When you are fully involved in an activity, you focus on what part of fulfillment comes from a conscious contact. Your intuition can result in positive or negative thought beginnings in your mind. Your problem is to believe and use it rationally in making decisions. Each day you are bombarded with decisions, making your whole life with decisions because it is your life partner. Most people's response is "It is my common sense."

But to everything Jill had to endure and later speaks of, her confused intuition of life with John was not right. Jill still, even today, visualized a pure happy life with John. Jill really only saw the positive because of her co-dependency not to be left alone. John was very intelligent and recognized Jill's weakness of loneliness. From that moment on, it was John's sword to wave above Jill's head and at times it would come too close. Jill's physical wound would heal but never healed emotionally from the beginning. Some would believe it was because she never had a chance. Jill started to be truly intuitive and much more. You look subconsciously in 360 degrees for all the information around your thoughts—most commonly called your sixth sense, instinct, gut feeling or intuition. There is a difference between rational reasoning and intuitive decision-making. For the most optimal decisions, try to use both, a combo that compliments each other.

Your lesson is to ask yourself, what is your excuse for not living the purpose of your souls' embodiment of your living human self? Ask yourself how you want to be remembered by your family after death. Do you really want to leave behind something memorable even for strangers to admire and use for self-fulfillment. Answer is a "yes" and you will find guidance towards your life's mission.

It is born within you to want. We want happiness, good friends, affection, adventure, health, a nice place to live and we have to balance our needs with our wants. We see our neighbor with everything and for us it is a challenge and a frustration. Living life in such degrees can be depressing and a leave a feeling of hopelessness, even suicidal feelings. We turn to others like our spouse, family, religion, even the internet to find answers. It is the power of visualization that pulls us forward.

It is time to explain to you what visualization is. Everyone has this natural ability. It is like daydreaming, and a movie flicks in your mind and becomes your imagination. If you see your mind positive which is what you should be seeing anyway, the desire will be to feel good about yourself. As well, there is certain music or a poem that inspires you to feel better about yourself, that is inspiration: a form of visualization. We all do visualize, and it would be great if we all knew this is what we are really doing for ourselves and others.

It works exactly as when you were a child and got what you wanted: the bicycle you dreamt about for Christmas morning. In your mind it was very clear, even to the color of the paint you wanted. You were dreaming and day dreaming so hard it made it as if it were real. This is what we call the momentum of achieving through either thought or even some action like giving a hint during dinner. This is a powerful process that can move you from negative thinking to positive thinking at an unconscious level.

Visualization then really is your power of thought. When you have a conversation with anyone other than a priest, people are usually negative because they are afraid to even think, day dream about success. As humans we do not want continuous disappointment and disbelief in our dreams. Sometimes we feel all we have are our dreams. To dream happiness and never achieve it, we lose faith in our visualization. And sometimes even when we get what we want, we fear its loss. Like some who win the lottery and keep working for fear it can all be lost. This is a learned attitude, probably as a child because the results of wanting things always turned out negatively. However, we forget that as a child we did not base things on our own ability to achieve but on someone else's.

We worry and doubt and our thoughts cause negativity. To replace that with joy and determination and "never let go," use your mind positively. This mind thought is our boundary; it is what our life encompasses. Boundaries limit possibilities by saying "We cannot." We need to learn to get out of the box in our minds, project our thoughts, visions, and emotions and we then realize how powerful this is in creating. Negative thoughts and emotions result in negative living. Positive thoughts and emotions give us positive living. Your thoughts and visions transform energy into a reality. It is the same as speaking to you, your mind conversation. If you negatively say you are ugly, "I feel ugly," then you will frown and others will see you as negative. But through a different imagery and emotions, we can use positive energy to bring positive reactions into our lives.

You are reading and wondering a daydream seems simple enough. But true visualization comes from living and feeling a thought. Experience a scenario in your mind of living what you are dreaming. You truly have to desire something; see it; feel the joy of your emotions and imagery and let all your emotions be positive. You must be aware of your thoughts, images, and the emotions that are attached, and what you are doing is visualization. It is very natural for all of us if we wish to; but do not force it upon yourself because then it is another task to do in a busy day. When just sitting still let your positive thoughts and emotions emanate through a mental image; a day dream and be confident, joyful so you see answers to questions and a life you need. Hopefully you can believe in your dreams but, yes, we know it is hard to do when you are faced with so many challenges. If you are fearful, stop the fears and think to understand what you are about and be a new self. Fears are natural and are ways of indicating doors you have not passed through yet, the point to new experiences that you should try to have. From here imagine the best and when you need to face reality and you can no longer daydream, remain happy.

Because not all is beautiful, sometimes you are faced with a crisis. You are in it, nowhere to go but to accept the situation. Then to help visualize where you would rather be and act if you wish, instead of giving more fuel to your negative emotion.

You may say, "I have no true friends, no one to count on." But life is your friend because you believe in yourself and your dreams; you stay positive as well accept the parts of life with thankfulness still, as you know there will be not only goodness, but also badness and sadness. Life is your true journey and it belongs to no-one else. Once you accept these points your life will change your living experience. Life has a flow like a small stream, sometimes if it runs too hard it will overflow and fear with worry will embrace you. But look at it knowing it will change. Embrace the moment for what it is. When you have acceptance and gratitude, you will begin to see people in your life are there for a reason. Part of all this is your need to be the one to take action, to achieve your objective, your momentum to manifest what you feel as an inner urge to do something. Action is the pleasant physicality you will have to enjoy and to make your dreams. A simpler way to understand is to see yourself doing what you enjoy. Do not focus on what you do not want to do or what you hate. All of this would be seen as a negative image. Create a momentum like a smile, living and feeling the change you see in your thoughts. This way you are avoiding saying it will never happen. Doing avoidance, you will convince yourself it will never happen and then your life's plan just becomes harder.

There are no rules. The only rules exist only in your head and they are as real or as false as you believe them to be. You truly are the creator of your Life living experiences.

End of Life living lesson: Visualization will help.

Life living lesson: You can create and live your reality

An understood point of the human being's makeup is that nobody can ever determine with complete certainty whether any part of their world experience will come into play and whether it will be good or bad for their growth forward. Individuals can only express for themselves whether the truth that appears true will be true for them only and not necessarily for anyone else, like a partner. There will always be a degree of uncertainty in any relation. Do you believe your thoughts are reality or did you create them? Does it really make sense to convince you to believe something that may or may not be true? How do you know when to stop believing? Maybe it will happen when you see it is true, but is your truth an external quality. And we all believe reality is mostly subjective, hence your thoughts are your truth. In turn, your thoughts affect reality—they are creating it. Your own thoughts contribute to shaping the world around you. If you think of peace, your life will be more peaceful.

Our own beliefs help to remake reality. In a relationship, if you believe there are problems, you have reshaped it to address possible problems. Believing is seeing. If in reality we must see, not just think it, and then we need to somehow choose thoughts responsibly because they are affecting our world. In fact, we are the choosers of the type of reality we actually want to live in. In order to use your thoughts to create, you must then believe it is conceivable to create such things. To think of this, you should believe that our own observation of our lives will influence our future reality as it unfolds. It is obvious that you are capable of interacting with the world with your directness. If you make a decision to do something and then do it, your thoughts are affecting reality by your actions.

Your beliefs are also what make you be what others see every day. If you go to college every day, it is because of your actions, not because of the universe. You have an impact on the world. While at school, this is your job and while doing this, you neglect to do different work. Your beliefs about reality will be reflected by your actions, even if it is very subtle. Your reality is shaped through your actions and impacts on everyone who comes into contact with you.

Your thoughts can change reality through conscious or subconscious actions. You as a person, your actions act upon the whole world. For example, you talk to people, move something around, you make changes in simple living things, and this is what makes you effective in helping to change the world around you.

Our whole life is needed to understand that our beliefs are decisions. They are choices evolving from your beliefs and hence you are creating your own reality. It is important to note, your thoughts can and do impact reality, so we need to choose the beliefs that give us what we wish to create. You believe your relationship should be happier; you think of ways to make it real and you make the decision that will impact on your reality.

We lose our power simply by living in fear—fear that if you believe in this ability you will not be able to understand or deal with the outcomes, leaving you overwhelmed with new responsibility. Why shake the boat? Because we need a new and better experience, every emotion we have is a belief. We are free to stop the fear, because fear kills your opportunities to change your reality.

It will take time to first believe that your thoughts are capable of having a significant impact on your reality, and then own the responsibility you created for yourself. But when you feel successful, this is what you have done, and unselfishly. Ultimately it is a choice. You have to choose to believe and then live this way.

Individually we make an impact firstly with ourselves and then impact others around us. Your effects may seem small but remember if consistent in anything, that thing will become cumulative. So, if one person can have an impact by believing, then it is possible many people will do as well and accomplish if they choose to serve the greatest good of all. As in every American beauty pageant, the contestant always quotes, "world peace". Remember you to be observing yourself as well as others. You can choose to make a bigger impact and provide more impact if you choose to do so. And because you use your beliefs to let more powerful decisions come true you do not give yourself greater responsibility. You can give up your power of thought but not your responsibility. You want to relinquish your power, just believe you do not possess the power.

Your personal development is a part of your thoughts and beliefs. If you want to grow then choose your greatest beliefs. It is your choice

Live in the Present and Learn Valuable Life Lessons to Improve Any Relationship

to grow rapidly, to grow peacefully and enjoy your life and this will all be your experience.

For a relationship to grow each must believe in the same thoughts, have their goals and chose the responsibilities of a prosperous life. To grow you need to grow by living and your expectations and when needed do not live in fear of changing your expectations. Follow your most positive expectations and make your behavior work with your expectations. Let the life you planned unfold, and if you decide not to then someone will be very frustrated.

As you follow through on your expectations you most likely will see a need to change part or all of your ideas. Do not be afraid, take control of your thoughts and do with a conscious change. You will lead your relationship into a path of growth. Learn to alternate between what you brought into your life and are experiencing to a different conscious change, a different experience which ultimately gives the most growth and the richest life experience.

You see your relationship as a representation of two different people's thoughts. These thoughts, when portrayed in reality, are what make your relation what it is. If you both hold thoughts of love in your consciousness you will perceive a loving relationship. If you believe you are attractive, your relationship will see that attractiveness. If you are negative, they see conflict.

You want to improve your relationship. Ask yourself what that person represents. If you hate another person, it's only because you hate the part of yourself that person represents. If you love that person, it is because you love the part of yourself that person represents.

If you wish to attract loving relationships into your life, and then identify the qualities you desire in others and learn to love and accept those same qualities in yourself. This will become your truth and your expectation. If your relationship is having trouble and if you want to improve it, then identify what that person represents to you and direct your focus on improving your relationship with that part of yourself. The harder you work at this, the better it will be with this person, life will improve.

End of Life living lesson: You can create and live your reality

Jill was ready and with full thoughts of herself. She wanted to leave all suffering and negative emotion float away in a helium filled balloon, disappearing over the waters, never to be found again by anyone. Jill wanted no one to ever feel such hurt. It was the end of suffering through her emotions, and what others were seeing on the outside was a woman who had integrity now lost to her. She still hurt, with physical pains from stress, emotional hurts that her friend Lori coached her to see the pains of suffering were now to be over. Jill's suffering was due to another individual in her life, John, and even with him still not here he had a control over Jill that was about to dissipate.

Jill, in her struggles, was looking for peace and calm wherever she could tap into. She wanted to move forward this time with no mistakes, no shaking from a rocky boat but moving as smoothly as a sail boat on a windless sea. She knew that the only way for her to move forward was to clear her mind of negative and useless ideas. She finally realized what she was doing wrong to heal. She had to stop searching from the outside and look within and with helpers: religion, the universe, and spirituality.

Jill had to start with her lack of self-confidence, self-esteem and find the determination to replace her losses. Since she was a teacher, it was like a power point slide show inside her head and of all the slides she must complete. She felt like she was grading herself using the achievement levels, barely passing to excelling in the course. Her course was to visualize and use her intuition all supported by religion, the universe and spirituality. Jill finally realized she was not alone. There are so many others who suffer as she does and worse. The clear point though: each will find support from different areas and each will see their issue in a different light. Jill stopped with all the doctors looking for the magic pill of which would only mask the disease of depression, anxiety and stress. For each it would have a different reaction and for some, a way out of their hole to a better place. Jill now knew what really does work is taking charge of your own life. We see ourselves sometimes as a paradox of life, what we take or do to help does not fix things, even though it should. We are left to our own devices of healing the hurts. Recognize the hurts, thoughts, and replace them with positive affirmations. Then she must move forward in a way to reinforce those positive thoughts and make them her, Jill.

Prayer was first in the morning and last at night with both hands crossed over her heart. It gave Jill a sense of touch from somewhere, pleasant, warm, and comforting. Find your physical heart's location and as Jill started, placing all your vibration thoughts to that place—the physical you. Bounce your thoughts up to the universe and all its power there for you to feel and grasp. Jill felt she was starting at the right place, the starting gate, waiting for the gun shot to echo through her charged muscles and then with her force, explode forward in her mind to be the winner. Be a winner in your thoughts, behaviors, emotions, feelings and be a new you, a never ending learner like Jill.

Jill would feel her ears and visualize the sounds of life coming in all for you to experience. Jill learned to feel passion in her tongue to extract every amazing flavor of every morsel as she fed his physical self. In the eyes of the beholder is the nose. Jill's nose was in search of bringing a pleasure of smells activating the brain receptors. The smell to Jill now of something as small as a rose brought her the feeling of love. Dinners are being prepared, and before you actually see them, your sense of smell lets your taste buds begin evaluating the pleasures your stomach will experience. Jill was feeling alive and with her own reflection in the mirror she almost did not recognize herself today. There were no rose colored glasses for Jill anymore, but pure reality of the beauty of living as a complete loving of oneself. Jill was soon ready to move forward.

Jill always wanted to free fall backwards into a trusting set of arms. She wanted to experience the freedom from any interference from life and feel the magic of being alive, a living energy force against a materialistic world. Jill now knows there is peace in life and you control how much and in what form it shall be. For Jill, after suicide attempts, this was the beginning of her "me" in reality, that her body with its soul is alive and she must be her soul's guardian.

Jill will ward off any more attempts of control, either physical or emotional, or any lack of belief of who she is as a person. She will thank spirituality through daily prayer that keeps her soul well, and she always will be a learner.

If you have a comment or question, contact:
learn.valuable.lessons@gmail.com

CPSIA information can be obtained
at www.ICGtesting.com
Printed in the USA
LVOW10*0934280518
578629LV00011BA/281/P